NO
BACKUP

NO BACKUP

MY LIFE AS A FEMALE FBI SPECIAL AGENT

ROSEMARY DEW

and Pat Pape

CARROLL & GRAF PUBLISHERS
NEW YORK

NO BACKUP
MY LIFE AS A FEMALE FBI SPECIAL AGENT

Carroll & Graf Publishers
An Imprint of Avalon Publishing Group Inc.
245 West 17th Street, 11th Floor
New York, NY 10011

Copyright © 2004 by Rosemary Dew and Pat Pape

First Carroll & Graf edition 2004

Library of Congress Cataloging-in-Publication Data is available.

ISBN: 0-7867-1278-3

Designed by Paul Paddock
Printed in the United States of America
Distributed by Publishers Group West

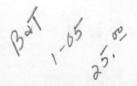

To Special Agents L. Douglas Abram and Livio A. Beccaccio, both of whom died in the service of mankind, and to my children, who gave more to the FBI than I did.

Acknowledgments

I would like to acknowledge my husband, Ian M. Dew; my mother, Eadie Newell; my agent, John Talbot; my editor Philip Turner; and my friends Bessie Means, Cheryl Pellerin, Bill Matens, Dan Ruben, Bill Carter, Mike Wyatt, Eric Washburn, and Helen Engle, all of whom devoted countless hours to helping me put this book together.

CONTENTS

A Good Idea Gone Mediocre

Make sure you get exactly the right kind of car. According to instructions it has to be a black four-door sedan. Don't come back with a yellow convertible, for God's sake! Inside, there must be two black umbrellas and two envelopes containing exactly the road maps and brochures relating to the area through which the trip will be made. The same stuff in each package. This Cadillac must be meticulously clean. Especially inside. Dirty upholstery or dirty ashtrays will not be tolerated. Callahan suggested that the agent chauffeur carry a dust cloth in the glove compartment and on occasions when the Director and Mr. Tolson leave the car for any periods of time, the agent should occupy himself with dusting the car's interior.

Instructions to agents hosting a visit from J. Edgar Hoover
Joseph Schott, *No Left Turns*

J. Edgar Hoover was a meticulous man. He'd learned to categorize and catalog when he worked at the Library of Congress from 1912 through 1917, and he used those skills to create an organization of strict rules that conformed to the order he preferred. Dubbed G-men by "Machine Gun Kelly," who in 1933 is alleged to have shouted, "Don't shoot G-men," as agents closed in to arrest him, Hoover's carefully selected agents were righters of wrongs, pillars of the community, men you could count on to get the job done.

Hoover understood public relations, how to manipulate the Bureau's image and how to showcase his G-men in the best light. In 1950, he started the Ten Most Wanted Fugitives Program and, five years later, he worked with newspaperman-turned-author Don Whitehead in the writing of *The FBI Story,* which later became a movie starring Jimmy Stewart. The subsequent television series, *The FBI,* starring Efrem Zimbalist Jr., premiered in 1965 and ran for nine seasons, locking in America's image of FBI agents as handsome, brave, and flawless. Hoover's savvy established the FBI as the best investigative organization in the world, and when a G-man strode upon the scene, there was no question about who was in charge.

So why has there been a stream of negative headlines about the FBI over the past decade or so? Accusations that September 11 terrorism information was not acted upon because FBI headquarters couldn't connect critical pieces of evidence? Documents withheld in the Oklahoma City bombing case that delayed the execution of convicted terrorist Timothy McVeigh? A high-ranking FBI agent jailed for destroying controversial Ruby Ridge documents rather than passing them along to defense attorneys as required by law? The famed FBI laboratory charged with fabricating findings that impact more than three thousand criminal cases? FBI agents convicted of espionage, murder, theft? And how could these national heroes and defenders of civil rights, lose so many discrimination suits to their own colleagues and former colleagues? The answers to these questions are complex, but the key lies in the very system that was created to ensure perfection. It also lies in the historical context in which the Bureau evolved.

Despite Hoover's obsession with airtight investigations, recently botched Bureau business—much of it played out in the news media—indicates that standards have slipped. To make matters worse, a number of FBI agents have testified before Congress that they were threatened and retaliated against for attempting to improve the system by conducting thorough internal investigations. In August 2001, special agent John E. Roberts said that his wife, an FBI support employee, had been "hounded from her job" in the Boston division and that his attempts to win a promotion had been rejected fourteen times because he had accurately reported his findings in the FBI's internal investigation of management actions taken at Ruby Ridge.

In response to Roberts's testimony, Democratic senator Patrick J. Leahy of Vermont said, "It appears from this that the 'good old boy' network has been allowed to persist at the FBI. It serves to protect some senior FBI executives from the same scrutiny and discipline applied to rank-and-file agents . . . This double standard is unfair and demoralizing."

I served for almost thirteen years as a special agent of the FBI, three of them as a headquarters supervisor and three of them as a field supervisor, and I know it to be a fear-driven, image-conscious organization. Hoover's compulsive need to appear perfect in the eyes of the public, coupled with the increasingly difficult, sometimes impossible demands that came with the agency's expanding jurisdiction, led to the edict that making a mistake was not an option.

Over the years, the Bureau has become a Stalinist absurdity that eradicates dissent, along with truth and integrity. And so, the G-men have morphed into yes-men, creating a world where "different" equals "bad," and mistakes are hidden in the code language of Bureau-speak. Behind the facade lives a dysfunctional family of agents willing to undercut each other for imagined steps up a golden career ladder. Oddly similar to the Mafia families it has investigated, the Bureau demands that its problems be kept inside the family. Revealing FBI family business to outsiders may not mean death by a hit man's gun but, inside the Bureau, enforcers of the unwritten code of conduct had no second thoughts about making a whistleblower's career a living hell. There's a saying among agents in the Bureau—"affix blame and bayonet the wounded"—and they aren't kidding.

Agents have to know how to work the system in order to get cases noticed and to advance above the rank of GS-13 (the highest level of promotions given automatically according to the number of years an agent has served). It started with Hoover and continues to this day. It has culminated in FBI director Robert Mueller's call for an extensive reorganization of the FBI, and, in November 2001, he felt it necessary to distribute an agency-wide memorandum extending his personal guarantee of protection for FBI whistleblowers.

Louis Freeh, who directed the FBI from 1993–2001, recognized that the Bureau's internal affairs were a problem. A former agent, he knew firsthand what was going on in the FBI workplace. Early in his directorship, he established the "bright line" policy, specifying that agents were not to lie under oath, cheat on vouchers, steal, or falsify government documents, among other things. It is significant that he would feel it necessary to reiterate to federal law enforcement officers that they could "expect to be dismissed" for such law-breaking activities.

Many agree that the system is broken, but there is a somewhat logical, if perverse, progression to the way things worked in the Bureau up to and after the September 11, 2001 terrorist attacks. The paradox is that the same strict system that birthed this legendary agency also allows mediocrity and error to thrive. While the majority of agents are honest and hard working, the culture that perpetuates the status quo has outlasted four directors since Hoover. Reorganization and new technologies are called for, but these changes cannot reverse problems that are culturally ingrained. To identify the changes that will make a difference in the future, as well as those that will prevent this closed society from slipping back to its old habits, one must first understand the FBI's culture, policies, and practices in the context of history.

For me personally, the system failed in not ensuring a professional atmosphere in the workplace, and, in a larger sense, the system has also failed the public, by setting the stage for the major blunders in investigations and prosecutions that have been publicized since the mid-'90s. This, then, is the story of a system that evolved through history, of what it was like to be on the inside, and what steps should be taken to make the FBI the agency the public once thought it was—the agency America needs it to be in years to come.

PART I

PROLOGUE

T hat crisp fall day in 1978 was my first chance to prove myself as an FBI agent. It was a textbook kidnapping and extortion case: An elderly man was missing, and an unknown male had telephoned the victim's daughter, a bank manager, demanding a $100,000 ransom and threatening to kill her father if she didn't cooperate. So there I stood, dressed in the daughter's clothes and clutching a paper bag stuffed with shredded copies of *The Berkeley Barb*, which was supposed to look like a bag full of ransom money. This was the day I would demonstrate to my colleagues and myself that I was worthy of my oath to protect and serve.

Over and over, I reviewed the plan the FBI team had set in motion just two hours earlier. I would drive the daughter's car to the opening of a blind alley in downtown Oakland, get out, walk down the alley, toss the bag in the back of a burned-out Chevy, then get out of there. No muss, no fuss, no complications—at least that's what I hoped. While I changed clothes, some twenty FBI agents and Oakland police officers positioned themselves to provide the backup that could save my life if anything went wrong.

My communications lifeline was a clunky portable radio that we called a "handy-talky." Its style shouted "cop," so I couldn't carry it into the alley. Instead, I'd count on my backup's eyes and ears to spot problems from well-concealed lookout points.

As I drove to the scene, I tried a radio check. To my horror, the prearranged channel was dead, so I flipped through the rest of the channels until I heard voices.

Relieved, I keyed the mike. "This is 2-2-9-2. I need some help out here. Do you read me?"

"You can't use this channel," came the response.

"You don't understand. I've got to drop some extortion money right now, and I need to let my backup know I'm going in."

"You are not authorized to use this channel."

Trying to stay calm, I rationalized: Two hours had passed, and everyone had had time to get in place. This was the FBI after all—J. Edgar Hoover's heroic G-men—things had to go according to plan. Then, just as I shoved the handy-talky under the seat of the car and prepared to drive to the alley, I heard a voice call, "2-2-9-2, can I help?"

Another agent had heard my transmission and volunteered to relay my message to the team. A minute later, he reported that the drop was a go, and I took off for the site, my confidence rekindled.

I'll never forget the scene. High-rise buildings framed the alley like a dark crevasse, and nearby streets were deserted, even though it was the middle of a business day. Bad sign, I thought. What did the locals know, that was keeping them off the streets?

As I walked into the dead-end alley, shards of glass crunched beneath my shoes and the acrid smell of urine filled my nostrils. Around me, broken and boarded-up windows peppered the facades of the old brick buildings. Here and there the boards were pushed askew, creating just enough room for a gun to poke through. Concrete stairways littered with trash led to below-the-street entrances and blocked my view to all but the first couple of steps. At the end of the alley sat my goal: the stripped-down, abandoned Chevy where I was to place the bag. It was the perfect spot for an ambush.

I quickly scanned the alley. I had decisions to make and not much time to make them: Where could I take cover if bullets started flying? What if someone was hiding in the backseat of the car? Someone with a gun? What if I was grabbed from behind?

My firearms instructors' adages ran through my head: Don't give up your gun, no matter what, and if someone with a knife gets the drop on you . . . run.

It was cold comfort, but I knew there was a team of experienced agents watching my back, ready to jump in and help if things went bad. I'd only need to hold out for a minute at most until the cavalry would arrive. In my head, I rehearsed a zigzag path out of potential lines of fire and told myself that if someone came up from behind, I'd stall, struggle, and wait for backup. My decisions made, it was time to get moving.

My borrowed clothes had left no room for the Bureau-issue holster, so I'd stuck my revolver in my waistband at the small of my back. As I grabbed the door of the abandoned car, my weapon shifted, and I feared it would slip through my skirt and bounce beyond my reach. But I leaned in, tossed the "money" into the blackened shell of the car, and headed out of the alley, weapon intact. As I moved away, my body was shaking, but I controlled my urge to bolt and walked briskly to my car—and safety. I was elated that I'd survived my first big operation and completed the mission.

The rest was anticlimactic. Like the other criminals I would meet over the years, this extortionist was no genius. When he showed up to collect his money, the FBI was there to arrest him, and as far as I knew, everything had worked as planned. I was feeling good about it until I overheard some agents laughing and joking at the extortionist's trial a few months later. That's when I realized they had been unable to see or hear me during the drop. Unless shots had been fired, no one would have known I was in trouble, and no one would have responded. What has puzzled me for the past twenty-five years is why no one had bothered to warn me when they relayed the go-ahead. Without that critical piece of data, the decisions I'd made for my own safety as I entered that alley could have gotten me killed.

Not much has changed since 1978. FBI communications still fail, and there are still agents who would laugh about endangering a twenty-eight-year-old rookie, who was only a couple of months out of the academy, by not warning her she was on her own once she reached that shooting gallery of an alley.

As an FBI manager, I looked back on this and other operations and wondered why there were no after-action debriefings, no backup plans to provide safety when communications failed. Today, the public knows the FBI is troubled, largely because of its institutional refusal to acknowledge and address systemic problems. But the situation is not hopeless. There are ways to make the FBI better, and my sincere hope is that this book will demonstrate to someone with the power and influence to bring about change, how reforming the FBI's culture is key to reforming the FBI.

Chapter 1

BARRIERS FALL

Let us face reality. If the credibility of the FBI is to be maintained in the eyes of the public, the lawbreaker, fugitive, deserter, and if we are to continue a flexible, mobile, ready-for-anything force of Special Agents, we must continue to limit the position to males.

FBI Memorandum to the Attorney General
May 19, 1971

Even today people tell me I don't look like an FBI agent. Well, it's true, I didn't don the traditional raincoat, wing tips, and snap-brim hat; but I definitely looked better than J. Edgar did in frilly things. When Hoover died in 1972, he was aware that women would soon be hired as agents. Some people believe that just having to face that fact finished him off.

To become one of the first women to serve as a special agent was not my lifelong aspiration, and I had no burning desire to break new ground for the feminist cause. Like many baby boomers, I was inspired by John F. Kennedy and hoped to make a difference in the world. Kennedy's challenge—"Ask not what your country can do for you. Ask what you can do for your country"—affected me deeply and, when I joined the Bureau in October 1977, I wanted to serve my country. The United States of my childhood was proud and patriotic. Throughout my school years, I stood with my classmates every morning, hands over our hearts, saying the Pledge of Allegiance; and during the Cuban missile crisis, I knelt in the halls of my Dallas, Texas, grade school with my hands clasped over my neck, waiting for the bombs to fall. I learned at an early age that my way of life was a prize to be protected by me and every American.

I remember when the Berlin Wall was built, and I saw newsreels of men, women, and children who had lost their lives trying to escape from East Germany to freedom. Both my parents proudly served as Naval Medical Corps officers during World War II and instilled in me the belief that our country, our government, would never do anything wrong. And so in 1976, though only a few women had been admitted into the exclusive club of agents, I applied to the FBI. With a personal sense of pride and duty, plus some girlish dreams of adventure, I believed I could make a difference.

The job had everything I wanted in a career: a big enough salary to support my children, a chance to use my education in Slavic languages, and an opportunity to serve my country. All this, with excitement as a bonus. It seemed too good to be true.

In the years that followed, I earned eight commendations from FBI directors and one letter of appreciation from the director of the U.S. Secret Service. I worked undercover against criminals, spies, and terrorists. Eventually, I became a supervisor at FBI headquarters, the seventh woman to attain that rank. I supervised big-name cases like the *Achille Lauro* hijacking and later supervised a terrorism squad and interagency task force in Denver. I had a no-bluff reputation and the support of some outstanding men and women, who would have followed me into hell. I even protected the president a couple of times at the invitation of the Secret Service. But up to my last minute on the job, in the eyes of many in the Bureau, I wasn't a special agent; I was a female agent, something much less than what the title "special agent" suggested. And let me just say now, all agents start out as gun-carrying field agents. There are no "administrative" agent positions where they stash the women, and we all carry the same credentials.

During most of my Bureau career, I was a single parent, raising my son and daughter alone. Looking back, it's easy to question what kind of a life I gave them. In San Francisco, a psychopathic ex-con stalked us and said my kids would be kidnapped. In Denver, white supremacists vandalized our home the night before a murder trial of Aryan Nation members. And me, well, I was always being called away for one emergency or another. No one would describe my family's life as charmed.

When I applied to the Bureau in 1976, I was twenty-six, divorced from a Foreign Service officer, and the unemployed mother of two. Originally, I had hoped to find a job in my hometown of Dallas, but my special talents—fluency in Serbo-Croatian, Russian, and Czech, which I'd picked up in college and from study abroad—were not in big demand. In fact, they were not in demand at all. For about a month, I naively thought my college degree would count for something, but in Dallas in 1976, if it wasn't banking or insurance, it wasn't hiring.

"Can you type?" was the 1970s personnel department mantra when interviewing women. (Even Sandra Day O'Connor, *magna cum laude* and a member of the editorial board of the *Stanford Law Review,* started in the typing pool.) Although I had mastered the hunt-and-peck technique, I could not type well enough to pass a typing test. In desperation, I began waiting tables in a steak house near the Apparel Mart at which President Kennedy had been scheduled to speak on the day he was shot.

Those first few months on my own were a massive plunge in prestige and in the way I was accustomed to being regarded. I was no longer Madame Foreign Service wife, who entertained diplomatic guests at black-tie dinners in Belgrade. Instead, I was a waitress who was summoned with salutations such as "Hey, chicky!" and treated to such nightly complaints as, "This steak ain't cooked right, sweetie," and "Where's my iced tea?"—all for $1.10 per hour, plus tips. Nonetheless, it was an honest income, and I'd always said that if I needed money to feed my children, I'd do whatever it took. Having no better job prospects at the time, I did what I had to do.

My journey to adulthood had begun in 1968 when I enrolled in the University of Texas at Austin and declared a biology major. Unfortunately, I couldn't master the mystical math that biological research required. At the same time, I was taking classes in Russian and Czech, which I enjoyed, so I switched my major to Slavic languages.

My interest in Slavic countries happened almost by accident. As a teenager, I traveled with friends to a rural area outside of Houston where everyone spoke Czech. I slept in my girlfriend's grandmother's attic on an overstuffed feather bed. The house had no air conditioning, but I didn't feel the searing southeast Texas heat. During the day, my friend and I picked cantaloupes and did farm chores. Some of the boys took us to swim in a nearby lake where rattlesnakes sunned themselves by the water, and the boys made a game of killing them by flipping rocks at their heads. This was one of the few dares in my life I didn't take. I wasn't interested getting that close to any viper. If you didn't kill them with the first whack, they coiled to defend themselves. I'd rather face a gun anytime.

The elderly Czechs who lived in the sleepy town maintained the traditions and language of their homeland. Their speech was pleasant to my ear, and for some reason, the words were easy to learn. I couldn't understand everything, but the conversations were animated with gesticulations, so I could guess the context, and everyone pitched in to help me.

The beauty and mystery I saw in their crumbling, sepia photographs deeply imprinted on my imagination, and these pleasant memories flooded my mind the day I noticed an announcement on the University of Texas's language department's bulletin board about a study abroad program in Zagreb, Croatia, which was then part of Yugoslavia. I jumped at the chance to travel and study, despite my family's concern that I would disappear behind the Iron Curtain, never to breathe the air of freedom again.

The idea of studying in a far-off place seemed romantic and challenging, so I applied for the federally funded scholarship and was accepted. The first phase of my big adventure was eleven weeks of summer school at Portland State University in Oregon, where I studied Serbo-Croatian and gained enough competence to scrape by in a Yugoslav university.

That summer in Portland was a turning point for me. It was there I met my future husband, Dick, a fellow scholarship student. He was handsome, smart, and five years my senior. He had served in the Navy during Vietnam and seemed a sophisticated man of the world to my fresh-from-Texas teenaged self. Even though he had a quick and somewhat frightening temper, I was a naive nineteen-year-old, blinded by his looks and intelligence. I felt confident that the love of a good woman (that would be me) could calm him down. My jokes made him laugh, and I told myself I could control his temper with my adoring and comical behavior.

The Yugoslavia I encountered was a giant step back in time, starting at the airport where we deplaned via wooden ladders, and continuing as we drove to the city through the suburb that was to become Anatevka, Tevye's village in *Fiddler on the Roof,* after the movie crew cleaned it up.

The sounds of locomotives filled the air for blocks around the train station: the mechanized screech of steel brakes stopping tons of power and the hiss of steam blowing clouds in the moist winter air. Trains were the circulatory system of Europe in the '70s, like the highways and airports of America, but more beautiful and symbolic of history—not new and shiny, but enduring. Twenty-five years after the end of the war, swastikas were visible beneath layers of paint on the sides of some of the older wooden boxcars, which the Yugoslavs couldn't afford to replace.

Public bathrooms consisted of two metal footprints in the floor with a hole in the middle, and people purchased toilet paper by the sheet. Chickens and other livestock rode on the trams along with their owners, and there was an ordinance against opening tram windows. I don't know whether this rule was law or custom, but I tested it once and was immediately chastised by a tramful of passengers. They believed drafts caused colds, which resulted in death. With the benefit of hindsight, I understand that their medical care system was vastly different from ours, and their citizens commonly died of what Americans would term minor illnesses. This, however, never occurred to me. Having just reached the ripe old age of twenty when I arrived in Zagreb, death was not real to me.

Nestled at the foothills of the Alps, the town of Zagreb had not been damaged by World War II, so it retained its romantic, Old World charm as opposed to other cities throughout Yugoslavia that had been razed during the war, then rebuilt in Stalinist gray-concrete dullness.

In 1970, about half of the women in Zagreb still wore native garb: black skirts, shawls, and scarves with white blouses. In addition, a blood-red embroidered scarf and an apron were commonly worn in the marketplace. Some men wore woven moccasins called *opanci*, which had a curled toe after the Turkish custom, though these were more common in Serbia and Bosnia.

I lived in a three-story house with Josip and Zagorka Kolar, respectively a Hungarian and a Serb, who treated me as if I were their own child. Josip's parents lived downstairs and Zagorka's mother lived upstairs. The house was built near the top of a hill and the architecture was the yellow rococo style that Peter the Great loved. My shutter-encased window looked out onto a scene from a 1940s spy movie. At night, the stone paths were lit with flickering lights that put off a glow not much brighter than gas lamps. I could easily imagine Ingrid Bergman running down the hill, through the mist of the park and into the arms of Humphrey Bogart.

The neighborhood had not changed much since the Austro-Hungarian Empire. In autumn, the trees turned brilliant hues of gold and red, and fallen leaves blanketed the sidewalks. Through gaps between the houses, I could see the spires of an ancient church with its Austrian onion dome, much smaller than the Russian cupolas I'd studied in school. There was a pleasant stillness about the street that stirred thought as I climbed that hill every day after class, writing stories in my head. The cool air was scented with burning wood and coal oil, and at times, the sky was gray with the residue that settled on the snow and in the lungs. There was also the scent of wonderful cuisine—grilling meats, browning onions, baking seeds, and popping corn.

The Kolars' house had many modern conveniences, especially considering that most of the other students boarded in houses where they had to chop wood to heat water for baths, or had no bath at all, which meant they had to use the public baths. The Kolars had a German device that heated water as it came through the shower, which meant that the hot water never ran out. They also had a full kitchen, wood and oil heat for the rest of the house, and even a washing machine. The washer didn't work, so they used it as a hamper to store dirty clothes—which was not unusual in communist countries.

Their attic was filled with treasures. Dried sausages hung from the ceiling, along with strange flags and bouquets of dried flowers. There was a wire dress form, and a multitude of books and storage chests. Zagorka's mother, Baba Mara, took me to the attic and showed me the contents of a chest. In it was her wedding skirt. She had woven the cloth, then stitched it by hand. The trunk also contained her husband's sword. He had been a cavalry officer, killed in one of the many wars between the Serbs and Turks, Germans, Croats, and others.

The harshness of life had aged Baba Mara beyond her years. A woman in her sixties, her back was bent and dark circles ringed her eyes. Her silver hair was always covered with a black scarf. She was soft-spoken and full of stories of her youth. She told me that, when she was growing up, it was not necessary for women to learn mathematics; instead, they learned to weave and to tat lace. She didn't like the shoddy materials that were sold in the stores and boasted that the fabrics she wove herself would last a lifetime. It was a point of pride that she did not need to buy new clothes.

She had a deep fear of Gypsies, communists, and werewolves, speaking of them only in whispers. There was not much I could do about the werewolves or the communists, but I did carry an empty wine bottle in my book bag to smack any Gypsy who might try to carry me off, though none ever did.

The Kolars had a television set, and we gathered as a family to watch various television shows. *Peyton Place* was popular at the time, as was *A Doctor in the House,* a wonderful British comedy about medical students in London.

Soviet television was dreary, and Romanian television was flat-out horrible. Polish television was artfully produced and interesting, if a little heavy. As the Polish language sounds something like a cross between Croatian and Russian, I usually caught the gist of what was going on.

The scholarship program that sponsored my studies included my books and a stipend of $45 per month. By local standards, I was wealthy. I enjoyed shopping in the outdoor food markets and going out for delicious meals that cost just a few pennies.

In the mornings, I strolled down the hill past the small park with weathered wooden and iron benches, to the square where I caught the tram. The scent of freshly baked bread—something I'd never smelled before—wafted into my nostrils, and I often stopped at a bakery to buy a little something for the ride. Each morning when I arrived at the university, I joined my fellow students to sip hot tea with rum before classes, yet another difference from the culture in which I was raised.

One of my fondest memories was the bus tour around Yugoslavia that the school arranged as cultural enrichment for the American students. The trip was a sensual confection. Slovenia was a forested extension of Austria. The Dalmatian coast bore an Italian influence, and I could see deep into its clear water, which was totally unlike the opaque muddy waters I knew from the Texas Gulf.

Serbia was my first glimpse of Stalinist architecture. Much of Serbia had been destroyed by the constant wars. The most recent conquerors had been the Nazis but, before them, the Ottoman Turks had attacked the cities and dug the saints' eyes from frescoes on church walls. Bosnia Herzegovina was the most mysterious of all. Its capital, Sarajevo, was not the modern city that lay in ruins on the evening news in the 1990s; this was pre-earthquake and premodernization for the Winter Olympics. Wooden houses jutted out over the streets in the old Turkish style, with latticed windows that had once shielded the harems from the streets.

I spent a couple of days on Lake Ochrid on the border of Yugoslavia and Albania. The crystal-clear lake looked as if a glacier had dug a hole only to melt into it, and I remember boys catching eels on their fishing lines. In the morning, I stood on a balcony and looked out over the lake toward Albania, and the surface of the water was covered in a brilliant pink mist. But, most of the time I lived in Zagreb, attending classes at the Filozofski Fakultet and riding the tram in the company of chickens, goats, and other livestock.

My biggest challenge when I arrived at Zagreb University's Filozofski Fakultet, was that I had studied only eleven weeks of Croatian language and was expected to study language, literature, history, and government—all in Croatian—on the university level. Classes were difficult at first. Nothing was taught in English. My Romanian class was taught in Croatian, Romanian, and French; unfortunately for me, the textbook had been published in France, thus the text was in Romanian and French. I was at a disadvantage because I had never studied French. In frustration, I dropped my Russian existentialist poetry class; existentialism is hard enough to contemplate in English, though I do love it now. My core classes were literature, history, politics, and the Croatian language.

As enjoyable as it was, Zagreb had a dark side. The more locals I met, the more stories I heard about political arrests and people who kept bags packed under their beds in case the police came for them in the middle of the night. These were stories that weren't told openly, but whispered in confidence when you got to know someone well. I didn't realize that I endangered myself by asking questions or that I endangered anyone who befriended me because I was an American, which automatically made me a bad political influence. Most of the realities of communism went right over my head until my diplomatic stint in Serbia five years later. In 1970, it was all an adventure to me, and danger was the last thing on my mind.

In February 1970, Dick and I married in Zagreb. Our no-frills communist wedding at the Zagreb town hall involved signing a few papers, then having dinner with our landlords, who had become dear friends.

Chapter 2

LOVE, HUMOR, AND OBEY

Love is patient, love is kind. It does not envy, it does not boast, it is
not proud. It is not rude, it is not self-seeking, it is not easily
angered, it keeps no record of wrongs. Love does not delight in evil
but rejoices with the truth. It always protects, always trusts, always
hopes, always perseveres.

Corinthians 13: 4-7
The Bible
New International Version

In June, our scholarship program ended, so Dick and I returned to
Portland, where our son Christopher was born in the fall. When I
went into labor, he decided he was not going to pay for a hospital,
so he dropped me off at the county hospital and went home to sleep. By
that time, the marriage was already beginning to unravel. I had gained
more than eighty pounds during the pregnancy, and Dick no longer
found me attractive. He had been ashamed of the fact that I was pregnant and chided me to "hold in my stomach." Also, his temper had
turned violent. Anything could set him off. He once kicked a cabinet
door off its hinges because he was peeling a hard-boiled egg and pieces
of the white were coming off along with the shell.

I could no longer make him laugh, and we fought all the time. Those
were terrible days, and the moment my son was born, I began to diet,
thinking that would make things better. Within four months I weighed

113 pounds, down from over 200. I had become anorexic and didn't even eat every week. The result was most unexpected: Dick became jealous of every man who even smiled at me, even grocery clerks who wished me a nice day. And the violence continued. If I didn't please him in bed, he slammed his fist down next to my head, and one night as we lay in bed he put his fist through the wall over my head because Christopher was crying in the next room.

In 1972, Dick became a U.S. Foreign Service officer and we moved from Portland, Oregon, to Washington, D.C. Life at home had become bizarre. Dick launched into tirades if he found I'd left the apartment. He claimed he was afraid that something would happen to me and said he didn't want me crossing streets by myself. Although he never hit me, he would pin me up against walls, throw things, break things, and punch the pillow beside my face. Life had become frightening.

My life with Dick was the beginning of my decades-long affliction: posttraumatic stress disorder or PTSD, known to most people as the flashback syndrome that many war veterans experience. It can occur from experiencing any event the victim perceives as life threatening, including natural disasters, violent assaults, rape, or surviving an accident or hurricane.

The PTSD sufferer relives the frightening experience through nightmares and flashbacks, has difficulty sleeping, and feels detached from the rest of the world. Emotional numbing is a common characteristic.

Still, in 1972, I stood up to Dick's protests and entered a graduate program in international relations and law at American University. By the second semester I was pregnant again. Our daughter Kendra was born in Falls Church, Virginia, while Dick was training at the State Department. When Dick arrived at the hospital, he told me that he had not wanted to leave class but his instructor had insisted. I was not amused.

Two months later, we were transferred to the embassy in Belgrade where Dick was to serve as vice consul. Though I enjoyed the diplomatic life immensely, there was little happiness at home. Dick spent his days and nights at work, and we hired a housekeeper to take care of the children. It seemed like such a luxury, but the result was that nobody needed me.

Belgrade was very different from Zagreb. Substantially damaged by the war, it had been rebuilt in a Soviet prefabricated block style that was devoid of character. The city was so heavily polluted in 1975 that the Yugoslav government admitted that living in Belgrade was as harmful as smoking two packages of cigarettes a day. The snows were streaked in hues of gray and black from the coal oil used to heat the buildings, and the streets were congested with cars. Politically, it had a more restrictive atmosphere than did Zagreb. I once entered a street where a soldier, who stood there with AK47 poised, told me I was not allowed. Believe me, he looked so serious that I beat a hasty retreat.

I had hoped to finish graduate school in Belgrade but, for some unknown reason, the embassy wouldn't allow wives to attend school at that time. I landed a job with the Fulbright Commission as a bilingual secretary, but the embassy also frowned on wives working outside the embassy, and I had to resign.

To entertain myself, I wandered the shopping areas for hours, but because it was a communist state, the stores offered virtually identical wares. Nothing but the open-air markets offered anything interesting, so almost every day I rode the trolley through the gray, pollution-drenched city past its expressionless postwar concrete buildings that were interspersed with ornate historic structures, hinting at the beauty that once was.

When at last I stepped down onto one of the town's many squares, I entered a world filled with crowds of shoppers, who elbowed their way to the vendor rather than stand in lines. But the sight was worth it. Tables overflowed with potatoes and other vegetables. Scattered about were splashes of color from rich red cherries, flowers, and yellow squash, but the fly-speckled, butchered animals that hung by their feet above the wooden vendor tables were a little hard to take. My purchases were wrapped in newspaper, and the chickens I bought for dinner still had feet. What is more, all their internal parts were intact.

Under the communist system, the public was allowed to ride the horses that raced at the track, and I took advantage of this communist perk. I would have never been able to ride horses of that caliber any-where else. When the weather got cold, I tried ice skating, but I was so clumsy that I bruised my protruding pelvic bones repeatedly and my doctor advised me to stop before I caused a serous hematoma. The high point of my week was a Polish television show called *Janošek,* which was about a Polish Robin Hood and starred a popular actor. All the ladies at the embassy "coffee" were abuzz the day after *Janošek* had removed his shirt on TV.

Speaking of embassy coffees, there wasn't much coffee served at those soirees. It was usually alcohol. I wasn't used to the amount of alcohol consumed on the diplomatic circuit, and it wasn't exactly what an already depressed woman needed. Not surprisingly, I spoke much better Serbian with a couple of glasses of wine under my belt, because I lost my inhibitions and my fear of making mistakes in the language. As a result, I took to the cocktail party circuit as if it were my life's ambition ful-filled. Finally, here was something Dick thought I could do well—dress up, munch hors d'oeuvres, drink, and make small talk with strangers in another language.

Everyone overdid the alcohol at the embassy parties. One British cav-alry officer had to be asked to remove his spurs at a black-tie affair. Feeling no pain and moving with boundless enthusiasm, he had spurred the other dancers as he'd spun his wife around the floor.

Then there were the dreaded congressional junkets. When a group from the Hill visited the embassy, all work stopped, and we became their hosts. One well-known congressman stayed drunk for his entire visit. He was quite a bit shorter than I and swayed back and forth toward me as we spoke. After a while, the sways became more pronounced and his nose came dangerously close to my sternum. This was due partly to his height and partly to the fact that he was directing all of his comments to my chest instead of my face. Just as I was fearing he would collapse into my décolletage, his aide, who'd probably seen this act before, dragged him away.

The following night at a state banquet, the same congressman sat, or rather slumped, in a chair next to Josip Broz Tito, premier of Yugoslavia.

When the congressman got up to speak (the getting-up part wasn't easy), he made a show of discarding his notes to speak extemporaneously. What a catastrophic idea! He opened by saying how glad he was to be in Czechoslovakia and ended with the toast, "Ziveo Tito, son of Croatia!"

Though he was born in Croatia, Tito had devoted himself completely to being a Yugoslav—not a Croatian—in order to unite his country into one ethnic identity. The congressman's toast was a dire insult, and as we've seen in recent years, ethnic slurs in the Balkans are not taken lightly, in fact historically they have been grounds for killing. He might as well have slapped the premier across the face—along with that of every other Yugoslav in the room.

On that same junket, the congressional wives visited the Yugoslav national museum. One of them got the idea that she could get a bargain on art and asked her host if there were any items in the museum priced under $10. This was the Yugoslav equivalent of the Smithsonian, and there was no gift shop. Again, the Yugoslav hosts were deeply affronted.

Believe me, when the wheels tucked into the belly of the plane that flew that group out of Belgrade, the entire embassy breathed a sigh of relief.

In January 1976, after months of shouting matches, accusations, threats, and tears, I told Dick I was taking the children and leaving him. Although he verbally agreed to the split, he did not return my passport, which was locked in an embassy safe, and no homebound plane tickets materialized. Without money of my own and official identification, it was impossible for us to reenter America.

We put on a smiling face in public, but the arguments continued behind closed doors. Eventually, I figured out the game: Divorce was bad for Dick's career, so he'd decided to stonewall and keep me there to host his parties.

Trapped and a little scared, I began making a pest of myself at embassy functions, an even larger threat to his career. One night at a party, Dick and I got into a major fight after a tequila shot-drinking contest with several Marine guards. Dick wanted to go home and I didn't. Alcohol had made me bold and, after a few harsh exchanges, Dick chased me out into the center of the embassy compound where there was a playground. I scurried to the top of the children's slide and managed to remove one of my boots before he reached me. Each time he grabbed for me, I whacked him with my boot. Naturally, we were the talk of the embassy for days afterward; but within days, the passport and plane tickets were in my hands.

Soon, I was back home in Dallas, alone with my children, with no job and $120 per month in child support. I was confident I could get a job—a good job. I foolishly thought I had something of value to bring to the job market—interpreter-level proficiency in an esoteric Slavic language, Serbo-Croatian. My college counselor had insisted it was a unique skill, and she was right. My talents were so unique that I ended up waiting tables in a steak house. One thing was clear: however difficult it might be to find the right job, I had to do it.

Nothing if not persistent, I phoned every federal agency I thought might need a Serbo-Croatian interpreter. The Department of State, CIA, and FBI were the only agencies that seemed even to know what Serbo-Croatian was. The State Department tested only one day per year in Dallas, and I'd just missed it. The CIA said they'd send me an application, but I'd applied there once before, and they had told me they wouldn't accept an application from a woman who didn't have a master's degree, even though they didn't hold men to the same standard. The agent who answered the phone at the FBI was enthusiastic, made me laugh, and was duly impressed when I described my language skills. I was intrigued when he told me the Bureau's jurisdiction included counterintelligence and counterterrorism. Up until then, I'd thought that was the CIA's responsibility. At the time, Croatians and Serbs were wanted coast to coast for bombings, murders, and kidnappings. My Serbo-Croatian skills were about to pay off.

I took all the required tests, then waited for a year, during which time the FBI conducted a routine background check to find out, among other things, why a nice girl from Texas had gone to communist (or as Hoover pronounced it, "commonist") Croatia on a scholarship to study the language, then back again later to Serbia as the wife of a U.S. Foreign Service officer. To my surprise, they called me in to report a delay, courtesy of my estranged spouse.

Dick and I were legally separated but hadn't filed for divorce. I had two good reasons: I didn't have the money to cover my legal costs, and Dick was thousands of miles away in Yugoslavia—out of sight, out of mind. I was too tired to do anything but work and take care of my children; and at that point, dating was of no interest to me. So, becoming Dick's first ex-wife was way down on my list of priorities.

Imagine my surprise when the FBI recruiter said something had come up during my security background check. Dick had informed them I was only looking for a summer job and would return to him in Belgrade in the fall.

Stifling my anger, I calmly explained that his story was not true—that, in fact, it was Dick's attempt to sabotage my chance to become an FBI agent. My protests fell on deaf ears. The FBI recruiter insisted that I submit proof that the divorce was final before the Bureau would process my application. I immediately filed but, by the time my divorce was awarded, the FBI was in a hiring freeze.

Having no idea when the freeze would end, and not really knowing whether I'd be hired anyway, I pondered my future. I considered careers where I might be successful and fields that offered me a chance to fulfill my desire to serve humanity while supporting my children at a point somewhere above the poverty level. I had always respected law enforcement, but I'd never even talked to a law enforcement officer, other than the FBI recruiter. In fact, my only indirect connection to a police officer was a former classmate, the son of J. D. Tippett, the Dallas police officer killed by Lee Harvey Oswald on November 22, 1963, the same day my inspiration, John F. Kennedy, was assassinated.

Perhaps the FBI application process gave me the push I needed to ditch my dream of a career in foreign languages and apply instead to the Dallas Police Department. During the police department testing and background verification process, I found an interim job teaching Russian at a private school. As it turned out, I actually taught physical education and answered phones instead, because there weren't enough interested students to make up a Russian class.

Nearly eighteen months had slogged by since I'd applied to the Bureau. The recruiter phoned intermittently to give me status reports on the hiring freeze and to request that I take more tests, since the Bureau had changed its entrance exams, but then I was called for The Big Interview at the Dallas Police Department. When the chief of police asked me whether I'd quit the police department to work for the Bureau, I admitted that I would. After all, the police department would pay me $14,000 to ride around in a patrol car alone on night shift, with a helmet and nightstick. The Bureau would pay $20,000, and it was predominantly a day job: I could actually see my children while they were awake.

"How long ago did you apply to the FBI?" he asked.

"It's been almost a year and a half, but they have a hiring freeze."

He shot me a patronizing smile and waved off my hopeful tone. I was hired.

A couple of months later—the same day my police uniform arrived—I received a letter offering me an appointment to the FBI Academy. The Dallas police sergeant who led my training class said that if I took the FBI job and failed, I'd never work in law enforcement in Texas again. Nonetheless, I burned that first bridge and accepted the chance to become an FBI agent.

There was a slight problem, though. I had no one to take care of Christopher, six, or Kendra, two, for the fifteen weeks I'd be in the FBI Academy. The Bureau wouldn't allow them to live with me at the academy nor permit me to live off-campus with them. I had no choice but to send them to stay with their father at the embassy in Belgrade and then practically push an ancient Toyota Corolla from Texas to Washington, D.C. I had no idea what awaited me there, but I was ready for my exciting new life to begin.

Chapter 3

WELCOME TO THE FBI

Keep a journal. You'll want to remember every bit of this.

**Supervisory Special Agent Livio "Al" Beccaccio's advice to me
in the FBI Academy**

On October 3, 1977, I arrived at the J. Edgar Hoover Building, where I raised my right hand and swore:

I will support and defend the Constitution of the United States against all enemies, foreign and domestic; that I will bear true faith and allegiance to the same; that I take this obligation freely, without any mental reservation or purpose of evasion; and that I will well and faithfully discharge the duties of the office on which I am about to enter. So help me God.

With that, I became the ninety-sixth woman to be sworn in as a special agent of the FBI. In my hands I held badge number 5655, and only the academy stood between me and the credentials that would allow me to carry a gun and make arrests. The dizzying pace had begun.

Still, even on that first day, there were signs of a huge discrepancy in the Bureau's reputation for efficiency and order and the way it conducted business. For example, when my class arrived at the J. Edgar Hoover Building, the guard wouldn't let us in. No one had told him that a new agents' class was starting, and when he asked to see acceptance letters, nobody had one. Ours was the first class of agents in more than a year, four women and seventeen men chosen from a pool of more than four thousand applicants, and the FBI had not sent out one acceptance letter on time. This was a hint of the inefficiencies in paperwork and accounting that existed in an organization that had built its reputation on attention to detail. In June 2001, Attorney General John Ashcroft described "massive holes in the FBI's command structure and in its record-keeping capabilities . . . " But on that fall day in '77, I had no idea of this as I waited to enter the J. Edgar Hoover Building.

Finally, our growing crowd of nervous recruits finally prompted the guard to make a call to the inner sanctum. Minutes later, a dark-suited man arrived and herded us into a hall featuring a massive oil portrait of a scowling J. Edgar Hoover. His eyes seemed to follow me into the auditorium where we were sworn in.

After the oath, there were a couple of speakers, but I remember only the announcement that a bus was waiting to take us to the FBI Academy on the Marine Corps base in Quantico, Virginia, thirty miles south of Washington. The recruiter in Dallas has never mentioned that I should be prepared to get on a bus immediately after the ceremony, so I had to cab it back to the State Department to pick up my belongings and my car. The bus left without me.

The agonizing trip through D.C. traffic was followed by a long haul down I-95 to Quantico. When I arrived at the academy, there were no parking spaces, so I left my car at the edge of the circular drive in front of the administration building. When I burst through the door, my class counselor, Livio "Al" Beccaccio stood before me, his arms crossed over his chest. Looking up into the stern face of this handsome, silver-haired former Marine who towered above me at about six feet, three inches, I was at a loss for words. Once an All-American in baseball at Florida State, he looked like a professional athlete in an impeccably tailored suit. Though he also looked like he could wipe up the floor with me, something about him hinted he was more amused than angered by my actions.

Shaking his head, he said he appreciated my desire to get started right away, but I'd better move the car or it would be towed. My classmates had been forced to wait for me, and they looked duly horrified. I had committed my first Bureau faux pas.

Years later, as a supervisory special agent (SSA), I attended a management training course during which all SSA participants completed a battery of psychological tests. The psychologist explained the results: The largest groups of supervisors fell into two major categories, "dominant" and "conscientious," with a third category, "steady," close behind. These groups are variations of iron-fisted, meticulous, and dependably conservative personalites. Put those traits together and they spell "J. Edgar Hoover." I tested as an "influencer." The psychologist described influencers as the small group of artsy types who drove the people in the other groups nuts. The parking incident was one demonstration of my influencer's ability to adapt and improvise, which the other groups typically perceived as taking risks.

My first official day as an agent was a blur. My classmates and I were swept through the induction procedures and then issued sheets, towels, gym uniforms, the FBI Academy rulebook, a multi-volume *Manual of Investigative and Operational Guidelines* (MIOG), and the *Manual of Administrative and Operational Procedures* (MAOP). We were instructed to stand against a wall while mug shots were snapped, producing the photos we would carry in our credentials for years. Then we were informed that class would begin promptly at eight o'clock each morning. Physical challenges and other exercises would often continue into the evening, and there would be an abundance of class materials to study each night.

The men's and women's suites were located on the same hall, close quarters for people under stress and an unfamiliar situation at a time when there were no co-ed college dorms or women on Navy ships. Roommates were issued alphabetically, except for the women. At that time, the Bureau hired a maximum of four women per class, if the class contained women at all. I've always suspected that this hiring decision was based on the simple fact that the rooms were suites for two that shared a bathroom with the suite next door.

My roommate was Pamela, an auburn-haired math whiz and Army brat. In our conjoining suite were two women from Valdosta, Georgia. Jean was a petite, soft-spoken high school teacher, who had learned about the FBI from a school career-day recruiter; and Betty was a former police officer, who was slender and about five feet, nine inches tall, with flaming red hair.

Al Beccaccio kept us moving that first day, and we obeyed his commands in awe. He was every bit the idyllic FBI agent, and we instinctively knew he was the one to emulate.

We walked down the winding halls of the academy, which agents call "the gerbil cage," clutching our bed linens and books in front of us like a bunch of college freshmen. As we hurried along, I studied the self-assured faces of in-service agents and cops who passed by, thinking someday that would be me.

That first night I lay in bed, staring at the ceiling of a room the size of a monk's cell. I had to be in class by eight the next morning, and I feared waking up at noon, alarm clock cradled in my arms with the ringer turned off, as I had done so many times in college. I also missed my children. We'd never spent a night apart until I headed for the academy. I assured myself that in only a few weeks we would be reunited, and that if I excelled and became a special agent, my little family would be set. This goal, which was so clear at the time, seemed worth any price. But I had no idea what I would ask my children to sacrifice over the next thirteen years, nor the personal price I'd pay.

After two weeks at the academy, I received a letter from my ex-husband, instructing me to immediately fly to Belgrade and pick up the children. "They are restricting my professional mobility," he wrote, adding that he'd been forced to hire a second housekeeper, as well as a chauffeur, to manage them. He said he was tired when he got home from work and these two "demanding children" didn't "understand" his problems.

Of course, there was no way I could retrieve them and keep my job. But, while I knew I had to look at our long-term future, every dream I'd had of Chris and Kendra spending quality time with their father evaporated. In its place grew a nagging guilt that I had failed them in some way, and I counted the days until we'd been reunited. I took solace in the fact that I'd never seen Dick be abusive to the children, yet I knew him too well to feel completely at ease about the time they were spending with him.

Chapter 4

LIFE AT THE ACADEMY

We are potentially the most dangerous agency in the country if we
are not scrutinized carefully.

Louis Freeh
"The Activities of the Federal Bureau of Investigation, Part II," House of
Representatives, Subcommittee on Crime, Committee on the Judiciary,
Thursday, June 5, 1997

F ive days after my appointment to the FBI, five days filled with
the panic of sending my children to Yugoslavia, packing everything I owned into a battered old car with more than 150,000
miles on the odometer, and driving from Texas to Washington, D.C., I
awoke at the FBI Academy on the U.S. Marine Corps base in Quantico,
Virginia. I'd been sworn in as a member of New Agents Class (NAC)
78-1—the first new agents' class that would graduate in 1978—and,
except for missing my children, I felt great. I was strong. I was independent. I was woman, hear me roar . . . or so I told myself.

That period at the academy was the only time in my adult life that
I'd lived without the responsibilities of my children. Christopher was
born in the fall of my senior year in college. Kendra arrived during my
second semester of graduate school. Despite the relief of being in school
without morning sickness or 2 a.m. feedings, keeping pace with new
agent training was like drinking cola from a full-open fire hose.

In 1977, the academy was actually two schools in one: the FBI and

National Academies. The National Academy provides senior executive training for U.S. and international law enforcement officers. Today, the Drug Enforcement Administration (DEA) also trains there, and the campus is vastly expanded; but in 1977 it consisted of only two dormitory buildings, a cafeteria, gym, swimming pool, library, chapel, auditorium, and some administrative offices. Outside was Hoover Road, where the agents-in-training ran every day. At the end of each run we had to hurl ourselves straight up a hill and climb ropes, sometimes hauling rifles on our backs. There was an obstacle course, as well as indoor and outdoor firearms ranges, plus skeet and rifle ranges. In this high-energy atmosphere, we dined to the booming sounds of nearby Marine artillery that rattled the cafeteria windows.

Days were crammed with legal, administrative, and criminal psychology classes, interspersed with physical training and target practice. Wearing conservative business attire, we sat alphabetically in class. While mental and physical stress was a mainstay of the program, there was no military-style marching in lines or standing at attention shouting, "Yes, sir!"

This was our indoctrination into the Bureau system—the clean, honest, and strict system of G-men. There had been a few changes in the years since Hoover had passed the baton. Men in the FBI were no longer restricted to a uniform of white shirts, white handkerchief in the suit pocket, wing-tip shoes, and snap-brimmed hats. By the mid-'70s, conservative navy blue blazers and gray slacks had become the typical FBI instructor's attire.

Al Beccaccio set the pace for the class. A great coach, Al insisted that we be the best class the academy had ever seen. He had ordered royal blue polyester gym uniforms for us, while the other classes, who began pouring in six weeks after we arrived, wore cotton. The cotton was undoubtedly more comfortable, but as Al said as he passed out the suits, "NAC 78-1 wins, but they don't show sweat."

Al always jogged out in front of the class, no matter how long the run or how good the runners. He encouraged us, corrected us, and made us want to be like him. Most of all, he made us want to be a part of the organization he called "the Bureau family."

Al believed that each person had something to contribute to the team and challenged us to use diversity to our advantage. Being accepted as part of the team—as one of the guys—is vital in law enforcement. Gradually, I was drawn in by the Bureau mystique, and I wanted to be part of the tradition, one of law enforcement's finest. And I began to believe that, not only could I be an agent, I could be one of the best. That was the mark Al left on each of us.

But Al was our class counselor and not one of our instructors. Sadly, as I was to learn, the instructors were not all Al Beccaccios. Virtually all-powerful, the instructors held our careers in their hands, and every word they uttered was significant, if sometimes disappointing. One speaker came in to lecture on undercover operations. Enthralled, I asked: "You've only talked about what men have done undercover. What operations have women been involved in?"

The cool, collected man twitched slightly and tugged at the knot of his tie. "Well, sometimes we use women as window dressing. It's not a bad idea to walk in with a doll on your arm. But you gotta tell her to take a powder when the business talk starts."

Other speakers felt free to tell dirty jokes, and it was not uncommon for them to preface these with, "I wouldn't usually say this around ladies, but since they want to work with us, they'll have to learn to live with it."

Those simple words spotlighted the women, separating us from our male counterparts and hinting that the men were free to say whatever they wished, and we would just have to bear it for the privilege of being in their workplace. More than that, it seemed that the purpose of the comment was to let us know that, as women in a male-dominated world, we would not be regarded with respect. Management—our trainers—had set the tone, a tone that had been passed from generation to generation through the academy.

The FBI Academy introduced me to many new topics, and one of them was dealing with rude male colleagues. While most of my instructors and classmates were complete gentlemen, a number of experienced agents, who had returned to the academy for in-service training, behaved like sexual predators.

The academy was my first taste of living in a fishbowl. The three other women recruits and I were surrounded by more than four hundred men, many of whom made passes. We couldn't sit down to a meal or walk down the hall without someone leering at us or inviting us for a drink after class, something for which we had no time or desire. They degraded us with their assumptions and, when they spoke to us, their eyes rested on our bodies, not our faces.

At the time, I thought these men were abnormal. What I didn't understand was that many men with whom I would work over the next thirteen years had also decided that women in law enforcement were either promiscuous or objects to intimidate. We were not individuals, and we were not law enforcement professionals. In their eyes, we were nameless entities who had foisted ourselves on their all-male playground, and they wanted us to pay a price for the privilege. The attitudes of these belligerent suitors/coworkers contributed to an atmosphere that declared, "If you want to work at a man's job, you'd better give up all expectations of being treated like a lady." Being from Texas, I knew something about snakes. These guys weren't like Texas copperheads that strike if stepped on; they were more like water moccasins that chase you for the sport of it.

A few instructors tested whether we would get insulted or cry if they berated us. One firearms instructor regularly stood behind me bellowing threats as I tried to concentrate on my target. He swore that, if I stuck out my rear end when I crouched into the combat shooting position, he would grab it. Since the secret of good shooting is concentration and since he knew I'd be distracted whenever he was behind me, I felt certain he wanted to sabotage my performance. With a wry smile, another firearms instructor told our class that the easy way to feel the holes in the gun cylinder when we loaded in rounds was to think of female genitals and pretend there was hair around the holes.

The majority of my male classmates were nice men, many of them were attorneys or ex-cops. Older and more laid-back than the average boot-camp recruits, the class was educated and highly competitive. A grade of 84 in an academic subject was a failure; two failures and you were out. Those who failed disappeared during the lunch hour. We never knew they were going, nor did we have a chance to say good-bye. We'd come back from lunch and find that the name tags on the desks had been rearranged, and the instructor would announce, "Mr. So-and-So is no longer with us," and that was it. By the time we got back to the dormitory, no trace of our former classmate remained.

The career of an agent was even more tenuous in Hoover's day. Agents who stood out from the crowd ran the risk of being dismissed, and, because of that, it was important not to attract attention to one's self. At the end of training school, it is the tradition that agents visit FBI headquarters, where they shake the director's hand. When Hoover was alive, that could be the last day an agent was on duty. If Hoover didn't like the way a new agent looked or something a new agent said, he would have him fired.

A story circulated that, as one new agents' class left the director's office, Hoover called the counselor aside and said, "Get rid of the pin-head." When the class got back to the academy, the instructors measured the head of each man in the class. To be safe, they fired the two with the smallest heads.

Our most stringent class was in federal law. Instructors emphasized that understanding law, especially what it takes to build a successful prosecution, set FBI agents apart from other investigators. As many widely publicized cases have shown, getting a case through the court system requires careful preparation. Agents who conduct their investigations as we were taught in the academy, without cutting corners, compile and present evidence appropriately. But sometimes the FBI screws up. For example, the law requires that the prosecution give the defense team any evidence that could clear the defendant. Sharing exculpatory evidence with the defense is basic legal procedure 101. The execution of confessed Oklahoma City bomber Timothy McVeigh was delayed when the FBI discovered that, due to document inventory mistakes, administrative screwups and field offices' failure to provide all documents to the task force, the Bureau had neglected to provide more than one thousand exculpatory documents for trial. The great cataloger J. Edgar Hoover must have been spinning in his grave over that blunder.

Strangely, the agent who confirmed this oversight in March 2001, did not report the problem to headquarters until May 7, 2001. He claimed that he planned to report the problem, but only after he determined the scope of it. This fear of admitting a mistake is widespread in the Bureau, although it was something I did not encounter until I hit the field. Unfortunately, it's a fear that tends to stalemate agents, leaving them incapable of making decisions or taking action. This was especially true of the agents who had served under Hoover. Fear has remained part of the FBI culture, and the result is that small blunders and simple over-sights easily fester into catastrophes.

Aside from in-depth legal instruction, our courses didn't attempt to make us the all-knowing investigators that Hollywood has invented. In fact, we only touched lightly on topics the public believes all investiga-tors know well. We received a single day of training on fingerprint iden-tification and conducting crime scene searches. We were told we could rely on specialists for these services in the field, but of course, I never met any such experts in a field office. Other courses included firearms, defensive tactics, field office administration (FBI communications), photography, and criminal psychology (my favorite). We had no training in felony car stops (stopping cars driven by criminals wanted for felonies, often after high-speed chases).

While learning to write FBI communications, we were introduced to FBI teletype language. There were no computer systems in the field when I joined the Bureau, nor were all field offices hooked into the FBI computer communications network when I resigned in 1990. Teletypes, therefore, were the fastest means of communication. In Hoover's day, Western Union charged the Bureau for each word in a teletype message, so a unique Bureau teletype language developed over the years to cut down on the number of words and save money. This new language com-bined words, such as "regarding my letter," into "remylet," giving the Bureau three words for the price of one.

Defensive tactics and physical fitness programs form a cornerstone of the FBI's mythical image of perfection, but for the most part, the tactics we learned had been around since the great man himself. Instruction focused on boxing, wrestling, and fancy "come-along holds" that only a magician with a highly cooperative arrestee could execute. This training was basically for show and not at all useful in real-life situations.

Physical fitness training was intense, challenging, and used as a tool to weed out candidates who couldn't make the grade. Physical standards were tough, but we only lost one classmate because of them—a man was booted out about halfway through the course when it became clear he would never pass the physical tests.

Interestingly, until just before I entered the Bureau, there was no forced retirement age for agents, nor physical testing for on-duty agents. Some agents stayed on the job into their seventies, and a few, including Hoover's best friend, heir, and confidant Clyde Tolson, actually tottered around with canes. By the early 1980s, annual physical testing for on-duty agents was mandated as a result of a 1970s class action suit brought by female agent personnel. The suit contended, among other things, that the physical standards upon which the Bureau dismissed people from the academy were not relevant to what agents encountered in the field.

For most of us, physical training and defensive tactics were the only tension relievers in the new agents' training program. I was in good physical shape by any standard and was a faster runner than many men. I had an advantage over some of my classmates, because I had competed in sports since the age of eight. As a child, I had competed on an Amateur Athletic Union swimming team for six years and was used to daily, sometimes twice-daily workouts that left me exhausted but knowing I could get up and do it all again the next day. Later, while attending college in Croatia, I was privileged to work out with the Croatian national youth fencing team, some of the best fencers in the world. My skills were not comparable to theirs, but I hurled myself at my opponents with such exuberance that the coach allowed me stay on, probably for his own amusement.

Those of my academy classmates who had never competed in sports did not know how to break their challenges into chunks that were small enough to conquer mentally or physically. This made the physical requirements seem almost insurmountable to them.

The training I received in the boxing ring offered me my first glimpse of the bureaucracy's tendency to overreact to an edict from FBI headquarters. The most famous overreaction story was that Hoover once scribbled "Watch the borders" on a memo that was passed to managers beneath him. Agents were immediately dispatched to the borders of the United States, when in fact it was a note to the secretary that she'd typed into the margins. Sure, it didn't make sense to dispatch the agents, but no one had the guts to ask the man what he meant because his disapproval could result in career-crushing punishment.

What happened in my class was equally ridiculous. A woman at the FBI's Washington field office, located in Anacostia in southeast Washington, D.C., had been robbed just before our class started. She was badly beaten and, sin of mortal sins, her credentials and gun had been stolen. This caused FBI headquarters to deduce that women were not accustomed to being hit in the face, so in order to "keep us safe," they made sure that our faces were pounded on a regular basis.

The face masks we wore for sparring were sized for men. Even the smallest mask was far too big for any of the women. You'd think that after five years of training women, the academy would have acquired protective equipment that fit us. However, the face masks we used were much too roomy and stood away from our faces, causing these so-called protective devices to become weapons against us. Every time an opponent landed a blow, the leather-covered metal mask flew back against our faces or teeth. It would have been safer to let the men hit us with their gloves. I still sport a cracked front tooth, which I acquired courtesy of a good punch that landed in the center of my facial "protective" equipment. Of course, each class of women had their own crosses to bear. In the early '70s, women trainees had to qualify with shorter-barreled guns than the men, a distinct disadvantage in accuracy.

What I objected to the most in defensive tactics training was the lack of instruction that would help counter a size disadvantage. Boxing and wrestling are the last things a smaller person should employ to fight off a large, strong opponent, and precision finger- and arm-twisting takedown or come-along holds assume a measure of control over the situation from the beginning. We learned none of the practical tricks that were taught in the police academy, such as if someone has your arms pinned to your sides, spit in his face and he will likely release your arms to wipe it off. One thing I knew by the time I graduated from the FBI Academy was that, if a big man got the drop on me, I'd better shoot him or get the hell out of there.

Time and experience have taught me that the real skill in law enforcement is not fighting: it's controlling a situation before it escalates to a physical confrontation. That is where women often outshine men, and it is something I wish we'd studied at the academy. This was an example of the Bureau's refusal to leverage the talents that women might offer.

Firearms training taught me more about the Bureau's culture than I wanted to know. The emphasis was on sameness in duty functions (except for the constant barrage of sexist remarks) and the way things had always been done. Blessedly, it is one area in which the Bureau has made substantial improvement. For example, there was no opportunity to simulate arrest situations, as is now available in the academy's mock city. Known as Hogan's Alley, the pseudo-city allows agents-in-training to experience what it would be like to chase a suspect up flights of stairs, be in the line of fire, and use a car as cover in a gun battle. My classmates and I didn't even move with our weapons, except to run down the firing lanes, though we did get one afternoon of shooting at an electronic "running man" target that zipped back and forth along a track. We trained with revolvers instead of automatic handguns because the prevailing opinion in the Bureau was that automatic weapons were unreliable since they can jam.

Firearms qualifications required proficiency with shotguns, rifles, M16s, and .38 revolvers. We were required to qualify with the .38 using each hand with a minimally acceptable score of 75 out of 100. With the exception of a few rounds in two positions on the course, the two-handed grip would not be allowed for years, although single-handed shooting requires much more skill, and for most shooters, is less accurate. With two-handed shooting, the aim is more predictable, which is what a shooter needs when there is no time to think and he or she must react on instinct. The two-handed grip also reinforces the strength of the weaker hand. When both arms are extended straight out in front of the body, the shooter will aim at the same place each time, and that place is basically wherever the chest is pointed. It is a simple, mechanical, and reliable aim. The Bureau did not institute two-handed qualifications for the field until the early 1980s. We were held to the Bureau's high qualification standards and told that we must shoot as well with one hand as other law enforcement officers did with two. Despite our logical protests about the accuracy of two-handed shooting, the instructors informed us that it was "not the Bureau way."

Shooting practice could be painful because my hands are small and bony, and the handle of the gun kicked back into my thumb each time I fired. Sometimes the gun handle rubbed skin off around my thumb, causing blood to trickle down my hand; and I often had visible subdermal hemorrhages in the webbing. To top it off, during one round of qualifications, a firearms instructor who had bullied many members of the class, followed me down the lane screaming, "Concentrate!" and grabbed the gun out of my hand to change my grip, which of course made concentration impossible. Fortunately, another firearms instructor called me and one other woman aside and took us to another range where we could actually concentrate.

Our final firearms qualifications were held outdoors during the blizzard of January 1978. Like a scene out of *Doctor Zhivago*, it was so cold that the man in the lane next to mine had icicles hanging from his thick, black eyebrows and beard.

One of my suitemates graduated with a patch on one eye and a cast on one leg. She'd been in the lane next to mine on a day when we shot hundreds of rounds. My gun built up lead deposits and was spitting lead with each shot. One of these pieces embedded in her eye, despite the fact that she was wearing eye protection. She ended up traveling to the hospital to have it removed and returned with an eye patch. Later, she broke her foot in the final two-mile run but managed to finish the course within qualifying time. The class fondly nicknamed her "the FBI poster girl." We all agreed that she showed more guts than anyone by running on that broken foot.

Because my class included some of the first women to become agents, we received a lot of media attention. One day when a national news station was filming our physical training, I was asked to demonstrate climbing a rope that hung from the gym ceiling. I was chosen because this had never been a problem for me, but on that particular morning, I happened to have put lotion on my hands.

I wrapped the rope around my foot and started the climb. Clasping the rope between my legs, I drew my legs up to a fetal position, then straightened them as I continued to grip the rope with my rubber-soled shoes. This move raised me about a body's length higher up the rope, and normally, repeating this process six or seven times took me to the gym ceiling. But on this day, I lost ground with each handhold, sliding down instead of pushing up. After slipping to the ground, I tried wiping my hands on my gym uniform, but the polyester didn't absorb the lotion, and my second attempt failed miserably, as well. Some of my male classmates were obviously irritated by the attention that the media gave the female recruits and believed we garnered some nebulous benefit from the extra attention. But, making a fool of myself on national news was no privilege.

I cried when I graduated from the academy, a place that had worked us so hard for fifteen weeks. I was leaving friends who had become family but was heading for my first field assignment with high hopes and tremendous enthusiasm. I was prepared to face whatever law enforcement threw at me.

My class had lost three men, but all four women graduated. Three years later, there were three of us left; six years after that, I was the lone survivor.

On September 17, 1997, a United Nations helicopter that transported twelve international officials on a peace mission in central Bosnia crashed into a fog-enshrouded mountain, killing all aboard. Passengers included Livio A. Beccaccio, then senior advisor to the deputy commissioner to the United Nations International Police Task Force.

I miss you, Al.

Chapter 5

MY FIRST FIELD ASSIGNMENT

The revolution is made by man, but man must forge his revolutionary spirit from day to day.

Che Guevara
Socialism and Man in Cuba

According to Bureau legend, there's a room at FBI headquarters where they keep a dart-throwing ape and a wall-sized map. Just before each new agents' class graduates, they give the ape a handful of darts with the new agents' names attached, and the ape throws the darts at the map. And that's the true story of how new agent field office assignments are determined. At least that's what I've been told.

As new agents' training nears the end, each graduating agent submits a list of three offices where they'd like to be assigned. On the day that our class assignments were revealed, we each received an envelope. One by one we stood before the class, told everyone our first choice, then opened the envelope and read the assignment. There was a contest to see who got the farthest from their chosen office. I came in second: I'd requested Washington, D.C. and was assigned to San Francisco; the guy who beat me had requested Albany but got San Diego.

Actually, it was immaterial to me where I was going. I was just happy that I had graduated from the FBI Academy; besides, it was all an adventure to me. I had a new badge, a new gun, and credentials signed by

Attorney General Griffen Bell, and I would forevermore bear the title of special agent of the FBI. So in February 1978, I hopped into my old Toyota and headed toward the City by the Bay.

Dick dropped the children off at my hotel the morning after I arrived in San Francisco and announced that he had to catch a plane right away. With that he left, and I had to call the office and tell them I couldn't report to work for a day or two until I could make arrangements for the children.

When I made it to the office two days later, I learned that I'd been assigned to the fugitive, military deserter, and background investigation squad. Apparently, no one was certain what to do with me. I was the fourth woman to have been assigned as an agent in the San Francisco division. Counting me, there were three left, along with several hundred men. The male agents were addressed as "Mr." and the clerical women were called by their first names and referred to as "girls." ("Have your girl bring the file to my office in ten minutes.") People in the office knew I wasn't a "Mr." but weren't sure whether to refer to me as a "girl," which seemed to make everyone uncomfortable. Still, I was thrilled for the chance to launch my career and provide for my children. With the fervor of youth, I was ready to show the Bureau exactly what women could do.

The first morning when I reported for work, I caused quite a ruckus. I made the mistake of signing in at the time I'd actually arrived, rather than two minutes after the last person on the book. One squad member grabbed the sign-in book and insisted that I change my time so that I wouldn't mess up everyone else's overtime. For some unexplained reason, Hoover had required special agents to put in an average of 108 minutes of overtime each day, for which they were paid "administratively unavoidable overtime," and this odd requirement had stuck. If you didn't average 108 minutes extra each day, you couldn't get the administratively unavoidable overtime pay that was automatically added to every agent's salary. But nothing in the Bureau was that simple, and "average" was the operable word for understanding the requirement. Agents had to ensure that the amount of overtime they clocked remained in the statistical quarters just above and below the office average. The problem was, of course, that no one knew what that magic median number was. Those who fell in the lowest quarter of overtime would be considered lazy. Those who fell in the upper quarter would be considered problems because they couldn't get their work done in the allotted time. Heaven knows, no agent wanted to be pegged as a problem.

I soon learned that it would be a hard road in San Francisco, but not because of the casework. My welcome from my first supervisor and one of the relief supervisors was identical: "We had one of you before," meaning a woman who had been a single parent and, in their collective opinion, hadn't pulled her weight in the overtime department. They made it clear that I would get no special considerations. I assured them and countless others who felt my performance was their business, that I would never ask for special consideration, and in the years that followed, I never did.

At first, my supervisor didn't assign me many fugitive cases, and when he did, they were deserters and escaped federal criminals who had committed bank fraud, not anyone who posed danger. Mostly, what I got were background investigations. I assumed this was because I was new and just learning the ropes. The difference in the treatment of men and women special agents was not apparent to me until a man, fresh from new agents' training, was assigned to our office. Unlike me, our supervisor did not give him a lecture about pulling his own weight, and he was immediately assigned to more heavy-duty criminal cases. No special considerations, huh? By then, I knew that I would get nothing but special consideration, meaning I would always be seen as someone forced upon the boys' club.

Secretly, I was furious, insulted, hurt, and discouraged. I was working hard to do a good job for the Bureau and to care for my family, and I never turned down a request to work overtime when other agents needed backup. I bore the onslaught of insulting remarks and innuendo, thinking my professional work would prove my detractors wrong and that they would learn to accept me. But little changed.

The background investigations I conducted were on people who had applied for government jobs. Background investigations were dull, and deserters were even more bland. Early on, I arrested my first deserter. A neighbor had seen him at his mother's house and reported him, so at about four o'clock one morning, six of us went to the house. The boy's mother answered the door and led us to the bed where her son was sleeping. I nudged him a couple of times and said, "FBI."

He sat up and rubbed his eyes. I said, "You're going to have to come with us." He just sat there, a kid not fully awake.

One of the guys with me said, "Get out of bed, son," and that was about it. We took him to the naval base at Treasury Island and left him with the Shore Patrol. At that point, the Navy was simply discharging deserters after we brought them in. So much for glamour and excitement. This was the reality of my day-to-day life in the FBI.

Workdays were arduous. Up at 4:30 A.M., I got the children dressed, fed, and deposited at a private school by 6:00 A.M. so I could be in the office as close to 7 A.M. as traffic would allow. I couldn't pick up the kids from school until 6 P.M., and if my job kept me even later than that, I had to find a babysitter who could pick them up. The problem was that the need to work late often arose toward the close of business, leaving me little chance to arrange childcare. If I were in the middle of something—say, processing someone into jail or conducting a search—and the clock struck five, I couldn't simply walk away. After a couple of months of living at this frantic, unpredictable pace, the children were exhausted and so was I.

It didn't take me long to realize that even chasing fugitives could be pretty ho-hum. There were no criminal geniuses among them. Mostly, we interviewed their families and friends, as well as neighbors who lived near their last-known address. Then we sat in cars, watching to see whether they'd come home to mama or a girlfriend. All of them came along quietly when confronted. It was a kinder, gentler time, I suppose, but it left me wondering why I was putting in those long hours. It was monotonous work, devoid of challenge, and I was bored. The drudgery of my duties and the relative insignificance of the crimes I investigated made me feel like I was wearing myself out for nothing. There had to be more. Even when I did well, I would be brought back down to earth by the reality of my work environment: One day, I had made two arrests and was feeling good about myself. I was standing alone in the squad room when a supervisor from another squad came over and said he needed someone to help pick up a prisoner. I volunteered that I'd be glad to help. Without hesitation, he responded, "No. I want a man."

My chosen career brought with it duties one won't find in any special agent job description. One of these was my first experience guarding a female prisoner. She had been taken into custody after storming the Nicaraguan consulate with some male companions and holding the consul hostage to get press attention. The FBI Special Weapons and Tactics (SWAT) team broke through the door, rescued the consul, and arrested the hostagetakers. This irate young woman complained to me she saw no reason for the FBI to use such force. "We passed out a note that said we weren't armed," she said with disdain.

I wanted to tell her that she should have passed out a second note that said they weren't lying, but I restrained myself. Apparently, she believed that law enforcement officers should risk their lives based on the declarations of kidnappers. Her misread of the situation didn't stop there. The agents who arrested her had not conducted a body cavity search, so I had to watch her use the toilet to ensure she didn't have a concealed weapon or other contraband. She seemed to think I was watching her for personal pleasure when, in truth, it was one of the most distasteful things I was ever asked to do. Later in Denver, my job responsibilities included supervising the drug testing of women in the office. Known to all as "the princess of pee," I served as the official witness as each woman urinated into little specimen cups. I attested to the fact that the specimen jar was warm when returned to me, described the color of the urine, and ensured that each woman placed a fingerprint on the seal of the bottle. And to think there are some people who believe my job was nothing but glamour and excitement!

The unexpected was often the hallmark of my arrests, like the time I went to an apartment complex with a fellow agent I'll call Wallace. We were there to arrest a fugitive named Ronnie, who had embezzled money or committed some other nonviolent crime, so this was no door-busting situation. Wallace knocked on the door and got no answer. I tried persuading Ronnie myself.

"Ronnie, are you in there?"

After a moment, a meek voice answered, "Yes, ma'am, I am."

"Well, you'd better open the door. We've got to take you to jail."

"Okay," he sighed. "Let me get my purse."

Minutes later, the door slowly opened, and Ronnie stepped out, a slender African-American man wearing a pair of loose silk pants and a coordinated shirt, with pink sponge curlers in his hair.

"I'm ready," he said.

At that point, Wallace, who was particularly religious, dropped to his knees for a quick prayer, and I cuffed Ronnie. Once Ronnie was in the car, Wallace began to chant, "God put those words in your mouth today, Rosemary. God put those words in your mouth."

I rode to jail in the backseat of the car, dabbing Ronnie's tears and assuring him that his makeup looked fine. Looking back, it seems that almost every man I arrested cried. Perhaps it was a macho thing about being arrested by a woman. Or maybe it was just a kinder, gentler time.

I am reminded of the many memoranda Hoover and his executives wrote that "justified" banning women from the special agent ranks. A common theme was that men could not have confidence in the women who would have to back them up in dangerous situations.

> Each Special Agent must have the confidence in himself and in each fellow Agent that each is able to dissuade against violence but prepared to act swiftly and surely should defense of one's self or fellow Special Agents be necessary. Dangerous assignments often develop spontaneously. The response by our Special Agents must be quick and is frequently military in nature with one man, supported by others, making the initial move, such as forcing entry into a room or building where dangerous resistance is expected and must be forestalled or otherwise dealt

with to protect the lives of the raiding party. He must have supreme confidence in his associates and inherently greater confidence will be associated with well-trained men.

It seems doubtful that Hoover had the likes of Wallace in mind when he wrote those words.

Little about my new career was like the movies. For example, arrests never go as smoothly in real life. In 1979, I was with a few agents who were sneaking into an Oakland neighborhood to arrest a male fugitive who was reportedly armed and dangerous. I'd left the car, shotgun in hand, and was tiptoeing toward the house when a portly agent named Tom accidentally leaned on the horn as he was getting out of the car. Then he tripped and fell on the front steps, dropping his gun, which clattered as it slid along the concrete walkway into a bed of ivy. As Tom scrambled after it, I held in my laughter and pressed my back against the wall by the front door, shotgun hugged tight to my chest so it couldn't be seen from the front window.

As funny as this scene was, it was also dangerous. We had a schedule to keep, because other agents planned to break through the kitchen door in the back of the house as we came through the front, and that left little time for Tom to chase his gun across the lawn. In addition, this was a tough part of Oakland, where the population was often armed and probably would not take kindly to a strange woman with a shotgun on a neighbor's front porch.

Finally, Tom and I were on either side of the doorframe awaiting the signal to go in. He tried the handle and found that the door was open, so we slipped in and moved through the house to the areas we'd been assigned. Two more agents came through the back door, as I moved to the rear of the house where I found a door just slightly ajar. I tapped it with my foot, and it opened. Swinging the shotgun to my hip, I moved in. There was a woman sitting up in the bed at the far end of the room.

"Keep your hands where I can see them," I said.

"I'm not going to fight you," she whispered, her arms across her nude chest.

"That's good," I said, moving in closer and snatching the pillows from the bed, so I could see any weapons she might have. I moved back toward the closet to make sure no one was hiding in it. "Just stay where you are . . . Where's your husband?"

"Shower," she said. Her voice was toneless, defeated.

I rummaged through the closet to make sure he wasn't in there, then grabbed a robe and moved back to the bed. "I'm going to let you dress, but you have to do what I say."

"Okay."

"I'm going to pull these covers back, then I'll give you the robe. You just stay right where you are."

"Okay."

I leaned in, grabbed the edge of the bedcovers and tossed them back, then caught my breath as a small child's head emerged. Before I could speak, an agent stepped into the room.

"We're clear out here. You can let these two go," he said. "The guy was in the shower. Didn't even hear us coming."

I learned a lot during my assignment in San Francisco. There, I discovered that criminals are not the masterminds we see in the movies, and bank robbers are the dumbest of all. Imagine planning a crime knowing that your picture will be taken, there will be plenty of witnesses, someone will set off an alarm, you won't get much money, and best of all, the money you get will contain an exploding dye pack that will turn you green, red, or magenta. That's why bank robberies have the highest solve rate of any crime the Bureau investigates.

One agent told me about a robber in San Francisco who had cerebral palsy. He could walk, but not fast, and he could barely control the muscles in his hands well enough to hold the robbery note between two fingers then drop it onto the teller's counter. The note read, "I've got a gun. Give me all your money."

Oddly enough, he was successful in a string of robberies. What worked in his favor was the fact that the tellers were trained to give robbers their cash without confrontation. Of course, the tellers were able to describe in detail how the man had struggled to get a grip on the bag of money and how difficult it had been for him to make his way to the street where his sister waited in the getaway car. The sister was sure a jury would let him off because of his disability. She was wrong.

Unlike most other law enforcement officials, FBI agents do not have assigned partners and are free to assist on a colleague's cases, as long as their own work doesn't suffer. Eager to learn more, I volunteered for new assignments when opportunities arose. No one on my squad seemed particularly interested in working with me. Eventually, I found work and someone I enjoyed working with when Megan, one of the other two women in the division, invited me to assist on some of her domestic terrorism cases.

Megan joined the FBI the first year the Bureau hired women agents. Tall and blonde, she was a sweet woman, who was a couple of years older than I, married with teenage children, and very much a lady. She was secure in her job yet cautious in her dealings within the Bureau. She listened to my problems with patience and encouraged my ambition. She taught me a lot about getting along on the job, including many Bureau do's and don'ts: never criticize the Bureau in public; don't tell anyone about your private life; and even neighbors can cause you problems if they report something about you that the Bureau views as derogatory, such as a man leaving your house late at night. This was useful, if bizarre, information about the intrusive grasp of the organization in which I was trying to build a career.

Megan and I had a lot in common. In addition to being working moms in a career dominated by men, we had entered law enforcement at an interesting time in history. Together, in 1978, we investigated the Prairie Fire Organizing Committee. The group was the political arm of the Weather Underground, a radical antiwar group that had split off from the Students for a Democratic Society (SDS) in 1969 and was part of what was termed at the time the New Left, a modern-day anarchist movement. Our job, Megan's and mine, was to seek out fugitives connected with the Weather Underground's criminal activity, which included bombings, assault, and armed robbery. (It was common for terrorist groups to bankroll their activities with robberies.) We expected to find them among their Prairie Fire companions, who were known to have offered support in the past.

It was, in fact, an interesting time to be in law enforcement, especially in San Francisco, and my time working these cases sparked my imagination. By 1978, American involvement in Vietnam had ended, but many organized groups remained in strong opposition to the U.S. government. Lynette "Squeaky" Fromme and Sarah Jane Moore, followers of convicted murderer Charles Manson, had each attempted to assassinate President Ford in San Francisco. It seemed that everyone was getting into the violent protest act. Just two years earlier, however, a national outcry against U.S. intelligence agencies' investigations of American citizens had resulted in Attorney General Edward H. Levi's 1976 guidelines for security investigations, which restricted FBI intelligence-gathering activities and ensured a Department of Justice review of FBI operations. The guidelines ended warrantless wiretaps, as well as clandestine searches, known as "black bag jobs." While it made cases harder to investigate, I was fortunate to learn the ropes in this atmosphere. Despite the negative factors I sometimes faced on the job, work like this undercover gig helped compensate and kept me hoping that the atmosphere would improve.

FBI agents in the Bay Area knew how far the anti-government groups were willing to go. The Berkeley FBI office had been bombed during the Berkeley student riots, which were led by such groups as SDS. Fortunately, the bombing took place at night and no one was hurt, but, as a result of these attacks, most agents investigating the New Left took it as a personal commitment. All of these things came together to create the mood at the San Francisco FBI office. The threat of violence was so real that we had to get down on the ground—suits and all—to check underneath the Bureau cars for bombs before we opened the doors, and I must admit cringing just a little each time I turned the key in the ignition of an FBI vehicle.

The Weather Underground was responsible for a number of bombings, but the most famous was the bomb that exploded on March 6, 1970 in a Greenwich Village apartment, killing the four Weather

Underground members who were in the process of building it. The bomb was supposedly meant for an Army dance at Fort Dix in New Jersey. This setback did not stop the Weather Underground. According to *Prairie Fire: The Politics of Revolutionary Anti-Imperialism,* written by self-avowed Weather Underground members, the group committed a number of violent acts between 1969 and 1974, including at least twenty bombings at universities, police stations, courthouses, the U.S. Capitol, police cars, offices of departments of correction, the Pentagon, military draft and recruiting centers, National Guard centers, and the San Francisco office of U.S. Health, Education, and Welfare.

On September 4, 1975, the group claimed credit for bombing the Kennecott Corporation in Salt Lake City, Utah. A Weather Underground "press release" said the attack was perpetrated in solidarity with the Chilean people because Kennecott was receiving money from the Pinochet military dictatorship in compensation for the government's nationalization of the mines. On February 3, 1977, almost one year before I arrived in San Francisco, the group bombed the San Francisco office of the U.S. Immigration and Naturalization Service. The group also claimed responsibility for twice bombing the statue that was erected to honor the Chicago police officers killed in the 1886 Haymarket anarchist bombing.

The Weather Underground did not go the way of Flower Power and the disco craze but continued operating into the '80s. In 1981, members of the Weather Underground and several other radical groups established an organization called the Armed Resistance Unit. On October 20, 1981, three members of the Weather Underground joined forces with a member of the Black Liberation Army to rob a Brinks armored car of $1.6 million in Nyack, New York. Eventually, the four were arrested, but not before a security guard was killed at the scene, as well as two police officers in a roadblock shootout at the entrance to the New York State Thruway. In November 1983, the Armed Resistance Unit car-bombed the Senate chamber at the U.S. Capitol and, in January 1984, bombed the FBI office in New York City.

With a resume like that, the Weather Underground and its offshoot organizations were of serious concern to the FBI. Megan and I were given a stakeout assignment at a roach-infested apartment in the Mission district of San Francisco.

Most of the time, we crouched in uncomfortable positions and peered out through an opening in the curtain of the apartment's bay window. Our backs ached, and we munched on candy bars, promising that someday we would go on diets and return to our regular exercise programs.

Through our binoculars, we watched people go in and out of the apartment across the street at about the same rate as customers shopping at a 7-Eleven store. As they entered and exited, we radioed their descriptions so that FBI agents in nearby cars could track them as mobile surveillance targets. During slack times, we talked. Megan was an expert on Prairie Fire's activities.

They were followers of Che Guevara, the medical-doctor-turned-revolutionary who had fought alongside Fidel Castro and helped bring communism to Cuba. They were middle class and college-educated, but they perceived the federal government's intentions as evil and launched protests on a variety of issues, ranging from the war in Vietnam to workers' rights.

This was my first long-term surveillance, and it was a cerebral experience, as surveillance often is. When you're on surveillance, you can't move around, read, or watch television, so thinking and talking fill the tedious hours. I'd read the files, but still, I wondered what sort of people these Weather Underground members really were. The group's stated goals were altruistic, similar to the premise of communism; and, like communism, their methods had nothing to do with altruism. War protesters who killed seemed hypocritical to me, and, having lived under communism in Yugoslavia, I knew firsthand that it was a paradise only for that scant upper echelon in power.

As a student in Croatia, I had tried my hand at political protest. Zagreb, the town where I had lived and studied, had appeared quiet and conventional in 1970, but it had been nothing of the sort. Revolution had been brewing. The Croatians had wanted to secede from Yugoslavia, and Croatian students had been vocal supporters of secession. I had attended student secessionist rallies but had had no understanding of what was really happening. I'd seen protest marches and listened to all kinds of rhetoric at the University of Texas. I had laughed that off as a bunch of hippies making a show of themselves. When I had heard Croatian students demanding that everyone speak *Čisti Hrvatski* (pure Croatian), I had no idea they were willing to die for it.

Historically, the return to a pure Croatian accent had been the harbinger of a return to Croatian nationalism. A month after I'd left the country, Yugoslav soldiers surrounded the university and arrested everyone they could catch, whether or not they'd been involved in antigovernment activity. Therein lay one major difference between our two systems.

One morning, Megan and I were on our way to the apartment when we discovered posters all over the barrio that read: "Women of the FBI are in the Mission." The posters warned that two FBI agents were spying on innocent people. Because the Weather Underground's preferred method of attack was explosives, the bomb squad had to open the door to our undercover apartment so we could retrieve our equipment. And that was the end of the surveillance.

The next day, I was back in the office when an agent from my squad summoned me to his desk. He'd been nice to me, and I liked him a lot, so I trusted what he said.

"Listen, Rosemary," he said. "I've got some advice for you."

"Uh-huh," I said, standing before him, as there was no extra chair.

"Some of the guys have been talking about you working with Megan so much."

"What do you mean?"

"Well, what's up with you two?"

"She has interesting cases, and she let's me work with her," I said with a shrug, wondering where this conversation was going.

"Here's my advice. Stop working with her. The guys are beginning to think you can only work with women."

"I'd work with anyone who asked. If they want to work with me, why don't they ask?"

"That's not the point. All I'm saying is that there's a perception you don't want to work with the guys."

I told Megan what was going on and took her advice to work exclusively with my all-male squad. For years, I avoided the company of other women in the Bureau and acted pleased when men told me that they'd never worked with a competent woman until me. I knew that wasn't true, and I felt patronized, but I was clinging to whatever positive reinforcement I could get. What it really did was reinforce the subtle warning that I shouldn't associate with the other women lest I be deemed guilty by association. The result was that I was pushed further from a potential support group, and I missed getting to know some exceptional women.

Ironically, my experience seems to mirror a quote from *Prairie Fire: The Politics of Revolutionary Anti-Imperialism*: "Our intention is to engage the enemy, to wear away at him, to harass him, to isolate him, to expose every weakness, to pounce, to reveal his vulnerability."

That, it seems to me, was exactly what many male agents did to women in the FBI. By then, I understood the FBI's caste system. I knew that I would always be a "female agent" first and a "special agent" second, treated with disdain, sexually harassed, and denied the opportunities and privileges accorded to male agents.

Even today, I can't describe the feeling evoked in me by that term—female agent. It makes me think of the story of special agent Martha Dixon Martinez, who was killed on November 22, 1994, by a gunman who opened fire in the Washington, D.C., Metropolitan Police Department, where she was working on a joint police-FBI task force.

In dedicating the Martha Dixon Martinez FBI Field Office in Pittsburgh, Pennsylvania, in 2002, Director Mueller said:

Martha was an outstanding Special Agent. She was smart, talented, and hardworking. She was SWAT certified and trained in electronic surveillance. She did exceptional work across a range of violent crime and drug investigations. And on that dark day seven years ago when she came face-to-face with danger, Martha was as strong and courageous as they come. She went down fighting, making the ultimate sacrifice to protect her partners in law enforcement. In both life and death, she epitomized the values that the FBI stands for—fidelity, bravery, and integrity. She is a credit to this city, to the FBI, and to our nation. And we are honored that this facility now bears her name, an enduring monument to her legacy of service and sacrifice and an inspiration to us all.

Martha Dixon Martinez was a seasoned agent with a glowing record, her reputation above reproach. She did it all, and well. Her husband had a chance to speak about her in public and to convey the things he knew she'd want the world to remember. One thing he said was that she "was very much an agent. Not a female agent, but an agent. It mattered to her to be seen that way."

Whether male or female, law enforcement officials have suffered at the hands of Hollywood and fiction writers who have glorified the cleverness of criminals and depicted law enforcement personnel as people who either never make errors or are incompetent chuckleheads. Law enforcement officers aren't MENSA members with access to technology well beyond the state of the art. No police officer or FBI agent can acquire all the information that is needed to conduct an investigation with just a few strokes of the computer keyboard. Let's face it. Cops are just regular people. Some are brilliant; some are not. And the idea that FBI agents jump into helicopters and fly out of their jurisdictions to conduct investigations whenever they want, or that law enforcement officers open up evidence files to private detectives, is pure celluloid fantasy.

Just as criminals are usually not brilliant, agents are not all-powerful. This fact was impressed on me when a man started showing up at my Sausalito apartment, about four months after I arrived. The man had mental problems and had been jailed repeatedly. I met him when he knocked on my door and told me he was a friend of the landlord's, that he had once lived in my flat, and that the landlord had told him all about me. Before I realized what was happening, he'd stepped into the apartment and pulled a gun. All I remember was telling my children to go to their rooms and talking as fast as I could for the next hour or so.

The man believed that the CIA, National Security Agency, and Nicaraguan terrorists were following him. What he wanted from me was protection. After a lot of talking, I convinced him that I couldn't help him unless I phoned my office. The Bureau sent out a couple of agents and the local police, who held the man in jail overnight, then released him. The police assured me the man was a well-known nuisance and wouldn't come back. But instead of disappearing, the man began showing up on my porch every day, armed, waiting for me to return from work and provide him with the protection he felt he required.

My colleagues gave me all kinds of advice, starting with: "You're an agent, shoot him." The person who blithely offered that tip also warned me to drag the man into the house after I shot him, because California law prohibited a person from using deadly force to defend himself from an intruder unless he'd first retreated to the farthest corner of his house.

One day, my stalker confided that he had bad news: a Nicaraguan terrorist had found out about me and wanted to kidnap my children. I looked up the name of this alleged terrorist and found a dozen files on him. The children's school installed a panic button that could ring the police department, and Megan and a male agent offered to take turns staying with me in their off hours. No official FBI assistance was offered.

I was on my own in the ludicrous position of being a law enforcement officer who could get no help from law enforcement, and I found myself disassociating from reality. Since it appeared there was nothing I could do to change the situation, my conscious mind decided everything would be fine. Fully into denial, I dulled my emotions in my personal life, just as I did on the job, but I couldn't control what happened physically. I didn't sleep at night, and each creak of that old wooden house sent me flying out of bed. My startle reaction was so strong that my flailing arms sent files flying from my desk if anyone walked up behind me at work.

Around that time, I received a call from the head of the Berkeley Resident Agency, a small office in San Francisco territory, and was offered a transfer, which I gladly accepted. This was not only fortuitous for my family's safety, but it was a good opportunity for a fresh start, and I hoped to find more interesting work in Berkeley, where radicalism and espionage flourished.

Feeling no guilt about breaking my lease, as the landlord was the one who had told the stalker about me, I packed up my children and moved to Walnut Creek in East Bay, just across the Bay Bridge but far enough from the stalker to feel safe.

About a month after we moved, the stalker situation was over: the man was arrested for writing bad checks. It seems he'd decided to run for governor of California and had called a press conference at a large hotel in downtown San Francisco. When he couldn't pay his hotel bill, the San Francisco police arrested him. He then subpoenaed me and about twenty other law enforcement officers he'd been menacing over the years to testify *in his defense.*

The state of California had a write-your-own subpoena packet that could be used by anyone who wanted to defend themselves in court, and the stalker wrote one for everyone he knew. My subpoena was *duces tecum,* meaning I was supposed to bring the files concerning the terrorist to court with me. Those files were classified, and I couldn't testify to their contents in an open court without a lengthy approval process. The Bureau told me to cite a couple of precedents but offered no legal support. One of the agents from my office, a man who had a law degree but was not admitted to practice in California, marked some precedents in a book and volunteered to sit with me in court.

The San Francisco assistant district attorney met me and the other subpoenaed officers in a room. He planned to ask the judge to declare the defendant incompetent to defend himself and request that he be assigned a public defender. The assistant DA warned us that the judge loved colorful characters and probably wouldn't force counsel on the defendant.

Later, when the assistant DA returned from the judge's chamber, he was barely suppressing his laughter. It seems that things had been going fine for the defendant in chambers until the judge had said something he didn't like, whereupon my stalker had jumped up and emptied his briefcase over the judge's head. The assistant DA assured us that the stalker was in jail and that we'd never be subpoenaed again in this case.

In Walnut Creek, my family was finally free of the man who had terrified us for four months. I enrolled the children in a small private school and slept with a gun in my bed for the next eleven years.

Chapter 6

A New Meaning to Undercover

Doublethink means the power of holding two contradictory beliefs
in one's mind simultaneously, and accepting both of them.

George Orwell

1984

I t was in Berkeley that I first began working undercover, something
I did off and on for my entire FBI career. I often posed as a prostitute, teamed with an agent named Winston, who pretended to be
my pimp. Winston was a soft-spoken, gentle African-American man,
who was married and had a couple of children. He was not at all pimp-
like, even with the stereotypical panama hat, bright suits, and flashy
Cadillac that he drove. I tried my best to look sexy, wearing short skirts,
high heels, and form-fitting blouses. Such outfits left nowhere to con-
ceal a gun, that's for sure, but I didn't complain because no one was
telling me to "take a powder" as I'd heard in training school. Despite the
prostitute gig, I felt respected.

Winston and I spent our late afternoons and nights in East Bay bars
that were patronized by fugitives or people suspected of gambling violations. There were hints of drugs and organized crime, as well as Black
Panther fugitives.

Advocating revolutionary black nationalism, Huey Newton and
Bobby Seale had founded the Black Panther Party in 1966. Other
famous members were Eldridge Cleaver, Stokely Carmichael, James

Forman, and H. Rap Brown. While African Americans served alongside Caucasians in the U.S. military, their civil rights in this country were still nascent in practice.

In 1965, Malcolm X had been assassinated in New York City. A month later, Dr. Martin Luther King led the historic march from Selma to Montgomery to protest discrimination against African Americans in voting registration, a move that pushed the Voting Rights Act of 1965. The next year saw race riots in Watts and Los Angeles and Ku Klux Klan attacks against African Americans and civil rights workers in the South. Raging against this atmosphere, the Black Panthers wanted amnesty for all African-American prisoners, as well as exemption from military service and wide-ranging welfare benefits. To accomplish their goals, they advocated violence, and that's where the FBI came in.

The Panthers were busy in 1969. A shootout at Panther headquarters in Sacramento resulted in injuries to thirteen police officers. Eldridge Cleaver took off for Cuba, and two Black Panther leaders were killed in Chicago when police raided their apartment. In 1971, Bobby Seale was convicted of contempt of court, and H. Rap Brown was convicted of armed robbery. By the mid-1970s, the Panthers were not in the news as often as they once had been, but the FBI wasn't giving up, so Winston and I were assigned to see what we could see.

At the start of each evening, we studied photo spreads until we felt we were familiar with the faces, then we hid them in the Cadillac and drove to the first bar. We'd walk in, order a couple of drinks, and strike up conversations with anyone who'd talk to us. Later, we'd go home and write up what we'd heard. We couldn't be too aggressive or nosy undercover because someone was bound to question our motives. We tried to blend in, so the bar patrons wouldn't hold down their voices around us. If anyone appeared interested in doing a little business with Winston (and consequently, me), he would coolly wave the potential patron away and say, "She's with me tonight, baby."

Often, Winston and I just sat and talked so that everyone at the bar got used to us. In the end, every time we thought we had a hot one, it turned out to be another undercover cop.

There is a science to undercover behavior, but I'd had no training and didn't learn the rules until much later. I was pretending to be a prostitute, but because this role was not within the realm of my experience, all I could do was make assumptions: In my mind, a prostitute would be bold and direct. As a result, I looked people in the eye when I spoke to them and attempted to be outgoing and flirtatious. Alas, staring someone down so they don't think you're afraid is a typical cop thing to do, and it probably blew my cover as often as not.

Also, with my limited experience in law enforcement, I assumed that criminals were tough and aggressive. Had I known better, I would have realized they can be anxious, paranoid, and evasive.

My time with Winston gave me a small taste of the prejudice with which people of color lived every day. One evening, Winston and I began our rounds at a new bar. As we walked through the door, the jukebox blared "Take This Job and Shove It," and we knew we were in the wrong place. T-shirted white men with pendulous bellies hanging over their belts, glared at us, making it clear what they thought of an African-American man being with a white woman. I was ready to turn around and walk out, but Winston gently prodded me forward.

We deposited ourselves on barstools, and Winston ordered a gin and tonic in a tall glass. The waitress was curt and brought his drink in a small juice glass. Conversation had ceased the moment we appeared, and by the time our drinks were served, every eye in the house was on us. We spent an uncomfortable forty-five minutes trying to make small talk with the waitress, bartender, and the patrons who sat near us.

No one wanted to have anything to do with us.

The waitress was peddling homemade candles, and Winston bought a couple on the way out. Even in this tense situation, he actually felt sorry for the waitress and wanted her to have the money.

No matter how good an FBI agent might be undercover, it was never as good as having someone on the inside, and the Black Panthers were not an easy party to crash. While our Black Panther search was neither deep cover nor particularly successful, it was still dangerous work, because we had no backup or communications with the office. The only weapons we could carry were the five-shot chief special revolver that Winston hid in his boot, plus knives that he had in his pocket and I carried in my purse. Since I'd never been trained to fight with a knife, I might as well have been carrying a hatpin.

Without emergency communications, if something happened to us, it would have been hours before anyone noticed we were missing. In fact, my babysitter, who spent the night at my house and knew only that I'd be home before sunrise, would probably have been the first to suspect something was wrong.

Still, I was young and brave and believed the Bureau wouldn't put me in a needlessly hazardous situation. The more time I spent in the Bureau, the more outlandish I realized that assumption was. My experience with Winston was the only perilous undercover work I ever agreed to do without some provision for communications, or at least someone who would follow-up and make sure I was still alive at the end of my shift. But in my Berkeley days, I didn't permit myself the luxury of worry. I did what I had to do and was still idealistic enough to think I could change the world. When it came to supporting two children, posing as a prostitute for the FBI paid better than waiting tables in a Texas steak house.

Later, when I was assigned to the Washington field office in Washington, D.C., I worked counterintelligence undercover cases involving national security. These experiences were far more fascinating than the criminal undercover cases where I first honed my skills. The foreign intelligence officers whom I investigated were interesting and intelligent— just the sort of people I'd have wanted as friends, if only I'd met them under different circumstances.

Undercover work gave me a special kind of self-confidence that is useful even today. Almost without fail, if I act as if I know what I am doing, no one questions my actions. I learned not to volunteer unnecessary details and not to carry every conversation. As obvious as it seems, not everyone who works undercover realizes they can gather more information if they keep their mouths shut. Instead, they're so busy trying to make the target like and accept them that they miss important facts.

Being a woman was an advantage in undercover situations, especially for a woman of my vintage, raised in the South in the '50s and taught to hang on a man's every word. It may have been passé behavior by the late '70s, but that old habit served me well. Allen Dulles, the former head of the CIA, said in *The Craft of Intelligence* that officers need to learn when to keep their mouths shut. So listening was a relevant art.

While I had great luck convincing my targets I was genuine, third parties could cause problems. When working undercover on the East Coast, I often claimed to be from northern California, since it was an area I knew reasonably well. One night in 1983, I was working undercover at a large private party and former President Richard Nixon happened to be there. I escorted the people I was with into the reception line, and when it came my turn to shake his hand, he struck up a conversation with incredible skill. A genuine politician, he made me think that he truly cared about talking to me. Then he asked where I was from, and I replied, "Palo Alto."

Unbeknownst to me, that was the first district in which he was elected, and he wanted to reminisce with me: "Was this place or that still open?" etc. I was out of my league in the lying department, and I stood there stuttering. Nixon was obviously used to awed political groupies, and he graciously covered the conversation for me before moving on to the next person. I was impressed, not only with his skill, but with his gentlemanly ability to rescue a tongue-tied admirer.

Sometimes I worked so many undercover cases at once, it was difficult to keep my identities straight. To solve that problem, I came up with my own special system. Whenever I had multiple phone lines in my house, each tied to a different identity, I had the phones installed in the top of a closet so my children wouldn't answer them by mistake. Then, I put three-by-five-inch card under each phone that said: My name is . . . I live at . . . My job is . . . I was born . . . I met you . . . etc. Whenever the phone rang, I picked up the card and held it in front of me to ensure there were no slipups. One of the Bureau psychologists taught me to envision these cards while I was meeting people undercover. If I concentrated, I could read the cards in my mind.

As fascinating at it was, undercover work could also be highly stressful. There were quite a few agents who claimed undercover work was their downfall and their assignments left them emotionally damaged. I knew two agents who had nervous breakdowns in the middle of undercover operations and required intensive psychiatric help.

Perhaps the most spectacular and public of those who believed FBI undercover work marred their mental processes forever is Eugene Bennett, whose FBI-agent wife had a well-publicized affair with best-selling mystery novelist Patricia Cornwell in the mid-1990s. In fact, Bennett claimed that the combination of years of undercover work and the fear that his children would be exposed to lesbianism drove him to attempt to murder his spouse and her minister.

On January 29, 1997, the *Washington Post* headlines read: "Defense Says Ex-Agent was Driven Insane by Work, Worry."

> Describing the case's twisted details as straight from a B movie, Weingarten [Bennett's attorney] characterized his client as a once-successful undercover agent who was damaged mentally by years of trying to outsmart criminals by pretending to be one of them.
>
> "The FBI has learned to its horror that undercover work is not only physically dangerous but dangerous to agents' mental health," Weingarten said. He said that "240 felons were brought to justice as a result of [Bennett's] efforts." The FBI fired Bennett after he was arrested and convicted of falsifying expense reports.

Bennett is only one of several FBI agents who have been convicted of crimes after working undercover for extended periods of time. By the mid-'80s, the Bureau had hired contract psychologists, who counseled undercover agents at Quantico. I attended a lecture during which one of these psychologists gave hints on how to relieve tension when working undercover. His advice was to masturbate. I got up and left the room.

Chapter 7

BOYS' CLUBHOUSE: NO GIRLS ALLOWED

When I became Director, I established certain "bright line" rules regarding conduct. These rules, strictly enforced, quickly had the desired effect.

Statement for the Record of Louis J. Freeh, Director Federal Bureau of Investigation on FBI File Management Before the House Appropriations Subcommittee May 16, 2001

While I adjusted fairly well to the ups and downs of life in the Bureau, I also developed some bizarre behaviors of my own. As a novice agent, I exhibited what police psychologists call the "Jane Wayne" syndrome. It has been described as "the tendency of some female rookie police officers to use excessive force to try to live up to preconceived 'tough-guy' images." Although I never tried to man-handle anyone I arrested, I did fit the mold of a rough, tough daredevil. One symptom of this was showing off my athletic prowess. A fellow agent once bet me $50 I couldn't hold one leg up to my hip and do a one-legged, deep knee bend, touching the bent knee to the ground, then standing upright again. I won.

Another symptom was my vocabulary, which could have made a sailor blush. To appear strong and able to take what was dished out, I laughed off whatever anyone said to me. If an agent made a crude remark, I responded with something cruder. Most of my male coworkers made it painfully clear that no female agent could expect to be treated like a lady—far from it—and I was afraid to demand respect or even show that their behavior bothered me, because I knew they would see it as a personal weakness and redouble their efforts. Instead, I tried to blend in with the crowd and beat them at their own game. Looking back, I often seemed to be standing on the sidelines of my own life watching a woman, who looked like me, behave like a macho jerk.

In San Francisco, being one of three women on duty among hundreds of men meant I was forever onstage. Any mistake I made was magnified and discussed throughout the office. My clothing, my makeup, my hair were constant topics of discussion, with the majority of the men in the office believing it appropriate to comment to me directly regarding my appearance, pro and con.

There were no social boundaries. I was expected to be one of the guys, and then some. The truth is, there were always strong policies on the books against discrimination and harassment within the FBI. They just weren't as strong as the good ole boy system.

The worst experience I had during my years in California (in fact, one of the worst I've had in my life) was when a supervisor from Oakland, a middle-aged man whom I will call Benny, phoned me at the office one afternoon and said he had to discuss an undercover case with me. He said he couldn't discuss it over the phone and had to run off to a meeting, but that he lived near my house and would come by there to give me the details that evening.

That evening Benny called twice from a restaurant to say that he had been delayed. I could tell by his voice that he was getting drunk. Finally, he showed up at my house late in the evening, blessedly after my children were asleep, thrust a bottle of wine into my hand, and suggested that I pour us a couple of glasses. I left him in the living room and went into the kitchen. Shaken that he'd arrived inebriated, it took me a few minutes to find a corkscrew and a pair of clean glasses.

When I returned, Benny was standing in my living room totally nude, his clothing scattered around the floor. As I stood there flabbergasted, this potbellied, middle-aged man threw his arms around me, kissed me and announced that there had been "chemistry" between us from the first moment we'd met. I felt powerless in my own home and terrified that he'd wake the children, who would witness this spectacle. All I could think of was to keep him quiet and get him out the door as quickly as possible. My foremost thought was to protect my children and survive this demeaning experience with a shred of dignity.

Pushing him away, I tried to defuse the situation by making him laugh and handing him his clothes. Luckily, he was drunk, because it quickly became obvious that there was no way he could fulfill our chemical destiny, and his embarrassment was more persuasive than anything I said or did. After a few minutes that seemed like hours, Benny pulled himself together and went home to his wife, and despite his persistent telephone calls, I never agreed to meet him or work with him again. Eventually, he was promoted to deputy assistant director of Inspection Division (internal affairs) at FBI headquarters.

Years later, I ran into Benny at FBI headquarters in Washington, D.C. He had obviously recovered from the embarrassment of that dreadful night because he leaned toward me and whispered that there was still "chemistry" between us.

The entire time Benny was in my house that night, I'd felt guilty, responsible, and just plain stupid, as if I'd unwittingly done something to make him think I found him desirable. It was demoralizing and paralyzing. Like a bad dream, the scene haunts me even today: Whenever I think about what happened so many years ago, twinges of helplessness and shame wash over me. I grill myself with the same list of questions again and again: Why didn't I do this? Why didn't I do that? Did I allow him to get away so he could exploit other victims? And sadly, every emotion is as fresh as it was that night. But in my fantasies, I am not the amiable woman with the soft voice and agreeable sense of humor; I'm strong physically and emotionally. This time I slap him and kick him out of my house—all the things I wish I'd been able to do at the time.

By the end of these mental review sessions, my heart is pounding. If I can't force myself to think of something else, I'm pumped with adrenaline for hours and have nightmares for several nights in a row. This experience and my reactions are a part of me, now and forever.

When I share this story with friends, they are puzzled. "Why didn't you just shoot him?" they ask, but to my then-twenty-seven-year-old mind, it wasn't so simple. Aside from the ramifications of shooting a respected law enforcement officer in my living room, drunk and nude or not, there was much more to consider: my children seeing their mother in a humiliating situation and the fear I'd sacrifice my family's income, not to mention seeing the hopes and dreams for my career go down the tubes. Somehow, fear of rape fell way down on the list.

That night killed my desire to be part of the Bureau "family." The next morning, I took a senior agent into my confidence about what had happened and asked how to go about reporting Benny. Without hesitation, he told me to keep my mouth shut and not to draw attention to myself.

I'd been in the FBI almost a year by then, and I already knew how the system worked. I never suspected that my FBI career would reinforce my PTSD, nor that the PTSD would make me an easy emotional target. When I got the appointment to the academy, I felt empowered by my new career choice, as if I had the ability to right wrongs and protect others and myself, a feeling I'd lost during my marriage. Within a year, that thought had faded.

During my first few months on duty, I'd watched the male agents ostracize the agents who joined in a class-action suit that alleged discrimination against women on the job. Even though the women won the suit, the men openly accused them of being whiners who wanted special privileges. My male coworkers spread cruel rumors about them and felt it was their right to know whether I would stand with the women or the men in court. I was notified that I could claim status as a member of the class as soon as I graduated from the academy, and I did a lot of soul-searching before removing myself from that suit. I wanted to be loyal to the Bureau, my new employer, and I also knew enough to keep as far away from Equal Employment Opportunity (EEO) suits as possible. I was wrong, but the reality was that my sexist coworkers were the same guys who were supposed to cover my back in arrests and undercover assignments. I needed them. In the FBI, there's a pack-of-wild-dogs mentality. You either belong to the pack or you're torn apart by it.

Chapter 8

LIFE IS STRANGER THAN FICTION

It's not the large things that send a man to the madhouse. No, it's
the continuing series of small tragedies . . . not the death of his love,
but a shoelace that snaps, with no time left.

Charles Bukowski
The Shoelace

B y the end of my first year, I had serious doubts about my chosen
career. Many times since, I have pondered why I stayed. I know
that one factor is that I still had a lot of fight left in me. I was
twenty-eight, energetic, and ambitious. Also, my primary goal was to
provide quality of life for my children. Since I thought of quality of life
in a monetary sense when I was young, I feared losing the job that supported my family. In hindsight, I can also see that I felt trapped.

If nothing else, the situation taught me not to be judgmental about
another's mental state. I remember the people we joked about at the
office. "Crazies," we called them: people believing they were being controlled from outer space, who walked into or called our office wanting
the FBI to do something about their problems. There was even an elderly woman in San Francisco who occasionally dropped into our office
and disrobed in the reception area because she believed her clothes had
been implanted with listening devices.

Such stories may seem humorous on the surface, but these people
were genuinely frightened, and there was little we could do but suggest

they talk to a doctor. We couldn't force them to seek medical care unless they were a danger to themselves or others, and most weren't. Some agents told them to ground themselves by attaching strings of paper clips from their clothing to the ground so that the space signals would pass through them. Foil hats were another common suggestion. These creative remedies actually made many of them feel better for a while. One man I knew wore a bucket on his head whenever he went outside. It was his own invention, and it worked for him. Unfortunately, foil and paper clips did nothing to deflect my trials.

There are few stories as horrifying as the first high-publicity case that I worked in my career. In November 1978, while assigned to the Berkeley Resident Agency, I got the call to interview former members of Jim Jones's People's Temple, and I still remember my impressions of those few people who escaped with their lives from the Jones cult.

On November 18, 1978, the news broke that the bodies of approximately nine hundred suicide and murder victims, members of Jim Jones's People's Temple, had been discovered rotting in the torrid heat of his Georgetown, Guyana, agricultural commune. Jim Jones was a cult leader, who, according to news reports, had forced his followers, men, women, and children, to drink poisoned Kool-Aid. Those who refused to drink the liquid had been either injected with poison or shot.

The camp operated under heavy guard, whom Jones called the "learning crew" and "public service unit," and there was a three-foot-high "punishment box" used for solitary confinement. The work of the commune was little more than forced labor, and people lived under constant threat of punishment or death for disobedience. To keep the people sleep-deprived and submissive, Jones required them to attend nightly sessions where he lectured for hours about his paranoid view of the enemies who surrounded them. Jones also enforced regular suicide drills during which his followers had to drink from cups of what they thought was poison liquid.

Congressman Leo J. Ryan, along with some staffers and news reporters, arrived in Jonestown on a fact-finding tour at the behest of worried families of Jonestown residents. After attempting to hoodwink the congressman about what was really going on, Jones finally barred him from the camp. As the congressman's party attempted to board a departing flight, a truck full of Jones's followers opened fire. Soon Congressman Ryan, three newsmen, and an escaping cult member lay dead. After that, the suicides and mass murders began—children first. Jones himself died of a gunshot wound to the head.

The Ryan assassination fell within the Bureau's jurisdiction under the Congressional Assassination Statute, so another Berkeley Resident agent and I were sent to the Human Freedom Center in Berkeley, a halfway house for former cult members. Our instructions were to interview anyone who would talk to us about Jim Jones and his activities.

I arrived at the center in the evening. News cameras were set up everywhere. It was the first time I'd had microphones shoved in my face and questions fired at me faster than I could answer them. It didn't really matter, because I'd been instructed not to talk to the press about what I was doing there.

"Who are you with?" a reporter shouted, stepping in front of me as we attempted to get by.

"Hey, back off," said the agent by my side. "She's with me."

"Well, who are you with?" the reporter asked.

"I'm with her," the agent fired back, and with that, he grabbed my arm and we bolted through the crowd and into the center.

Inside were people of varying ages. I spent most of my time with a couple that appeared to be in their sixties. They had been searching for a sense of belonging when they'd fallen under the captivating spell of Jim Jones. Their story, which seemed so bizarre at the time, was the same story that has been told by many cult members since: they had been held in the grasp of a charismatic leader, controlled with threats and sleep deprivation, and had been willing to die for what they believed the leader offered. What is even more difficult to accept is that they had been willing for their children to die, as well.

"Father—that's what we called him—beat us in front of the congregation," said the gray-haired woman. "He made me stand up in front of everyone and defecate into a plastic bag."

She sighed and her husband, a blue-eyed man with salt-and-pepper hair, patted her hand. "I don't expect you to understand," he said to me. "He made us work all the time, but wouldn't let us sleep more than four hours. Pretty soon we didn't know what we were doing."

"I just thought I was bad, so bad that I needed something harsh to test my faith," the woman broke in, her hand in her husband's as tears seeped from the corners of her eyes.

"What could you possibly have done to deserve that kind of treatment?" I asked.

"I don't know," she sobbed. "I just knew I wasn't good enough. I had to do something to pay for my sins or I'd never make it to heaven. I thought Jim Jones knew the way."

"We all thought that, for one reason or the other," the man said. "And he offered us a tough road to redemption. Made us work hard for it. That's all I can tell you. We were so tired all the time. We just couldn't think straight, I guess."

They seemed to be average people, except for the fact they'd lived in an abusive cult led by a dangerous megalomaniac. They'd been attracted by the promise of altruistic work, such as caring for the poor. At one time, Jim Jones had been the darling of San Francisco. When he moved his temple from Indianapolis to San Francisco, he opened a free health clinic and a drug rehabilitation program. In 1976, he managed to get himself named chairman of the San Francisco Housing Authority. These accomplishments gave him credibility as he set out to recruit pliable followers.

At the time of that interview, I asked myself naive questions, the result of a narrow understanding of the realities of life: Why didn't they just leave? Couldn't they see the impact on their children? Now, older, wiser, and more secure, I've asked myself the same questions about my almost thirteen years in the FBI.

Chapter 9
BACK IN THE USSR

> During those years I experienced many conflicting feelings, but the
> dominant one was that of amazement.
>
> **Eugenia Semyonovna Ginzburg**
> *Into the Whirlwind*

I n September 1979, the FBI transferred me to the Defense Language
Institute (DLI) in Monterey, California. My assignment was to
study Russian, so that I would be a more competent foreign counterintelligence investigator when I returned to the field after school. DLI
had moved to Monterey in 1946, five years after it had been founded in
San Francisco as a secret language school to teach Japanese to a few carefully chosen U.S. soldiers, most of them of Japanese ancestry.

Monterey is a beautiful, beachside community south of San Francisco. All I had to do was live there, go to school, and enjoy my life.
Unfortunately, finding housing was a bewildering challenge. In 1979,
Americans were heavily into the "me" era, and much of the Monterey-
area housing was restricted to people without children. This was just
months after the "Twinkie defense"—insanity from a junk food sugar
high—was successfully argued to mitigate the fact that San Francisco
supervisor Dan White, an anti-gay conservative, had shot and killed
Mayor George Moscone and openly gay supervisor Harvey Milk at San
Francisco's city hall. So who was I to question that a law wrought by the
California legal system might not make sense?

One realtor told me there was no housing within my price range because I needed a three-bedroom apartment.

"Oh, no," I said. "My children can share a bedroom."

"Not in this state," she said, almost spitting her words at me. "We have child abuse laws, and children of different sex cannot share a bedroom!"

"They're not teenagers," I protested. "Christopher will be eight this month, and Kendra's just three."

"The law is the law," she sniffed.

When I tried to rent a house in nearby Carmel, the realtor said she'd have to ask the neighbors' permission before we signed the lease. The neighbors said "no."

Finally we found a two-bedroom apartment in an area called Seaside. Apparently, the child abuse laws were different there; or perhaps the complex was unaware of them because they never objected when I told them I had a son and a daughter. It was a nice apartment complex and less expensive than the ones that had rejected us.

The Russian course at DLI, comparable to thirty-six hours of college credits at the University of California at Berkeley, gave me a graphic illustration of what it was like to live under the Soviet system. It also revealed far too many parallels between the Soviet and the Bureau ways of doing things. It started with orientation when administrators attempted to instill fear by saying, "Look to the right, look to the left. One-third of the people around you will not graduate with you." Exactly one-third failed.

DLI was an academic challenge, and I often studied past midnight, memorizing text and dialogues because the instructors insisted that we memorize every word in our textbooks—not just the vocabulary assignments. Although I was conversant in Russian, the vocabulary at DLI was largely military, and that was new to me. Since I'd studied Russian in college, I figured the course wouldn't overtax me, and it was, in fact, the first and perhaps only year I was able to relax and spend time with my children during daylight hours. We went sightseeing around one of the most beautiful coastal areas in the United States and took long walks on the beach to watch otters, seals, pelicans, and gulls. We enjoyed simple things. I cooked, and we ate dinner before we were too tired to enjoy it.

For me, living in laid-back Monterey and attending DLI was easier than the two previous years had been. I traded the erratic hours of case-work for predictable school hours: 8:00 A.M. to 4:00 P.M. I no longer had to wake up at 4:30 A.M., and the children didn't need as much before-and-after-school care, which reduced our cost of living. Still, for the first few months, I felt nervous and agitated for no reason at around 4:00 P.M. Finally, I realized I was replaying old mental tapes from my former field office job, which demanded I start scrambling for a sitter about that time every afternoon. What a relief I felt in not having to deal with those uncertainties every day.

The most useful thing I learned at DLI was not advanced Russian. What I took away was a snapshot of Soviet life and some insight into what motivated the Soviet people. In later years when I worked coun-terintelligence, these insights were invaluable.

Our primary teachers, Mrs. Galkina and Mrs. Lipilis, were recent Soviet Jewish immigrants. They had been told by their Ukrainian Chris-tian supervisor, whom we nicknamed Frau Blucher after the acerbic character Cloris Leachman played in the movie *Young Frankenstein,* that if the class grades went down, they'd be fired. Since this sort of threat was commonly made and carried out in the Soviet Union, they took it seriously. What else did they know?

On top of that, Frau Blucher set up our instructors for disaster. The books we used had been revised so that they no longer coordinated with the tests we were given. Other teachers knew about the change, but Mrs. Galkina and Mrs. Lipilis had not been informed. Consequently, we were tested on material that we hadn't covered in class. Our teachers were frustrated and frightened, and several U.S. military personnel who failed the course suffered severe career setbacks. In fact, one was transferred from intelligence work to a job driving trucks. The parallel with FBI life was that the school was a place that offered no avenue for redress and quashed all suggestions for change.

Mrs. Galkina was a beautiful young woman with deep brown hair that hung in waves past her shoulder blades. She had been educated in Moscow. Mrs. Lipilis was a sweet and patient Lithuanian, whose speech had a soft, poetic lilt that I tried to emulate. Petite and white-haired, she worked with a few of my classmates who didn't have an ear for the language and never showed frustration when she said one thing and the students parroted back something barely reminiscent of the sounds she'd just made.

As the months rolled on, however, we began to see signs of strain in both teachers. They seemed angry when they returned our papers and the class grade average had fallen. Mr. Dubavik, an elfin instructor who could make us laugh as he drilled us in the vagaries of Russian grammar, revealed what was going on. It was a shocking display of prejudice that Frau Blucher was perpetrating against the Jewish teachers and we were powerless to stop it. I reported the problem to the local FBI office, but there was nothing anyone could do. The instructors were not FBI employees. They worked for the Department of Defense, and the Bureau was nothing more than a customer.

Frau Blucher was as distorted in appearance as she was in thought. She painted on huge black eyebrows, achieving a Groucho Marx look, and then added an abundant amount of blood-red lipstick. She and I had a steady stream of confrontations over the way she graded my papers. The test question would ask that we translate, for example, "I am going to the store." There are several ways to translate this sentence in Russian, since variations of the Russian verb "go" imply either a round trip, one-way trip, future trip, trip in process, as well as on foot or by vehicle. If I used the verb for a trip in progress, she marked it wrong, saying she was thinking in future tense when she wrote the sentence. When I argued it was impossible to derive that from an English sentence out of context, she'd chide, "You have to understand the Russian psychology!" How similar this was to the way ideas were dismissed in the FBI because it was "not the Bureau way."

Mr. Dubavik told me Frau Blucher graded my papers down because I confronted her in class on points of grammar. So she'd decided, unknown to me, to test me twice: once during the test and once when my test was returned. When I found the questions she'd erroneously marked wrong, confronted her, and won the argument as to why she should restore my points, she would give me my true score. Though at times she made my life miserable, in a way she did me a favor. I never trusted the Soviets again.

Because I'd majored in Slavic languages and had known Slavs from several countries, I was something of a Slavophile. My year at DLI cured me of that. It taught me to better understand the deceptions that Soviet society imposed on people and the societal need to lie in order to get by. I also discovered that, in the Soviet culture, telling a lie is not the breach of trust it is in America. The Soviets lied whenever it suited them, and if they got away with it, they felt a sense of achievement as opposed to guilt. It was a way of getting by, surviving, making do—things all Soviets understood and appreciated. Because I learned this, I was a better Soviet affairs analyst when I finally started working Soviet counterintelligence matters.

Finally, one of our primary teachers, on the verge of tears because the class average had slipped, demanded to know why we didn't cheat. This question shocked the students, most of them military officers and FBI agents, each of whom had been carefully chosen to guard the nation's secrets.

Her hands clasped before her as if in prayer, she leaned across her desk. "If you reached this level in the Soviet Union, you'd know how to cheat and cheat well," she said. "Write on your hands, on the bottom of your shoes. Put a piece of paper up your sleeve."

We stared blankly as her eyes reddened. "It's not the same there," she sighed. "It didn't matter how much you studied. It only mattered whether you passed the political exams and who you were. Sometimes you were marked to fail the political exam, which equals failing everything."

That was the profound sadness and craziness of the Soviet system. Communism was based upon the ideal concept that each person would have what he or she needed. In practice, it was an elaborately propagandized system where some were more equal than others. When the Soviet government took an action, the subsequent press releases always justified it based upon elaborate policies and laws.

This also was the Bureau system I'd come to know. It didn't matter how well your work was rated. You were accepted or not for reasons beyond your control. The Bureau's rules and policies were carefully contrived to show that everyone was equal. There were written procedures for everything, and everyone received training in these rules. The promotion process looked equitable, but often, before the voting members walked into the room, the fix was in.

Chapter 10

FIDELITY, BRAVERY, INTEGRITY

When a Central Intelligence Agency officer, Aldrich H. Ames, was arrested as a spy for Moscow in 1994, critics questioned how the agency could have allowed his espionage to go undetected for nine years. Officials at the Federal Bureau of Investigation helped fuel the criticism with complaints that the C.I.A. had failed to share sensitive information, stifling the investigation.

James Risen
Gaps in C.I.A.'s Ames Case May Be Filled by F.B.I.'s Own Spy Case
New York Times
February 21, 2001

When I graduated from the Defense Language Institute in September 1980, I was transferred to the Washington field office and assigned to one of the Soviet counterintelligence squads. Finally, I was getting somewhere. Not only was I working in Washington, D.C., the nation's capital and the area where I wanted to live, but I was assigned to the office that conducted some of the best counterintelligence in the Bureau. I was going to be part of an illustrious team.

I found a comfortable town house in Annandale, Virginia, and enrolled Chris and Kendra in private schools, hoping the smaller classes would ease their transition. We joined a local Lutheran church, and I felt that we were set. It wasn't exactly the "Leave It to Beaver" lifestyle, but it was comfortable and as close to normal as the family of a single FBI agent was going to get.

As I set out on my morning commute to the Washington field office that first day, I expected to see an impressive edifice like the J. Edgar Hoover Building downtown. Instead, I found a bleak white, rodent-infested, high-rise built on a landfill known as Buzzard's Point, located in a corner of Anacostia in southeast Washington.

Only supervisors had offices, and hundreds of people, including me, were packed into open bullpens. We'd been assured that the U.S. General Services Administration (GSA) was attempting to find another location for the field office, but that search had been going on for about ten years and it wasn't looking good. However, the anticipated move gave officials a great excuse not to repair the existing facility—why sink resources into repairs and maintenance when we'd be moving anyway?—so, the building slowly crumbled around us.

The view from my squad area was of the Anacostia River, once labeled one of the ten most contaminated rivers in the country. I could also see some type of quarry, which I watched with curiosity throughout my four-year assignment. The laborers were digging all day, but the site never seemed to change. My colleagues joked that the workers filled a barge, which floated away at close of business each day, and that, after we went home, a second shift of workers put it all back. It reminded me of casework in the Bureau—if you closed a case one day, you got two the next.

The city had never bothered to cover the old trolley tracks that ran down the center of the street in front of our building, and metal objects from the tracks worked their way to the street's surface. Flat tires were a daily occurrence. There was no parking for nongovernment cars near the building, except for a narrow strip in front and "the mud lot," an unpaved patch of bumpy ground on one side of the building that flooded when it rained. Employees had to be at work no later than 7:00 A.M. to get one of these prime spots. Whoever ran late and had to park farther from the building could count on at least their car's battery being stolen. A friend of mine had so many batteries stolen that he set up a surveillance, caught the teenaged thief, then arranged a "protection" deal. For the next two years, the agent paid the boy $10 a week not to steal his battery and to make sure no one else did.

Nearby was an electric power plant, and beyond that, a residential area composed of deserted-looking buildings, several of which were still occupied. Here and there windows were broken or boarded up, creating a surreal, war-zone landscape. Also in the vicinity were a couple of abandoned warehouses, and a few blocks away, stood some shabby bathhouses where male prostitution was rampant. All this was dangerous territory to traverse.

The field office agents worked without effective equipment. There were no computers, and all record searches were done by hand. Our federally provided autos were rolling wrecks. Once, when the SWAT team was called out on an emergency, the first car in line, its lights flashing and sirens blaring, broke down at the exit ramp, blocking everyone else until the agents got out of their vehicles and pushed it aside.

Despite the run-down conditions, the work made me happy. Generally, counterintelligence work consists of surveillance, interviews, developing assets (informants), recruiting foreign spies, undercover gigs, and extensive file reviews. FBI counterintelligence agents have duties similar to CIA officers overseas because the FBI, rather than the CIA, has primary jurisdiction in the United States. My former life as a diplomat's wife, combined with my knowledge of Slavic languages, gave me a certain advantage in my new assignment compared to those who'd had little exposure to foreign cultures and ways of thinking.

Until early 1980, women had not been allowed to work on criminal squads in the Washington field office. Fortunately for me, counterintelligence was where I wanted to be. My squad, Counterintelligence 2 (CI-2), had about twenty-five agents, including two other women. As I was being introduced around the open squad room, one of the agents announced that he kept the "flow chart" for the women in the field office, so I should let him know when I was on my period. That was my introduction to the men I would work with, and it set the tone for the rest of that assignment. By then, though, I knew the game and laughed off the remark, assuming yet again that acceptance would come when my male colleagues got to know me.

These were challenging times in the nation's capitol. In 1980, the Washington field office began the first prosecutions under Abscam. The name "Abscam" came from the phony company the FBI had set up— Abdul Enterprises—to catch bribe-taking congressmen and senators. The bribes came from undercover agents posing as wealthy Arabs, and everything from bribe offering to taking was captured on hidden video cameras. Florida representative Richard Kelly, for example, was caught on tape cramming $25,000 in cash into his pockets, then turning to an undercover agent and asking demurely, "Does it show?" On January 26, 1981, Kelly was convicted of bribery, conspiracy, and interstate travel to promote additional illegal activities. For some reason, an appeals court bought Kelly's entrapment defense, and his conviction was overturned.

Though the name "Abscam," short for "Adbul scam," was offensive to many Arab-Americans, the moniker caught on and was never changed. Later, the FBI gave sting operation members specially designed jacket patches featuring a cartoonish bee wearing an Arab headdress.

The cold war was raging and trouble was brewing around the world. In Iran, Islamic revolutionaries overthrew the government of Muhammad Reza Shah Pahlevi, who had left his country, allegedly on vacation, in January 1979 and never returned. On Oct. 22, 1979, the shah was allowed to enter the United States for gall bladder surgery, and, a few days later, in retaliation, a crowd of about five hundred seized the U.S. embassy in Tehran and held fifty-two people captive in the building for 444 days. They demanded that the U.S. return the shah, but the U.S. refused. Then-President Jimmy Carter halted oil imports from Iran and froze Iranian assets in the U.S., but his efforts to free the embassy hostages were fruitless. In 1980, after Ronald Reagan was sworn in as president, the hostages were released. That same year, the shah died in Egypt. Everyone involved in international relations, especially the intelligence community, was edgy.

Every embassy in downtown D.C. housed foreign intelligence officers, making Washington a center for intrigue. One of the best ways to find out what's happening in the enemy's camp is to recruit their intelligence personnel to work for the U.S. government, either as defectors or to remain on duty at their embassies where they can pass information through documents or verbally. Electronic gadgets are fun, but there's nothing more effective than having an insider who's on your side. This is the ultimate accomplishment in what is termed "human intelligence" in the spy business, and during my assignment in the Washington field office, I was involved in a number of recruitment/defection operations. A great deal of thought and planning went into each recruitment effort. To kick off one of these operations, we carefully analyzed information on foreign diplomatic personnel to detect weaknesses that might make them want to commit treason. Working undercover was one of the many ways we gained access to them. Once we identified targets, we offered incentives for them to provide us with what we needed.

Not every pitch was a home run. Soviets, for example, often redefected, as did Vitaly Yurchenko, a high-ranking KGB official, who walked into the U.S. embassy in Rome seeking asylum in 1985. During his brief career as a defector, Yurchenko unmasked such notable American spies as Edward Lee Howard, a CIA officer who managed to escape while under FBI surveillance and make his way to Moscow, and Ronald Pelton, a National Security Agency employee. Some say that Yurchenko was a false defector planted by the Soviets to give up information on Howard and Pelton, to protect a more important recruit: Aldrich Hazen Ames, a CIA counterintelligence officer convicted of spying for the Soviet Union and, later, for Russia. As chief of counterintelligence at CIA, Ames had access to information that told the Soviets who among their own was talking to the U.S. government, or, as the Soviets called us: "the main enemy." Looking back, one wonders whether he also protected FBI supervisory special agent Robert Hanssen, who was later exposed as a traitor, as well.

After just three months on Uncle Sam's side, Yurchenko redefected. As easily as he'd walked into the embassy in Rome, he walked away from his U.S. government keepers in a Georgetown restaurant, and two days later, held a news conference from the Soviet embassy, where he claimed he'd been drugged, kidnapped, and held against his will in a secluded CIA "safe house" in Virginia.

As far as the intelligence community is concerned, the success or failure of a defection has little to do with whether the person redefects. Success is gauged by the information the defector shares or the disruption caused to the opposing intelligence service, which doesn't know what details have been revealed or what they have to do to counter the loss. Although redefection may cast doubt on the veracity of the defector's information, all such information must be verified through independent investigation anyway and is used in its raw form only for investigative leads.

I've heard agents brag about how they cleverly talked someone into committing espionage but, in truth, you can't convince someone to betray their country. The best you can do is realize an individual is predisposed and provide the opportunity when he or she wants to cooperate. The Soviets and the oppressive regimes of communism tended to provide the impetus for Eastern Europeans to defect. The Eastern Europeans were, by and large, ideological defectors and did not expect to be treated like royalty by the U.S. government. By contrast, Soviets wanted money and lots of it. For them, ideology had little to do with switching sides.

The average Soviet defector believed living in the U.S. meant they would never have to work again, and they'd be treated like kings forever. But it wasn't always smooth sailing. American society often overwhelmed them—not just the material abundance that caused them confusion and frustration when choosing from twenty different brands of toothpaste, but the darker side of capitalism, such as crime and poverty. A Soviet woman once told me that her government was much kinder to its people because it didn't force bad news on them via the media.

Getting permission to approach ("pitch") a foreign diplomat for recruitment required FBI headquarters' formal approval, a process that was usually handled on paper. When I wanted to pitch a potential source, that process included a personal interview with a deputy assistant director, although such interviews were not required of men in the same situation. The deputy assistant director told me they were seriously considering my request; however, they'd never permitted a woman to do such a thing in the past, and if I failed, they would never allow a woman to try it again. Not only was this an unprofessional comment, but it put unnecessary pressure on me, making an already difficult task even harder. It was the FBI's managerial tradition to use whatever had gone wrong in 1950 as an excuse to deny operational ideas thirty-five years later. I certainly didn't want to be the well-remembered test case used to bar all women from conducting the full range of investigations for decades to come.

Fortunately, I was successful, but once the woman I targeted had defected, I was moved out of the picture. My supervisor decided I would not participate in debriefings, which was the customary procedure. Instead, I was told to baby-sit the woman's child. As if that wasn't bad enough, one of the debriefing agents, whom I'll call Perry, snapped his fingers at me whenever he wanted me to come talk to him. He did this in front of the defector and the second debriefing agent, Max.

Perry's behavior prompted the defector to assume I was a servant, and she, too, snapped her fingers when she wanted my attention.

I explained to my supervisor what was going on. After he stopped chuckling, he said, "You know, I was planning to write you up for an incentive award, but if you're going to take that kind of attitude, I won't."

Shocked, I said, "No incentive award is important enough to make me put up with being demeaned like that. Tell Perry to treat me like a professional."

"You have to have thick skin," he said. "You'll never make it in this organization if you don't."

And that was the end of it. Once again, management had set the tone.

Back at the safehouse, the defector acted giggly and cute around the men, like a flirtatious teen, but there was a manic edge to her, as well. I knew she was lonely and confused, and I tried once or twice to discuss the psychological pain she must have been feeling. Due to the tone that had been set by Perry, she continued to regard me as a servant and wouldn't take me into her confidence.

Even back then, I'd had extensive volunteer experience with people in psychological need. Since the age of thirteen, I'd volunteered my time to be with children and adults who had mental and emotional handicaps. I knew how to listen and guide conversations in directions that promote healing. I served for years as a peer grief counselor for families and coworkers of officers killed in the line of duty. I stepped with ease into the role of FBI critical incident (posttrauma) debriefer, with the letters of commendation to prove it. But in the case of this defector, prejudice once again wasted my time and talents, as well as the taxpayers' money.

Within a few days, the woman I recruited decided to redefect. One morning, Max reported for duty and found her packed and ready to leave.

"I don't care what you do to me," she said. "Strip me naked and throw me out in front of the embassy, but I'm not staying with that man any longer."

"That man" was Perry. I have no idea what he did or said to her, but she echoed my sentiments exactly.

Even though she redefected, the case generated considerable publicity, disrupted her government's intelligence operations in the U.S., and forced them to regroup. Perry, Max, and I received letters of commendation from FBI director William Webster for our work on that case. Max and I shared an incentive award, while Perry received a separate, larger check. So far as I know, no one officially investigated what Perry had said or done to upset the woman to the point that she'd risk prison in her communist homeland to get away from him.

Considering the circumstances, that letter of commendation meant little to me, and apparently not much more to Max, who left the Bureau a couple of months after the redefection. Perry resigned from the FBI a few years later, following an incident in a stairwell when he tried to shove a young woman's hands down his pants, but not before he was exposed to a continuous flow of highly classified national secrets. A couple of years after that he was picked up by police in another state when he had followed a woman into her apartment, exposed himself, and left his FBI business card.

The next defection I worked on was more satisfying for many

reasons. It involved a highly placed Eastern European couple whose reason for defecting was not personal safety but a desire to speak out in a way that would attract world attention to life under Soviet occupation. The couple was charming, intelligent, and, unlike the Soviets I'd encountered, they did not want money; in fact, they tried to pay us for their food while under our protection. They gave up everything in the struggle to make their cause known, but this was not their first act of heroism. During their youth, they'd worked against the Nazis. He was a communist, she an intellectual with enough nerve to have rescued Jewish children from a wartime ghetto. She had been a teen at the time, and she would walk into the ghetto and come back out with a child in tow. By the grace of God, she got away with it.

My work during that defection won me a second letter of commendation from the director, plus a monetary incentive award. This commendation meant a great deal to me because of the people associated with it. Even the fact that it was addressed "Mr. Rosemary" didn't dampen my enthusiasm.

Chapter 11

FLEXIBILITY

Therefore the very basic tenet of our operations is flexibility, meaning flexibility in terms of the maintenance of a Special Agent staff of superbly trained, experienced and conditioned men we may deploy from FBI headquarters to meet changing emphasis and needs on a broad or national level, which Special Agents in Charge may deploy on a day-to-day or minute-to-minute basis in fast-breaking cases, and the deployment and flexibility dictated by Special Agents themselves singly or together during sensitive and critical situations, many of which are completely unforeseen, develop suddenly and defy preplanning.

Justification for Limiting the Position of Special Agent in the FBI to Males FBI Memorandum—May 19, 1971

The aging hotel in downtown D.C. was a sandy, chiseled edifice that had once been grand. On either side of the ornate brass doors were large planters, but cigarette butts grew from the soil instead of flowers. My spike heels clicked a determined rhythm as I moved across the dulled marble, and the lurid stares I encountered in the lobby told me I'd achieved the "working girl" look. Hopefully, I didn't look too pricey for the clientele.

The ominous creak of the elevator encouraged me to climb three flights of stairs, a decision that stretched the hem of my clingy dress and made me wish I hadn't chosen high heels for this job.

On the third floor, the scent of stale smoky carpets filled my nostrils, and as I neared the door, blaring music told me the joint was jumpin'. The undercover agent inside opened the door and whisked me to the bar. As he poured me a vodka and tonic, he whispered, "Corner behind you to the right."

I took a sip and glanced around. My eyes rested on a squat little man in an expensive dark suit. He had a balding head and a whimsical look on his face like a harmless character from a children's book. As the agent introduced me, the European kissed my hand and his eyes locked on my cleavage. He was in the United States on business. He wanted to find large-scale buyers for his pornographic films featuring children.

"Such a beautiful woman," he cooed. "I could put you in the movies."

"Really?" I batted my eyelashes and leaned toward him.

"Sure, perhaps we could talk later . . . alone."

"Perhaps," I smiled, all the while thinking, We'll be talking later, all right, when you're in jail. That's exactly where he'd be by the end of the evening, since this party was just window dressing for the sting. Once he made his deal with the undercover case agent, he'd be packed off to jail. The warrant for his part in this international criminal enterprise was already signed.

It was amazingly easy to deal with slime when I worked undercover. The difficulty was in dealing with their victims, such as the boy prostitutes who walked New York Avenue in downtown D.C. Under their tough facades, they were just children. Living with the fact that I'd never be able to help them turn their lives around was difficult enough, but having to look at photographs of the crimes of pederasts tore my heart. Pederasts are great catalogers; they love to photograph boys all soaped up in the shower and in pornographic positions. I couldn't disassociate these boys' faces from my own young son's, and I was never able to be objective. In fact, sexual exploitation of children is the only kind of investigation that still haunts my sleep at night.

The boy prostitutes on New York Avenue were runaways or "throwaways," ranging in age from nine or ten to about fourteen years old.

Most had been picked up by a "chicken hawk" (their version of a pimp) in a mall, video arcade, or bus station. The chicken hawk took them in, gave them food and drugs, and taught them to have sex with men. The boys called what they did "hustling," and many didn't consider themselves to be gay because they wouldn't take a passive role in sexual acts.

Though the neighborhood has been renovated since, in 1983 the boys lined up on New York Avenue near the Greyhound Bus Station and the Terminal Hotel, an area known as "the Meat Rack." They stood along the sidewalk as men drove by and looked them over. When a car stopped, the motorist would roll down the window and ask, "Want a ride?" Then the boys would go to the car to check out the trick and negotiate a price. If a deal was struck, they got in the car with the john and drove off. Sometimes potential clients simply walked up to them on the street and chose a boy to take into the Terminal Hotel. In 1980, Maryland congressman Robert Bauman was arrested after soliciting sex from a sixteen-year-old boy who was hanging around the area.

The agent I worked with was committed to getting these kids off the streets or at least eliminating their customers. He was an unassuming man, and the boys, knowing he was an FBI agent, cooperated with him. But they still talked tough in front of him and put on a show, strutting and bragging when they spoke. With me, they were just kids. They called me "the lady detective" and assumed I was with the D.C. Metropolitan Police Department. I never told them differently.

After a while, they'd all heard of me and would gather around when I showed up. Their conversations ranged from asking me to go to the movies with them to telling graphic stories of how their clients had hurt them. It was hard to quell the motherly pangs I felt when they confided in me. Some tried to shock me, and others worried that I was judging them, so I gritted my teeth and tried to show nothing but concern, although revulsion for those who victimized these children swept over me. Some told of being handcuffed or tied up and anally raped or beaten until they submitted to even more humiliating acts.

Anyone who thinks prostitution is a victimless crime has never spent time around those who sell their bodies for a living. Even now, I think about those children and wonder whether any of them survived. I know drugs got some of them, street crime got others, and the boys who left the streets have been replaced with new ones. It's a never-ending cycle of pain and abuse.

After six months, I couldn't watch it anymore. When I started having serious thoughts about how a slip of my finger on the trigger of my gun could rid society of some of the predators, I knew it was time to quit working "the Meat Rack."

Meanwhile, parenting my own children from my desk ten hours a day wasn't easy. By the age of eight, my daughter Kendra had developed innovative ways to work the system. I had a standing policy that my children could call me at work at any time and I would take the call. However, when I was out of the office, the radio room wasn't authorized to relay personal calls, except emergencies. So I told the kids to talk to anyone on the squad if they couldn't reach me. I assumed the agents could determine whether the call was an emergency.

One day I walked in and heard one of the guys talking on the phone, "Sure, you can have cookies, Kendra, and while you're at it, have some ice cream too." As it turned out, she'd been calling the squad a few times each afternoon trying to get anyone but me in order to request things she thought I'd deny her.

Chris, too, was learning to work the system. Once, when he'd gotten into a little tiff at school, his teacher sent him home with a note for me to sign. The next day, she called me to ask whether I'd seen the note. When I said I had not, she burst into laughter. The signature on the note Chris had returned read: "My mom."

Chapter 12

THE GOOD GUYS

The FBI is a unique organization comprised of thousands of devoted and capable public servants who live and breathe the agency's motto of fidelity, bravery, and integrity everyday. The FBI has a long and proud history, and it does many things well.

Statement of David M. Walker, Comptroller General of the United States before the Subcommittee on Commerce, Justice, State, and the Judiciary, Committee on Appropriations, House of Representatives June 21, 2002

FBI agents are not assigned partners; they choose the people with whom they will work. L. Douglas Abram was my partner and friend. He was broad-shouldered, graying, and was slow to anger. This soft-spoken man had been a pilot in Vietnam and served in a number of capacities as an FBI agent. He was a member of the SWAT team, a Bureau pilot, and a "sound agent"—one of the guys who runs the wires and plant the bugs—yet he told me his true dream was to become a cowboy singer, just to sit in front of an audience, play his guitar, and make people happy.

Doug and I worked a long-term counterintelligence case where we spent hours sitting in a car night after night with nothing to do but watch a house and chat. There were about thirty minutes of activity when we changed the tapes on our wiretap; otherwise, we sat on surveillance and talked about whatever ran across our minds. Unlike so many other men who used surveillance time as a chance to complain about their wives or flirt, Doug had nothing but praise for his wife and family. He treated me as an equal coworker and never made a pass at me. It just wasn't an issue. Writing these words, I realize how sad it is that a fellow agent who did not put the moves on me or look down on me was an exception. But Doug was exceptional in many ways.

Once, we were assigned a surveillance job in a run-down hotel. The plan was to rent two rooms and wire one of them for video and sound prior to a meeting between an informant and a pederast suspect whom we hoped to prosecute under the Mann Act (White Slavery Act). After the wire was installed, we could listen in on the meeting from the adjacent room, and as soon as the suspect said what we needed to hear, we would burst in and arrest him, as well as the informant. (The informant is always arrested so the criminal doesn't realize his "friend" or "business associate" is working for the FBI.)

That particular hotel was frequented by people of questionable intentions, so the desk clerk was suspicious when we asked to see floor plans. From his leering looks, he seemed to assume we planned to do something kinky, and he wanted to be part of our secret.

"Why do you need floor plans?" he asked.

"I'd just like to know how the beds are placed." Doug smiled, but color crept up his cheeks.

"Uh-huh." The clerk pushed the floor plans Doug's way.

"Uh, well, we're playing a joke on some friends," Doug quickly added. "Could we get the keys to these two rooms? We'd like to take a look."

"Okay, buddy, here're the keys," he dangled them just beyond Doug's reach like a dad lending the car, "but if you're not back in fifteen minutes, I'm charging you for the rooms."

Everything else went off without a hitch, except the informant couldn't locate our suspect that week, and we eventually gave up the surveillance. The entire time we were there, the desk clerk remained curious and tried to glean additional information. There is no telling what he assumed, since there were several men in the room with me at different times each night.

Doug introduced me to flying small planes. I never took a lesson or got a license, but I always volunteered for aerial surveillances. Sooner or later the pilot would get tired of "drilling holes in the sky," as they called the circular patterns a plane makes during surveillance flights. There was no autopilot on these planes, and, when the pilots took breaks, they sometimes let me take the controls and fly while they rested. It was more physically taxing than it looked. The slightest change in steering position meant a big change in course, so I had to hold things steady. Since many FBI pilots had flown in Vietnam and most were thrill seekers by nature, they showed me how to dive, pull up, and make the sharp turns that surveillance flying necessitated. Flying is a glorious freedom, and the small propeller planes allowed me to experience the power of the wind and other natural phenomena, such as air pockets that can make the plane plummet as if it's falling from the sky.

Mostly, Doug and I used aerial surveillance to track moving cars. A plane put us too far away to be noticed by any but the most vigilant suspects. It also meant we could carry out a surveillance over long distances and through secluded areas without being detected. But it wasn't easy to keep the correct car in view, especially at night. I had to lock my eyes onto the car or its headlights and not blink. If I looked away for a second, I lost it. It was exhausting.

Doug left the division before I did. The last time I saw him, he gave me a book on electrical wiring to commemorate the times we installed surveillance wires, and we shook hands good-bye. The office gossip was that we were an item, which is a sad commentary on the prevailing atmosphere where everyone minded my business. I am reminded of a quote from Justice Louis Brandeis in *Olmstead v. U.S.* (1928): "The right to be left alone is the most comprehensive of rights, and the right most valued by a free people." That right was what I gave up to be an agent.

By the end of my first year at the Washington field office, FBI no longer meant Fidelity, Bravery, and Integrity to me. The defenders of the nation's civil rights adhered to a double standard, and I knew it.

Chapter 13
CRUEL INTENTIONS

Once in a while you find yourself in an odd situation. You get into
it by degrees and in the most natural way but, when you are right in
the midst of it, you are suddenly astonished and ask yourself how in
the world it all came about.

Thor Heyerdahl
Kon-Tiki

The realization that I would never be able to improve my situation in the FBI crept up on me slowly. There was no blinding
light; it was more a long series of little defeats that left me less
willing to confront the problems and more resigned to living with them.
I was a single parent receiving minimal child support in one of the most
expensive metropolitan areas in the world, and I needed the income. I
also loved my work, but my coworkers drove me nuts.

In the early 1980s, while assigned to the Washington field office, I
complained to my supervisor about a photocopied cartoon pinned to
the bulletin board above the register where the agents signed on and off
duty every day. It was a drawing of a nude figure that was bent over with
its head stuck up its rear. The caption read, "A typical CI-2 female
Agent."

The first time I saw it, I ripped it down and threw it away. By the
time I signed out that night, a new copy of the cartoon was posted in
the same spot. I took it down every day for a week or so, but there was

always a new one to replace it. When I finally complained, I was furious. It was blatantly obvious that this sexist illustration was against the laws that ban a hostile work environment, and I marched into my supervisor's office, once again putting my faith in the system.

My supervisor, Jim, was an affable man, short, heavy, and never without a cigarette in his mouth. He had recommended me for several commendations, so I thought he respected my work. Still, I had a nagging fear he wouldn't understand why the drawing bothered me.

I closed the office door, and he looked up from the piles of paper on his desk, a half-inch of ash hanging precariously from the tip of the cigarette that dangled from his lips. His shirt was wrinkled and his hair finger-combed.

"Pull up a chair," he said.

We frequently did the *Mary Tyler Moore Show* Lou Grant/Mary Richards bit, so I pushed an ashtray where I thought the ash would fall and said, "You really shouldn't smoke, you know."

He laughed and crushed out the cigarette as I sat in the chair across from him. "Are you just here to be the guardian of good taste or have you got something to say?" he asked.

"I've got something to say."

"I was afraid of that," he laughed again. "Well, what?"

"I want you to talk to the guys about that damned drawing they put up over the register. I've got to look at it when I sign in or out, and it's not okay with me. In fact I think it creates a hostile work environment, which as you know, is against federal law."

"That's what this is about?" he asked, lighting up again. "Take my advice and forget about it. The guys kid me about being Greek, and I just let it roll off my back. Everybody kids everybody around here." Then he hit me with the usual, "You've got to have thick skin if you want to get along in the Bureau."

"Jim," I said, "I'm sorry, but being kidded about being Greek just isn't comparable to having a demeaning drawing about women posted in the squad room."

He put down the cigarette and clasped his hands in front of him on his desk. He pursed his lips and looked me in the eye. "We're friends, right?"

I nodded.

"Then take my advice as a friend: Get out there and laugh it off. If you complain, it will only get worse."

The sad thing was that I knew he was right, and I also knew that without his support, there was no use in carrying the complaint further. He was a powerful supervisor whom the front office trusted, and he would line up behind the men on this one. He just didn't get why I found the "joke" to be a problem.

He promoted me to relief supervisor soon thereafter, and it angered some of the guys. Two refused to speak to me, even about business, for the duration of my Washington field assignment; others made up a nickname for me: Kuntenführer. One complained to the supervisor because I wouldn't approve his paperwork, even though it didn't meet minimum standards. In fact, one of his rejected documents contained more than a hundred errors. Being tagged a "by-the-book agent" in investigations was considered an insult in FBI land, but it was one tag I was proud to wear.

Supervisors from other squads took the liberty of telling me they didn't believe in women working, much less as FBI agents. It never occurred to them—and they didn't care—that their actions and comments were inappropriate or that they were breaking the law with their antagonistic remarks.

That attitude toward women agents was rampant in the Washington field office. I once walked into a briefing in progress, and an agent rose to offer me his chair. The briefer, who was later promoted to assistant director, stopped in the middle of his presentation and chided the man for his action. "If she wants to be equal, she can stand," he said coldly. All I did was walk into the room; I didn't ask to sit down.

Another woman and I were assigned to a moving surveillance team that was scheduled to drive up the coast of Maryland. Someone asked the case agent who else was on the team, and the same man who'd harassed me in the briefing shouted across the squad room, "Six guys and a couple of cunts." No one even flinched.

I wondered whether situations like this occurred only in San Francisco or Washington. Or did they just happen to me? But I found it was endemic to the FBI system. A supervisor in New York was testing a closed-circuit television surveillance system. The sensor was on the floor of his office and was set to beam a picture into the nearby squad room. He got a female agent, who did not know what was going on, to stand over the sensor, which transmitted a picture of her crotch to everyone in the squad room. This "prank" got him transferred to another squad, but he was not demoted.

There were a number of male coworkers whom I trusted. They could make cracks around me, and I laughed it off with no hard feelings. I had no qualms about a little ribald humor among consenting friends— consent being the operable word. In these situations, I understood their intent, and I knew they would stop if I asked. It was the people I didn't know and who assumed they could say whatever they liked who left me angry and humiliated. Once, I was sitting in the squad room at the Washington field office when an agent from another squad overheard me discussing the new wallpaper I'd bought for my house. His response was that I could probably "burn the wallpaper off the walls in bed." I don't even recall this man's name—that's how well I knew him—but the atmosphere in the Bureau was such that he felt free to make his offensive remark loudly enough for three squads to hear.

When there are hundreds of men in a work environment—men who feel free to let whatever transits their brains fly out of their mouths—a woman may hear these kind of comments several times a day, almost every day; and, each time, she is judged on her reaction: can she take it, or is she a humorless bitch?

This was the attitude some had toward racial minorities, as well. There was an African-American man on my squad, a true gentleman who never provoked anyone. Every time we made surveillance plans as a squad, an agent I'll call Martin suggested that the African American dress as a jockey and stand in the yard holding a lantern.

One of Martin's favorite tricks was to get a woman alone on a surveillance assignment and describe in great detail the sexual acts he'd like to perform with virtually every female who walked down the street. He did an imitation of taking off a large-breasted woman's bra and pretending to catch her breasts as they fell out. If you mentioned a woman in conversation, he'd ask whether she had "big ole good 'uns or good ole big 'uns." Asking him to curb his adolescent behavior only enhanced his pleasure.

Did his lack of respect for women affect operations? Martin joined one of my surveillances that occurred on a holiday. There also was a big football game that day. Since he saw me as powerless, he felt no qualms about leaving his assigned post to watch the game and taking the holiday pay. What happened when I reported it? To my knowledge, nothing. Did he receive holiday pay? You bet.

Martin phoned me a few years after I left the Bureau, when I was a program manager in a large consulting firm. He was job hunting, and we made small talk. When he asked how I was doing, I made the mistake of telling him I'd been prescribed medication for migraines. His immediate response was that my "underwear must be too tight." I ended that call as quickly as possible and marveled that he believed I might hire him or recommend him to other managers in my company. Like many special agents I ran across in my Bureau career, he was clueless about how his behavior was perceived by the outside world. The difference was that, this time, I was not powerless.

Chapter 14

New Lessons Learned

The thoughts of a prisoner—they're not free either.

Alexander Solzhenitsyn
One Day in the Life of Ivan Denisovitch

I was always interested in opportunities to learn new things and expand my investigative repertoire. For example, I wanted to get onto the terrorism squad and volunteered whenever the members needed help. Everyone I worked with from the Washington field office's counterterrorism squad was great. The hostage negotiators were assigned to this squad, and it was their work I wanted to learn.

I volunteered to participate in a hostage negotiator/hostage rescue team training exercise. The interesting thing is how real these role-playing exercises tend to become to those involved. There have been exercises where people were "held hostage" for days and actually experienced Stockholm syndrome—identifying so closely with the hostage-takers that they switch loyalties and take the side of their captors.

It takes a surprisingly small amount of intense fear to inflict substantial damage on the human psyche. In one hostage exercise, the FBI used civilian volunteers as "hostages." The volunteers had a general idea of what was going to happen and when they'd be released from the exercise, because they knew what day they were scheduled to return home. After several days as hostages, they were loaded onto a bus and told they were going to the airport to fly overseas. In reality, the exercise called for them to be rescued from the bus by a SWAT team. One of the "terror-ists" handed a hostage a box with switches on it and said that, if the bus were assaulted, she was to press the button and blow up the bus. The explosion, he said, would probably kill everyone. When SWAT agents boarded the bus, the volunteer hostage was pressing the button franti-cally and sobbing, "It won't work! I can't make it work." This how strong Stockholm syndrome can be.

My own experience portraying a hostage was surprisingly emotional for me, and the exercise gave me insight into what true hostages experi-ence. Susan, a fellow agent, and I were assigned the role of hostages, while two Spanish-speaking men pretended to be hostagetakers. This was the scenario: A group of people had been taken hostage during a bank robbery and was being held by a Central American leftist faction. The negotiators had to talk our captors into making concessions, such as letting each of us speak on the phone, the theory being that if they could get the hostagetakers to make small concessions, the big ones might come easier. Also, each concession made was a sign to the nego-tiator that he was earning the hostagetakers' trust.

According to the plan, Susan was supposed to be a diabetic who required insulin and food every few hours. She had no medicine with her, and, as the day wore on, she was supposed to get sicker and sicker. My assignment was to verbally assault the negotiators for not doing what our captors wanted, since their failure to cooperate prevented Susan from getting lifesaving medical attention.

While waiting for the negotiators to call, there was a lot of downtime. The agents playing the hostagetakers regaled us with humorous stories and the latest office gossip to pass the time, but we snapped into our roles when the phone rang. It was a great game.

Late in the afternoon, I whipped myself into a veritable frenzy when the negotiator called. I screeched into the phone that he'd better start helping us or he'd be responsible for our deaths. I went on and on about how his delays were causing us to remain captive, making it as personal as possible and threatening lawsuits. The negotiator let me continue the harangue until I couldn't think of anything else to say, then he spoke to me in a soft, calm tone. No one was more surprised than I when I burst into tears! I'd been drawn so strongly into my role that my emotions were raw. While I hadn't begun to sympathize with my captors, I was angry with the negotiators, as if they were intentionally withholding Susan's vital medication.

Playacting can be powerful. One of my friends, a supervisor in the FBI's Behavioral Science Unit, participated in a similar exercise. After a couple of days as an imaginary hostage, he became so agitated that other agents had to throw a blanket over him to restrain him until he calmed down.

Working with hostage negotiators was just one of many intriguing experiences I had in the Washington field office. Another occurred when I was working in downtown D.C. with a man from the terrorism squad and we received a call concerning the possible assassination of a diplomat. The diplomat had been shot twice in the head: once under the chin and once through the temple. He was in a car in a dingy underground parking lot downtown, his head thrown back, his mouth open, and his chin sagging to one side. The car and garage floor were a blackened sticky mess from the massive amount of spilled blood, and I'll never forget the smell. We couldn't account for all the bullets, so I accompanied the body to the morgue to witness the autopsy and take possession of the missing bullet as evidence.

Along with a homicide detective from the Washington Metropolitan Police Department, I donned a gown and gloves to join Dr. James Luke, then-chief of the D.C. Medical Examiner's Office, who performed the autopsy. The detective was experienced in such matters as these and had come prepared with a pack of spearmint gum and a cup of coffee. He also had a tuna sandwich. I must have been looking at him strangely because he said, "Get some coffee. Trust me. You're going to want something strong-smelling to hold under your nose in there." He handed me a stick of gum, and I put it in my mouth.

Dr. Luke explained everything he did as if he were teaching medical students. As soon as the doctor made the Y incision, which slashes the body from each shoulder to the center of the sternum, then straight down the body to the pubis, I understood about the coffee, gum, and sandwich. A stench filled the room that made me want to rush to the nearest waste can and vomit. It was the unsettling smell of death and decomposition that screamed, "Run! Save yourself!" Of course, I just stood there, chewed the gum, and tried to let the scent of peppermint fill my nostrils.

Dr. Luke removed the skin on the face and the skull—fragmented from a shot to the temple and one beneath the chin that had blown out his sinuses—looked like a jigsaw puzzle. He explained that, at that point, he couldn't rule out suicide, a statement I found puzzling.

Next, he removed the internal organs and examined them one at a time for chronic disease. The detective and I assisted him by weighing the organs, and he talked us through the procedure, explaining the rationale for each action he took. His professorial attitude helped me disassociate from the realization that we were dismantling a human being piece by piece. After about forty-five minutes, an officer arrived and told us the missing bullet had been located, so I was free to go. But I was too interested to leave.

In the end, the doctor's preliminary opinion was that the diplomat had committed suicide. Apparently, the pattern of shots in this case was not unusual for a suicide. The man had placed the gun under his chin but jerked his head back as he pulled the trigger. He ended up shooting out his sinuses, which was so painful that he finished himself off by shooting through his own temple.

A couple of weeks later, a man from the counterterrorism squad, whom I'll call Agent X, had to witness an autopsy. He fainted during the Y incision, cut his head, and had to get stitches. The other agents were merciless, especially since a woman had just made it through an autopsy without fainting. They put a sign over his desk that said, "Autopsy–1, Agent X–0."

This seemed smug coming from agents who did not have the guts to observe the procedure themselves.

Chapter 15

SMART WOMAN, ANOTHER FOOLISH CHOICE

I am amazed and astounded and completely at a loss to understand how a supposedly rational human being could commit an act of such colossal stupidity.

Letter of censure from J. Edgar Hoover
Joseph Schott
No Left Turns

I remarried in 1981. It was one of those "serial marriages" that police psychologists joke about; that is, making the same mistake over and over again. My son, daughter, and I hadn't heard from Dick in years when Alvie walked into our lives. What attracted me most to him was the way he treated my children. He played with them, joked with them, entertained them, and made them laugh. What a refreshing change. It had been a long time since any man I was interested in had accepted the fact that I had children.

Alvie was an Army officer when I met him, but he became an FBI agent a year after we married. Throughout the time we dated, there were hints that our relationship was doomed, but I chose not to see them. The week before our wedding, he phoned to report that his mother threatened to disinherit him if he married me, because they were Catholics and I was a Lutheran. He laughed about her threat, but things were never the same after that call.

We'd kidded each other before the marriage, but soon the little barbs we had thrown in jest weren't funny. After our kiss at the marriage altar, Alvie pulled away from me and said to the crowd, "Down, girl!" I just stood there, feeling hurt and demeaned, but it confirmed my worst fears—fears I could not face until the public humiliation forced the issue. All I can say is that, for me, there has always been a huge discrepancy between the logical abilities of my heart and head.

Within the first month of our marriage, Alvie, who was still in the Army, told me he was working late. There was an important inspection coming up and he needed to prepare. As the evening wore on, I decided to cheer him up with a phone call. His sergeant answered the phone and told me Alvie was at a party. That night when my husband came home, he was not wearing his wedding ring. He said, "It must have fallen off somewhere." I never saw it again.

Before the wedding, Alvie and I had wrestled playfully, but after our vows, as often as not, wrestling ended when someone got hurt. At first it was just me, but toward the end, he got rough with the kids, especially Christopher. Once this happened, our arguments turned to vicious fights, physical and emotional.

Soon after the marriage, I learned that making love could hurt too. Several times, Alvie forcefully raped me, and he made sure it hurt. I told him it hurt, which was obvious from the blood, and I tried to fight him off, but all he did was laugh. When I came home from work, I never knew whether I would face a violent night, and PTSD (post-tramatic stress disorder) took hold. Eventually, when Alvie attacked me, I was able to numb my body and disassociate from what was happening. But there is no way to stop the flood of terrifying images that still accost my mind.

The rapes were far enough apart, and I was so out of touch with my feelings, that each time it happened, I fooled myself into believing it wouldn't—couldn't possibly—happen again. After a while, I hoped I could drive him out of the house and out of my family's life. I was tired of being pushed around in every aspect of my life, and my once-tender feelings for him had turned to hate.

The numbing effect of PTSD was a protective mechanism, but it also contributed to my seeming inability to make the rational decisions that would have gotten me out of this situation. Even with the numbing and general disassociative thinking, I often needed several drinks before I worked up the nerve to go to bed at night. Although I no longer drink to go to sleep or feel safe, PTSD visions cause me to relive the violence of that marriage in my mind—even today. Safety, once lost, is a hard thing to recapture.

In addition to his physical attacks, Alvie went after my mental and emotional health. His habit of verbal put-downs reinforced what I heard all day at work, and I reacted just as I did at work, with smart-aleck remarks or stony silence. There was no escaping the harassment that chipped away at my self-esteem. Old demons reappeared, and I began a downward spiral that made me believe some of what he was saying and change things about the way I looked. Alvie had told me that only blondes were beautiful, so I bleached my auburn locks. He didn't comment for days. Exasperated, I finally asked him whether he liked the new look. He said, "Oh, I didn't realize you colored your hair. I just thought you washed it."

Alvie often showed interest in other women. One weekend we decided to get away and try to restore our relationship. We went out to eat in downtown Washington, D.C. After a lovely dinner, as we were walking back to our hotel, he became so engaged in flirting with a woman who was walking across the street that he tripped over a fire hydrant. All I could feel was shame. Mostly, I was ashamed of myself for getting into another degrading, abusive marriage.

Alvie and I lived together for three years, and, by the second year, my self-image was shattered. When I talked about leaving him, he would attempt a reconciliation. He would become apologetic and pitiful, like any con man, and I would give in and try again. The results were catastrophic to my psyche, especially with the negative reinforcements of my workplace.

So why didn't I, the gun-toting FBI agent, just pack up and leave? The question is simple, but the answer is complex. Basically, I felt worthless, powerless, and exhausted. I was a typical battered woman. That's the long and short of it.

Church was a safe, peaceful place for the children and me, although Alvie called us "heathens" because we didn't follow what he believed was the "true" religion. He was jealous of the time we spent at church and of the supportive people who befriended us there. On those rare occasions when he attended a church function, he made a point of embarrassing me. He wanted us to be too ashamed to come back, and he was almost successful.

As the director of parish education, I invited my husband to watch the children's Christmas show. Officiating was a female vicar, a third-year seminary student, who had a lovely, strong singing voice. But Alvie didn't approve of women at the pulpit, and as she was leading the procession of costumed children past our pew, she lifted her arms and said, "Everybody sing." Alvie turned to her and shouted, "Oh, eat me!"

There I was, the woman who was directing the religious education of the children in the church, and my husband was shouting profanities at the vicar. I wanted the earth to open up and swallow me, anything to get me out of there. Instead, I sat like an ice sculpture until the show was over. I walked out of church with numbed emotions, afraid to look people in the face, and hopeless about improving my marriage.

Those were tough years. In the Washington field office I had to work long hours, and the children needed me more as they approached adolescence. Chris began to sneak out of the house and skip school. I had no idea. His grades fell, and he complained about his teachers. Preoccupied with my own trauma, I didn't understand what I was hearing or recognize how hard our home life was for him. That was the beginning of what our family counselor called "teenage maladjustment." I blamed Chris' situation on his age, and thought I could make it go away if I just loved him enough. The fact that Chris and I got along so well allowed me to rationalize what I saw.

In February 1984, life changed for all of us. Alvie, by then an FBI agent, was shot while attempting to arrest a fugitive. We were well on our way to divorce, and the morning of the shooting Alvie and I had had another big argument. When he'd announced he would be working late, I'd told him he'd better eat before he came home because I wasn't cooking twice. Then, we'd both stomped off to our jobs, and I didn't see him or hear from him again until I got to the hospital.

It snowed that day, and I'd parked in the infamous Washington field office mud lot. That evening, as I approached my car I stepped into a hole, and my foot sank in until the icy water reached my shin. My windshield was covered in ice, and I didn't have a scraper. I tried to use a credit card to scrape it, but the card broke. When I finally got inside the car, I looked in the rearview mirror and saw mascara streaming down my cheeks, frizzy hair framing my face like a fright wig.

Rush-hour traffic was stalled in the snowy drizzle. I had to push someone's car to get it started again so vehicles could cross a blocked bridge. And as I fought to get home, I dreaded the inevitable evening argument. Angry words were the only kind Alvie and I exchanged anymore.

When I walked into the house, hoping for a few moments of peace before Alvie arrived, Chris said someone was on the phone. It was the special agent in charge of the Alexandria office, calling to tell me that Alvie had been shot. He described the wound as "not too serious" and said a police officer would be by shortly to take me to the hospital.

Numb, I sat my children down and told them what had happened. They were concerned, but calm. They would stay with another agent and her husband while I went to the hospital.

Soon two police officers arrived, and I invited them in. I asked them if they were hungry or would like a Coke. They said "no," and I asked them if they could wait while I cleaned up.

I went upstairs, plugged in my electric curlers, and washed the mascara off my face. At that point, I began to do what I can only describe as milling around. I walked from the bathroom to my closet several times. I paused in front of my closet and couldn't remember what I needed. I stopped in front of the mirror and stared. Exhausted and stunned, I went through the motions of getting ready, totally disassociated from the trauma. Finally dressed, I went downstairs as my friend arrived to pick up my children. I kissed the kids good-bye, then the officers drove me to the hospital.

There was a flurry of activity in the emergency room, and Alvie was acting extra macho. "I want a beer!" he shouted as I entered the room, but when the crowd left us alone for a minute, he whispered, "This isn't like in the movies. This hurts."

His arm jerked frequently, and I feared a spinal injury, so I pulled his doctor into another room to question him. The doctor didn't answer my questions to my satisfaction so, as we spoke, I began to back him up, pushing his chest with my hand. My personality had changed to a command presence, and, from then on, I wanted to run the show entirely. I didn't need help from anyone. I had no emotion and felt no fatigue.

Several agents arrived to announce that the two fugitives, one of whom had shot Alvie, were still at large, so the office needed to use the agents at the hospital in the manhunt. They asked if I needed anything. When I said "no," they left. Actually I didn't know whether I needed anything or not. At some point over the next few days, the special agent in charge said they'd worried about me at first, but then they realized that I was handling the situation better than anyone. What a joke!

I stayed with Alvie until the early hours of the morning, standing next to his gurney in the hall for what seemed an eternity, as he waited his turn in radiology. At 3:00 A.M., I went home and slept for about two hours, but I was still in my command mode when I returned to the hospital for Alvie's early-morning surgery.

While I was in the ladies' room, orderlies arrived and took Alvie away. When I found he was gone, I went down the hall by myself and located the surgical area. I saw a surgeon press a button beside the door, and it opened automatically. So I pressed the same button and walked up to a station that served as the command center for the operating rooms. A nurse asked what I was doing, and I told her I was there to see Alvie. She wanted to know if I was an agent or his wife. I flashed my credentials and said, "Both."

Another agent was scheduled to observe the surgery and to take custody of the recovered bullet, and my presence thoroughly confused the nurse. However, I walked past her and she didn't try to stop me. I stayed with Alvie like an emotionless bodyguard until they took him into the operating room, and then I went to the lobby and sat with a few friends.

There was a provision in the FBI manual to grant administrative leave with pay for agents affected by shootings, but my manager didn't allow me to take it. My supervisor told me I was "too high-profile"—whatever that meant—to get administrative leave benefits. He also commented that the mail clerk watched the agents' comings and goings and would probably complain. I was way too tired to even address why anyone would complain about an allowed benefit, and as a result, I was forced to take vacation time to deal with Alvie's shooting. I was the only agent at the hospital who had to take annual or sick leave to be there.

Alvie's surgery was successful, so I went to dinner with two of the women from the Washington field office. It was the first meal I'd had since lunch the day before. My friends knew something was wrong and weren't buying my command presence. High on adrenaline, I couldn't think straight and didn't eat, and I'd hardly given a thought to my children, because I knew they were being properly cared for.

Three days after the shooting, my pastor took me aside. We were alone in a room, and I don't recall what we were talking about, but I burst into tears—the only time I cried in front of anyone. Looking back, I see that I was concerned about how other agents would view my reactions at the hospital and judge me as to whether I were a good agent, based upon what they saw. Some were true friends, and some weren't. Some were what I would describe as "shooting groupies," people who just wanted to be near the action. One of those shooting groupies, who was never nice to me on the job, called me after midnight one night, claiming that was the only time he could get through. He never gave a thought to whether I needed sleep.

Alvie and I continued arguing even while he was hospitalized. Even in his drugged condition, he offered plenty of spiteful comments about my appearance. He said my eye makeup made me look like a raccoon, and when I couldn't give him a status report on the search for the fugitives, he looked me in the eye and said, "Then what good are you?"

Once he was released from the hospital, I was trapped. While Alvie was recuperating, I didn't have the heart to leave him, so I continued to take care of this man who had abused me—mentally and physically. But the truth is I hated touching him, and I hated listening to his put-downs, and listening to complaints of pain from this man who had laughed when he had hurt me. Then one evening in September 1984, nine-year-old Kendra came running to me, sobbing. Alvie had slapped her across the face for making noise. I didn't even ask him to explain; I just packed a suitcase, rounded up the children, and left, without so much as a backward glance. Alvie returned to duty, and I filed for divorce. We haven't spoken since the divorce was final.

Looking back on that period, I have many regrets. Dealing with my personal problems clouded my judgment and affected the way I dealt with my children. Although I had talked with them about the shooting, we generally had agreed that everything would be fine and had not gone into depth about how we felt. We hadn't really addressed what this crisis meant to us or how our lives had changed.

Five years later, I attended a presentation from the FBI's Post-Critical Incident Program, a group established to help FBI employees get through major traumatic events, such as line-of-duty deaths and shootings. Jimmy Carter, the presenter, talked about the Bureau's handling of shooting incidents and said if anyone wanted to discuss that subject with him, he'd be available after the program. Later, I practically pinned him up against the wall and gave him a five-minute blast about FBI policy versus reality.

That single conversation set me on the long road to healing. I began to talk to members of the program, and for the first time, I began to really talk to my children about the shooting. Five years after the incident, I learned that my children had seen newscasts about the search for the fugitives who had injured their stepfather. The media had used our names and printed our address, so some kids at school had told Chris and Kendra that the bad guys knew where they lived. Perhaps the most disturbing revelation was that Chris and Kendra had feared that I, too, would be shot. For years, my children had lived with thoughts that someone would kill them or me, and I had never made that connection.

When I asked them whether my job scared them, they each immediately answered "yes." This was the first time I realized how they felt about my work; but then, I'd never asked before.

Christopher looked at me and said, "I just wish I could be like you and never be scared."

I couldn't believe my ears! I'd been sleeping with a gun in my bed ever since the stalker in Sausalito pushed his way into our flat in 1978. I was so compulsive about it that I'd created a little ritual of checking the position of the gun over and over before I could fall asleep, as some people check their alarm clocks. I even slept with one hand under the sheet so I could get to the gun without letting an intruder see my hand move.

On the job, it wasn't acceptable for me to express or even acknowledge "feelings," known in law enforcement peer support counseling as "the real f-word." Unaware of how my mask of control affected my children, I had walked around in a psychological protective bubble that had shut out potential avenues of support, such as family and friends.

My best instinct had told me that if I pretended not to be afraid of anything, my children wouldn't worry. I had been so out of touch that I never realized they could be frightened for me. I never considered that they'd lost their father through divorce and feared losing their mother to death. They saw me being "brave" and assumed they had to be brave too. What Chris and Kendra drew from my behavior was that fear was an emotional no-no. Not only did they feel uncomfortable discussing their fears with me, they were ashamed they had fears at all.

Finally, the three of us sat down as a family and read the FBI's instruction book for handling shootings. I asked them what the FBI should do to help kids whose parent had been hurt. That discussion was cathartic for all of us. I sent our suggestions to John Otto, an executive assistant director who served as acting director of the FBI until William Sessions arrived. He ensured that the FBI adopted some of our suggestions, which made all three of us feel that good had come of our pain.

After that, I joined the Post-Critical Incident Peer Support Group as a debriefer. That association was valuable to me for the rest of my career in the Bureau and remains so today. I finally felt free to talk to friends made in the peer support group. While others on the job had summarily dismissed me when I tried to open up about how I felt, the peer support group didn't mind listening to me, and they didn't think less of me for showing what many other agents perceived as weakness. Critical incident debriefing taught me that it wasn't possible to shake off the pain and go back to work as if nothing has happened. In fact, studies indicate that law enforcement officers tend to resign within two years of a fatal shooting, if there is no intervention.

On average, twice as many officers take their own lives every year than are killed by others in the line of duty. Personally, I consider these suicides to be line-of-duty deaths that are a direct result of a job that piles on the stress and discourages healthy outlets. Law enforcement and other emergency service careers demand that people disassociate from the pain they see on the job and keep working as if nothing has affected them. You can bet that this carries over into their home lives.

Law enforcement families may experience the same stress reactions as the officer simply from learning about dangerous incidents, either from the officer or from the nightly news. Medical research has shown that children can even experience PTSD from watching catastrophes on television, such as when planes crashed into the Twin Towers in New York City.

Children in law enforcement families can suffer in many ways. Children get most of their ideas about law enforcement from what they see on television, and they use their imaginations to fill in information they don't have. They fantasize about what is happening to their law enforcement parent and sometimes imagine things far worse than reality. In addition, they may have traumatized parents who are emotionally or physically unavailable for them.

As part of the Post-Critical Incident Peer Support Group, I traveled to various offices after shootings to explain what had happened to my family and to listen to what others were experiencing. Each time was difficult, but it was gratifying to help people address their own and their children's needs, and it was important for me to talk about my own experiences.

Critical incident debriefing is exhausting. Some agents and I once served on a debriefing team after a tragic shooting incident involving the use of automatic weapons. Several men had died during that arrest, some with multiple shots that nearly severed body parts, including the lower part of one man's face. For two uninterrupted days, our debriefing team listened to heart-wrenching stories from the agents and their families. Late the last night, we returned to our hotel, thinking we'd grab a quick bite then go to sleep. We were walking down the hall of the hotel, each of us exhausted, dazed, and distracted. When we reached a wall at the end of the corridor, we stopped as a group and stood there staring at it. It was as if none of us knew what to do next.

Later, I participated in National Police Week activities. What the public sees on the news is the annual rededication of the National Police Monument in Washington, D.C., where the names of officers killed during that year are added to the memorial wall. Privately, I joined families, friends, and coworkers of officers killed in the line of duty, for special peer counseling. We met in groups to help each other through the losses.

For several years, I worked with adults but found that I was not strong enough to bear the grief of the mothers of officers. In fact, halfway through one group session, I ended up sobbing with my head buried in the shoulder of the woman next to me. For them, there is little comfort. A mother always feels the need to protect her children, and a child's death brings a unique sense of grief mixed with survivor's guilt. I could not separate my emotions from their grief, so I was no good to them. As they say in psychological counseling, you can either reach your hand into the hole to help someone out or get down in the hole with them. If you fall in the hole, neither of you is getting out.

As a result, I turned my attentions to the children of officers killed in the line of duty. I was more comfortable with them, mainly because their grief was mixed with childhood play. They could cry one minute and be outside playing ball the next. The trick is to understand how children work through grief at various ages, and guide them through the task. There are no magic words to make it all better, and, sometimes, listening in silence is the best gift you can give.

This work was the beginning of forgiveness for me. I'm not there yet, but I'm not as bitter as I was for so many years.

Chapter 16
LIFE IN HOOVERLAND

The political challenge of communism springs from Lenin's
conviction that power, not law, is decisive.

J. Edgar Hoover
A Study of Communism
1962

I n May 1985, I became the seventh woman in the history of the FBI
to be named to the post of government manager-14 (GM-14)
supervisory special agent. As a supervisor in the Intelligence Division (now the Counterintelligence Division) at FBI headquarters in
Washington, D.C., I was responsible for program management of cases
in the New York field office, the largest office in the Bureau.

A supervisor's survival at FBI headquarters depends upon the ability
to unravel the mysteries of Bureau administrivia. Early on, for example,
I noticed that one of the other supervisors read his communications by
placing a ruler under each line. I have an astigmatism that causes lines
to run together when I read and I often use a ruler to keep things
straight, so I wasn't curious until the day I heard him declare, "Aha! Just
as I suspected! These words aren't evenly spaced!"

I have no idea why he was so concerned about this, but I would have
hated to have been the secretary who had to retype the long document.
In the early '80s, the headquarters' typists were still using electric type-
writers and carbon paper, so retyping a perfect page was not a trivial feat.

Another day, I was sitting at my desk, pen poised to initial a communication, when from out of nowhere a hand appeared and grabbed the pen. Behind me stood my agitated supervisor, who handed me a pencil.

"Never use a pen to initial a headquarters communication," he warned, his eyes wide in disbelief, then walked away without further explanation, my pen still clutched in his hand.

Intrigued and amused, I consulted the agent in the cubicle next to mine. "Why can't I use a pen?"

With a knowing nod he whispered, "Plausible denial."

That was the beginning of my foray into the Hooveresque traditions and rules that make FBI headquarters the incredible logjam they can be. In those times, field offices sent in several copies of communications. Field copies could be white or blue, depending upon the type of communication, and there were generally two copies for FBI headquarters. The headquarters' file copies were supposed to be yellow; if they weren't yellow, they couldn't be filed unless the supervisor wrote "Treat as yellow" on them. There was actually a "Treat as yellow" stamp.

In the lower right-hand corner of each communication was a block stamp, which bore the date received and the supervisor's name. To send a copy of a document to the file, the supervisor was supposed to sign through the name and date, even though there was a space designated for the initials and the date, and it wasn't in that box. If you didn't sign through both, the paper came back to you. And finally, the mailroom penciled a diagonal T in the upper right-hand corner of certain outgoing communications. The T, as it turns out, stood for Tolson—Clyde Anderson Tolson, the associate director of the FBI who became the director upon Hoover's death. Tolson was Hoover's best friend and constant companion. They were so close, in fact, that Hoover left most of his estate to Tolson, and they are buried just a few yards from each other in the Congressional Cemetery in Washington, D.C. Tolson signed out headquarters communications with a big, canted T. Although Tolson died in 1975, the mailroom had never received authorization to send out communications without the Tolson T. So in the years that followed, they provided the *T* themselves in order to keep the mail moving.

Important communications had to be routed through the Reading Room, for proofreading. Its staff was always referred to as "little old ladies in tennis shoes," but that was just part of the mythology. In actuality, it was staffed with grammarians of various ages, and they were to have the final say on text. It is believed that, in Hoover's day, a supervisory special agent at FBI headquarters could be demoted for spelling errors. Such arbitrary beheadings for grammar were among Hoover's fear-instilling mechanisms.

Actually, I have a great deal of admiration for certain aspects of the system that Hoover created. Although the man was compulsively rigid in thought, his demand that agents demonstrate perseverance and precise attention to detail resulted in remarkable investigative work. The atmosphere that became his legacy is driven by fear, but he did clean up the corruption that characterized the agency before he assumed command in 1924.

Headquarters was a quiet and orderly place where the Legal Counsel Division wielded tremendous power. The Legal Counsel supervisors had to approve most major operational requests to ensure no law would be broken, and many agents lived in fear of them and their power. Personally, I found the Bureau's lawyers to be helpful. They taught me how to write documents correctly and how to better analyze the statutes so I knew what had to be included in my papers to the court. Despite their attention to detail, the attorneys were not always stuffy.

There is a story told about a new FBI attorney on his first day of work. He was acquainted with his supervisor's reputation for being particularly humorless. When summoned to the supervisor's office, he received a lecture on his grave responsibility to carry on Mr. Hoover's work and was questioned closely as to his moral commitment. At the end of the interview, the new attorney was asked to kneel and pray with his supervisor. Afraid of what would happen if he didn't comply, he got down on his knees, head bowed, hands folded, and affirmed before God his fervent desire to perpetuate Hoover's work. When he opened his eyes, he was surrounded by the attorneys he would work with, all of whom had participated in this practical joke. The real supervisor was away on leave.

Even the halls of FBI headquarters were steeped in mystery. There were transparent lines along the floor that marked a track for the mail robot to run on. To ensure that the tracks were not damaged, a warning was posted at intervals along the walls: "Do not step on invisible lines." Why the sign-maker did not see the illogic and humor in this, I'll never know.

The critical elements for my Intelligence Division performance review had what I always called the mind-reading element: "Anticipates supervisor's questions." Still, I enjoyed my time there. The Intelligence Division was a contemplative place that operated like a chess game. Much of my time was spent approving and coordinating operations and writing applications to the court for warrants, and I perfected the art of moving paperwork swiftly through the system. My there's-a-way-to-make-this-work attitude held me in good stead. No matter how much time it took to chat with people along the way, it proved more efficient to walk my paperwork through FBI headquarters whenever possible, rather than dropping it in the interoffice mail and waiting for a response. Some applications to the court required approximately eight signatures, including the director's, the attorney general's, FBI and Department of Justice legal counsels', and several others in between.

Aside from the elaborate approval process, certain personalities enjoyed slowing everything to a crawl. One unit chief I worked for frequently rejected paperwork without saying why. Supervisors received such written comments as, "It doesn't flow," "It's not convincing," or "There are three grammar mistakes in this communication. Find and correct them." These critiques were a throwback to freshman English and provided no guidance for improving the paperwork or getting the job done. One coworker submitted a communication fifty-four times before it was signed out. This could have been done in a single rewrite if he'd received proper guidance.

Because I encountered no prejudice of any sort at headquarters, I was infinitely happier than I had been in my field assignments, and my hope grew that the Bureau could be a place where I would be judged on my work alone. Nonetheless, it was an exhausting commute, and headquarters work took a lot of concentration. After a few months, I felt worn down and tried to pep myself up with Geritol tablets. I carried them in my purse so they would be within reach whenever I remembered to take them. Because headquarters personnel do not make arrests, I carried my .38 in my purse, instead of in a hip holster. One day, I went to headquarters' basement indoor range to qualify with my revolver. As 'we conducted the preshoot weapons inspection, I noticed that something was lodged in the muzzle of my gun. One of the firearms instructors had to use a pocket knife to dislodge the item that was jammed in the end of the gun. Imagine my embarrassment when he held up half a Geritol tablet!

I heard that story for years to come. Fortunately, as the story spread around the Bureau, no one remembered it had been my gun.

Some of my most interesting hours at FBI headquarters were spent analyzing historic files. I believe that the past foretells the future and that it is important to understand historic trends. I knew that the FBI hadn't changed substantially since Hoover's reign, and I theorized, based on my studies of the Soviet Union, that the KGB hadn't either. So, I read World War II–vintage files, where I often encountered Harold "Kim" Philby's green-inked comments and J. Edgar Hoover's blue scrawl on the same page. (Everyone else at FBI headquarters had to use black ink.)

Philby was an MI6 officer, which is the British counterpart to the CIA, and he spied for the Soviet Union from the 1930s until his 1963 defection. From 1949–51, Philby was posted to the British embassy in Washington, D.C. There, he acted as liaison to the CIA and FBI. The FBI began to suspect that Philby was a traitor in 1951, when Guy Burgess, who had been Philby's close friend since college and had lived with him in Washington, D.C., defected to the Soviet Union. Philby remained under suspicion, but not under arrest, until he defected. In the Soviet Union, Philby was revered as a hero until his death in Moscow twenty-five years later.

Another interesting MI6 connection was Duško Popov, a Yugoslav who became a British double agent and spied against the Nazis during World War II. Ian Fleming, author of the James Bond books, was an MI6 officer during the war, and many say that Popov's flamboyant personality was the model for Fleming's Bond character. The story goes that the Germans had given Popov about $80,000 to finance an operation in the United States. Fleming was sent by MI6 to safeguard the money, so he tailed Popov to a Lisbon, Portugal, casino. There, to Fleming's horror, Popov got into a macho contest with an ostentatious Lithuanian, who had said he'd match anyone's bet in the house, no matter what the amount. Popov plunked down $50,000 on one round of blackjack, just to show the braggart up. When the Lithuanian could not match the bet, Popov snatched his cash from the table and stamped off indignantly.

Popov took up residence in the United States, where he presented J. Edgar Hoover with an intelligence-collection questionnaire about Pearl Harbor, which the Germans had asked Popov to fill out for their Japanese allies. Hoover, instead, focused his attention on Popov's reputation with the ladies, including actress Simone Simon. Hoover went so far as to have agents follow Popov when he took a female friend on vacation. They were lying on the beach when FBI agents in suits walked across the sand and threatened to arrest him for "transporting a woman across state lines for immoral purposes." Despite the fact that Popov had been introduced to Hoover by MI6, Hoover tossed away this intelligence coup because of Popov's active social life.

In late September 1986, I took a lateral transfer from the Intelligence Division to a counterterrorism desk in the Criminal Division. Even though it was not a promotion, it was a chance to live my dream of working some serious counterterrorism cases, and I went after it. By then, I am proud to say, I was able to navigate my way through FBI headquarters and had become a supervisor who worked to facilitate field operations, not inhibit them.

Chapter 17

TERRORISM: A WALK ON THE WILD SIDE

The U.S. Government continues its commitment to use all tools
necessary—including international diplomacy, law enforcement,
intelligence collection and sharing, and military force—to counter
current terrorist threats and hold terrorists accountable for past
actions. Terrorists seek refuge in "swamps" where government
control is weak or governments are sympathetic. We seek to drain
these swamps.

Patterns of Global Terrorism: 1999
U.S. Department of State

B efore going to sleep on October 6, 1985, I'd turned the ringer
off on the phone near my bed in the basement of our Virginia
town house. The children were tucked in for the night on the
top floor, and when the office called during the early morning hours of
October 7, my daughter Kendra, now at the threshold of her teenage
years, did not feel like walking downstairs to wake me, so she told them
I wasn't at home. At breakfast, she announced "some guy" had called
from the office. I wasn't worried. I had never received an emergency call
since I had been at headquarters. Besides, I had broken a tooth during
the night, and getting to a dentist was the only emergency on my mind.

When I arrived at headquarters, the Emergency Operations Center
was in full swing, and I knew the dentist would have to wait. My supervisor handed me with a pager, one of two I would carry by the end of

this hijacking incident: one for the exclusive use of the executive assistant director for operations and the other for everyone else. I also had to sign a declaration stating I understood that, if a battery went dead or the pagers were in disrepair for any reason, administrative action would be brought against me.

After the tongue-lashing my supervisor laid on me for not being available by phone in the wee hours of the morning, I was put in charge of an international hijacking case in progress. On October 7, 1985, the Italian cruise liner *Achille Lauro* was sailing the Mediterranean Sea from Port Said, Egypt to Ashdod, Israel, when four heavily armed members of the Palestine Liberation Front (PLF), a Palestinian faction and sometimes-ally of the Palestine Liberation Organization (PLO), seized the ship and the 420 people who were aboard, including American citizens. Until that time, the PLF had been known mainly for unsuccessful airborne operations against Israel, such as dropping grenades from hot-air balloons and hang-gliders. The PLF had splintered into three groups, each known by its leader's name: Iraqi-backed Abu Abbas, Syrian-backed Talaat Yacoub, and Libyan-backed Abdel-Fattah Ghanem. It was the Abu Abbas faction that had pulled off the hijacking.

The hostagetakers, who had boarded the ship as passengers, demanded the release of approximately fifty Palestinians held in Israeli jails, and they threatened to kill the passengers and blow up the ship if their demands weren't met. A Swedish ham radio operator reported that the passengers were locked in their cabins and that the hostagetakers were going from room to room checking each passenger's nationality and religion.

Spokesmen for the PLO in Cairo and at the United Nations in New York claimed they had nothing to do with the attack; however, the hijacking occurred less than a week after Israeli Air Force jets had bombed PLO headquarters in Tunisia, allegedly in retaliation for the PLO's assassination of three Israeli agents on a yacht in Cyprus.

The *Achille Lauro* was only the second case in which the Bureau had taken extraterritorial jurisdiction—the June 13, 1985, hijacking of TWA flight 847 to Beirut being the first—and in this second incident, nothing went smoothly. The U.S. agencies that usually ran their own shows overseas, such as the State Department and CIA, weren't ready to give up what they considered to be their personal domains. Moreover, foreign countries felt pressured by the U.S. government over what they viewed as interference in their sovereignty and didn't welcome our presence. The laws we used were U.S. laws, not the laws of the countries where the hijacking and murder occurred, and there was no coalition of countries working together to make joint decisions as seen in the post-September 11 war on terrorism.

Logistics were another problem. At the time of the *Achille Lauro* hijacking, the Rome office covered most of the Mediterranean and the Middle East with just a few agents. Today the Bureau has more than 40 legal attachés assigned to embassies in foreign countries to smooth the way for law enforcement concerns, but, in 1987, the investigators deployed from the Washington field office had to talk their way into places in order to conduct their investigations. And, of course, since eastern standard time is six hours behind Rome, the Emergency Operations Center staff kept the poor legal attachés on the phone half the night, every night. The legal attachés still had to have the answers to Washington's questions as soon as the Italian government opened in the morning.

On October 7, sixty-nine-year-old American tourist Leon Klinghoffer, who was Jewish, was murdered, his body and wheelchair pushed into the sea while PLO and Egyptian government officials negotiated with the hijackers. The other hostages were grouped by nationality and held for fifty-two hours as the hijackers, ranging in age from sixteen to twenty-three, strutted about brandishing weapons and making threats.

Standing impotently by as we watched hijacking and murder play out on CNN was a terrible position for a bunch of law enforcement officers, who were used to pointing our guns and controlling situations. I felt helpless and angry, but it would not be the last time. It happened again in November, when Egypt Air flight 648 was hijacked en route from Cairo, Egypt, to Athens, Greece, by a group calling themselves the Egypt Revolution, who said they wanted to take the plane to Libya. Once the plane set down in Malta for refueling, the hijackers began killing passengers and throwing their bodies out on the tarmac. One American, Jackie Pflug, was shot in the head and thrown from the plane. She survived but, before the hijacking and rescue effort were over, a total of fifty-nine passengers and crew were to die. And Egypt Air flight 648 was not to be the last time I watched helplessly as Americans died in international terrorist attacks. In fact, it was to happen again and again through the hijackings and bombings in the mid- to late '80s. But back to the *Achille Lauro.*

On October 8, the *Achille Lauro* hijackers attempted to dock in Syria, but the ship was turned away. Next, it steamed toward Cyprus, but was refused permission to dock there, as well. On October 11, at Port Said, Egypt, the hijackers surrendered to the Egyptians in exchange for a pledge of safe passage.

At headquarters, we averaged fourteen-hour days coordinating logistics and legal matters, such as swearing out warrants, not to mention running interference in the many interagency turf battles kindled by the case.

One of the more pleasant testimonies of my career was swearing out the warrant for Mohammed Abu Abbas, who—under the guise of negotiating the hostages' release—actually supervised the hijackers' activities by radio. An assistant United States attorney and I drove to a judge's swank condominium complex in Washington, D.C. and sneaked in past a throng of reporters. I guess the fact that we hadn't slept well or eaten a real meal for days was an effective disguise, since no one in the press corps gave us a second glance. As I swore to the warrant, the judge's wife served us grapes and Stilton cheese with Carr's water crackers, probably the only food I had all week that wasn't out of a vending machine.

During the first seventy-two hours of the *Achille Lauro* hijacking, the Emergency Operations Center looked and sounded a lot like the New York Stock Exchange. People were standing and yelling into phones while we watched what was happening overseas on a series of television monitors. A deputy assistant attorney general sat in the Emergency Operations Center, helping us get the warrants together and handling other legal matters. It was a tense situation, and no one was allowed to make mistakes or care about their personal lives.

In the middle of all this, my daughter Kendra had her own crisis. As the headquarters case supervisor, I was seated in the center of the Emergency Operations Center, fielding phone call after phone call. Suddenly, an agent interrupted and said there was an emergency at home. My daughter was on the line. I practically hung up on our legal attaché in Rome to take the call.

"When are you going to cook dinner?" my daughter inquired.

"I'm afraid I'm going to be working late tonight, dear. The sitter will have to handle dinner," I said. "What's the emergency?"

"You need to come home right away because she can't cook what I want," she insisted.

"What do you want?" I asked.

"Grilled cheese sandwiches," she announced.

"Kendra, you know how to cook grilled cheese sandwiches yourself!"

"Nooooo," she wailed, "there's mold on the cheese."

The din in the EOC was so loud, I had to raise my voice so she could hear me. "Well, cut the mold off the cheese!" I said, emphasizing each word in frustration.

Suddenly, the EOC hushed. Everyone stopped and stared at me, then burst into laughter.

Except for that brief moment of levity, there was little to smile about during the investigation. Despite requests by the U.S. and Italian governments to hold the hijackers for trial, the Egyptian government—claiming it was unaware that an American had been killed—released them to the custody of PLO members in an Egypt Air plane. On October 11, Abu Abbas and the four hijackers boarded an Egyptian plane and fled to an undisclosed destination. The plane was refused permission to land in Tunis and Athens, and was just south of Crete when four U.S. Navy F-14 fighters from the USS *Saratoga* intercepted it and forced it to land at the U.S. Naval Air Base in Sigonella, Sicily.

The Italians took custody of the four hijackers but allowed Abu Abbas, who was carrying an Iraqi diplomatic passport, to board a waiting Yugoslav JAT Airways plane, despite the U.S. warrant for his arrest. Though the United States government asked the Yugoslavs to hold Abbas for extradition, the Yugoslavs recognized the PLO as a nation and extended diplomatic immunity to Abbas because he carried an Iraqi diplomatic passport. They released him to PLO custody instead.

We sent FBI agents to help the Italians put their prosecution together, and the hijackers were tried there, which was just as well because, as it turned out two were minors, and the likelihood of minors being successfully prosecuted under United States federal statutes was doubtful at the time. In June 1986, the Italians convicted Abu Abbas in absentia to a life sentence.

The Italians also issued warrants for sixteen others involved in the planning and execution of the hijacking, but only the four who were taken into custody at Sigonella were convicted in court. Majed Yussef al-Molqi, the twenty-three-year-old leader who was convicted of killing Leon Klinghoffer, was released from an Italian prison on a twelve-day furlough in 1996 and never returned.

In the end, the FBI filed its voluminous investigative case for future reference. FBI director William Webster described the *Achille Lauro* hijacking as one of the historic events of his administration. As for me, three weeks after the hijacking, I finally got my crumbled tooth to a dentist. He performed gum surgery to remove the tissue that had grown over the fragmented tooth because I'd waited so long, then he fit me for a crown—my only souvenir of the case.

The United States warrant against Abbas for piracy, hostagetaking, and conspiracy was dropped without an indictment, because the case was not considered strong enough for successful prosecution in the U.S. But the incident was never forgotten, and, in 1991, the story morphed from news and law to culture when a controversial modern opera entitled *The Death of Klinghoffer* had its premiere.

On April 14, 2003, Abu Abbas was captured by U.S. forces in Baghdad, Iraq. Truth be told, my immediate thought when I glimpsed the captured Abbas on CNN was not one of triumph over a hard-fought case. My first thought was that he'd gotten old.

Chapter 18

ROCKY MOUNTAIN HIGHLIGHTS

There was an atmosphere of endeavor, of expectancy and bright
hopefulness . . .

Willa Cather
My Ántonia

ecember 1987 found me driving into Denver with my children and all our worldly possessions in tow. I was the newly
appointed squad supervisor of the Denver field division's
counterterrorism, counterintelligence, and background investigation
squad. Again, it was a lateral transfer, but supervising a squad was a necessary step on the FBI career path and an experience that I relished.

Sitting at my desk in Washington, I'd fantasized that the mile-high
city would be a pleasant assignment where nothing happened, a place
where I could ski and hike and enjoy a laid-back lifestyle with my kids.

As it turned out, Denver was a major hub of white supremacist
activity and domestic terrorism, especially crimes perpetrated by skinheads and Aryan Nation members who roamed the streets. The FBI had
vigorously investigated white supremacists since just after World War I,
when the Bureau used the Mann Act to arrest and prosecute Louisiana's
KKK "Imperial Kleagle," Edward Y. Clarke.

The Ku Klux Klan was founded by six Confederate soldiers in
Pulaski, Tennessee, on Christmas Eve, 1865. It was intended to be a
social club but quickly became the white-sheeted and -hooded band of

terrorists that the name now evokes. The Klan quickly grew in numbers, but by the 1870s had declined due to internal squabbles over leadership. It almost disappeared, but was revived in 1915 and grew to national prominence by the 1920s, when millions swelled its ranks. Many lawmakers, including governors, senators, and congressmen, led the Klan during this period. Targets of its hate were blacks, immigrants, "immoral" women, and members of non-Protestant religions, such as Jews and Catholics.

When the FBI stepped into the picture in the early '20s, there were no good federal statutes for prosecuting white supremacists. The FBI was not able to arrest Louisiana Klan leader Edward Clarke for murder or racial violence, but they were able to get him on morals charges. Finally, in 1923, he was indicted for taking a woman across state lines for immoral purposes. Clarke pleaded guilty to the charge and paid a $5,000 fine, which doesn't seem like much considering the number of murders he was implicated in, but the case threw the Klan's leadership into turmoil. The Klan has always represented itself as a moral crowd, steeped in American family values, and the intense publicity about the case stirred disunity and resulted in the Klan's decline in political power.

As I packed up my office for the move to Denver, I felt reluctant to leave FBI headquarters, an emotion that surprised even me. I was proud of what I'd accomplished there. I'd supervised some outstanding international investigations, and I'd been a facilitator for field operations instead of a roadblock. Facilitating field operations had been my major goal when I decided to go into management in the first place, and now I hoped to use my knowledge of the headquarters process to smooth the way for my new squad's operations.

When I left headquarters, my supervisory responsibilities were divided among several new desks, an indication of how much work I'd handled by myself. The section chief who wrote the recommendation for my Denver application said, "I can't believe I'm doing this. I'm cutting my own throat."

My first impressions of Denver were the magnificent Rocky Mountains toward the west end and the graffiti spray-painted on buildings all over town: "Rosie is a bitch." I supervised a squad and four resident agencies (small FBI offices within Denver territory)—Colorado Springs, Pueblo, Boulder, and Fort Collins—though only two at a time. Colorado Springs was the largest resident agency within Denver's territory, which includes Colorado and Wyoming.

My employees gave me nothing but support, and they were repeatedly commended in inspections for developing some of the division's most outstanding cases. An example was a years-long sting, code-named "Operation Aspen Leaf."

The counterintelligence agents in Denver had come up with an innovative idea to stem the illegal flow of embargoed technology from the United States. Working with U.S. Customs agents, they established a storefront in Golden, Colorado, called Technology Specialists, Inc., and advertised it as a fledgling import/export business.

The first few months were spent launching the new company. The agents had to establish undercover identities and learn the import/export business, as well as everything about embargoed technologies that could not be legally shipped to certain countries. Like any fledgling business operators, they had to get credit references and set up the office, while sending mountains of paperwork to FBI headquarters to justify each expenditure. Once the operation was up and running, they mailed "letters of introduction" to businesses suspected of illegally exporting American goods to foreign countries.

It's an interesting legal challenge to carry out a sting operation without crossing the lines of entrapment, but the FBI had learned a great deal since the Abscam congressmen, who in 1980 were charged with taking bribes, got off without punishment.

In order to succeed, the agents had to follow guidelines that seemed silly at times. When customers asked the company to break the law, the undercover agents were required to tell them that the request was against the law in the U.S., then the agents had to ask—in writing—what the customer wanted them to do next. The customer basically had to give the agents written directions on how they wanted them to break the law. The agents were not allowed to make suggestions. Altering shipping records to disguise contents or destinations was a common way to hide the crimes.

The illegal diverters of technology wanted to ship items through neutral countries to end-users in communist countries. The bogus Technology Specialists, Inc. shipped customers a few products, such as defective parts for night-vision devices, but we couldn't actually ship anything that might be useful to a hostile country in a war against the United States. However, prosecution was not based upon how dangerous or important to defense the shipped item was; it was based on whether the item was embargoed.

There were ups and downs during the three-year life of the sting and changing laws made certain prosecutions impossible. In the end, the undercover agents invited five foreign nationals to meet them in San Juan, Puerto Rico, with the promise of a Caribbean cruise paid for by Technology Specialists, Inc. The suspects, four West Germans and an Austrian, were sent one-way tickets and told they would pick up their return tickets in San Juan. Instead, they were awakened in their San Juan hotel rooms at 5:00 A.M. and dragged off to jail. I had flown in with the undercover agents to be the liaison between the United States Attorneys as the situation evolved during the postarrest interviews. However, I got into a bit of an altercation with the special agent in charge of San Juan, who decided that instead of serving as liaison, I should perform the nonsupervisory duty of guarding the female prisoner. I refused, and a standoff ensued. This time, I prevailed.

After appearing before the magistrate in San Juan, the prisoners were transported to Denver, where they appeared before Judge Richard Matsch, who later presided over the Timothy McVeigh trial. Eventually, the five foreign nationals entered plea bargains in exchange for information and were deported to their homes in Europe—and freedom. And that's how it goes in real life cases, no matter how hard you work or how right you are.

The Denver field office was also a key player in the 1989 FBI/Environmental Protection Agency (EPA) raid on the Rocky Flats. Located about sixteen miles north of Denver, the plant was built in 1951 to make plutonium "triggers" for atomic bombs. Rockwell International, Inc. managed the site for the Department of Energy, and there had long been rumors of contaminated soil and water around the facility.

The FBI called it "Operation Desert Glow," evoking the glow of a nuclear hotspot. After a two-year investigation, our team of approximately one hundred FBI and Environmental Protection Agency agents descended upon Rocky Flats and began an unprecedented search of this highly sensitive facility. Since we had to ensure that no evidence was destroyed, we arrived without warning. The grounds were owned by the Department of Energy, but run by contractors, and the ubiquitous signs that warned trespassers would be shot on sight were not a joke. The Rocky Flats guard force was better equipped, trained, and paid than any SWAT team in the United States, and they weren't amused at our arrival.

As law enforcement officers, we were accustomed to making swift entries for raids, but there were so many of us trying to get through the gates at once that we created our own traffic jam. Mike, one of the agents from my squad, had to get out and put his former-traffic-cop skills into action to get the cars out of gridlock and into parking spaces.

From its earliest days, the Rocky Flats plant had had an uneasy relationship with its neighbors, due to the fact that its operations were cloaked in secrecy. Additionally, there had been two hazardous fires, one in '57 and another in '69, caused by ignited plutonium. Both had been spectacular conflagrations, and the public had feared that these had been chain reactions releasing nuclear matter that had contaminated the atmosphere as well as the water and soil in the vicinity.

In fact, after the second fire, citizens had demanded that soil in the vicinity be tested, and the tests had confirmed dangerous levels of radioactivity. Over the years, the government spent millions buying up land around the site. That act physically isolated the plant but didn't fully address the problem of radioactive particles that might be carried in the air. Because of this fear, local environmentalists dubbed the plant a "creeping Chernobyl," and their concerns were not far-fetched; in 1987 Rockwell International had admitted that the ground water was contaminated. Our search for improperly handled hazardous wastes and media reports of outdated, ineffective equipment at the plant renewed public outcry and fears.

I was in charge of the emergency operations center during the Desert Glow raid. My job was to coordinate the activities of agents from both the FBI and EPA, who conducted the physical search. It also was my responsibility to ensure that classified evidence was not mishandled.

The facility's grounds covered approximately 9.65 square miles. Because the plant housed dangerous nuclear waste products, agents had to be trained to use respirator suits in case they needed to enter contaminated areas.

The operation was complicated due to the facility's size, the presence of classified information, and the federal statutes being applied in the case. This challenge was not made easier by the FBI case supervisor, whom I will call Darnell, who constantly tried to undermine my authority and belittle my work. It started the night before the raid when, as introductions were being made around the table, he announced to a meeting of high-ranking representatives of the Departments of Energy and Justice, the U.S. Attorney's Office, and the EPA that none of them was to listen to me because I had no experience in criminal cases. When I pointed out that I had in fact been a supervisor in Criminal Division at FBI headquarters, which I noted he had not, he continued his unprovoked verbal assault. The assistant special agent in charge of my office sat silently beside us and said nothing to stop Darnell.

As the search progressed, I worked closely with the case agent, whom I'll call Tony, helping him to prepare logs and summaries to send to FBI headquarters. I knew what the supervisor at headquarters would need to keep abreast of the case to get legal process when we requested, and I shared this knowledge with James. In fact, I came in early and stayed late to make sure everything was taken care of, even though the overall responsibility for the case was Darnell's. Of course, Darnell was nowhere to be seen after hours.

As if Darnell had nothing else to think about, he continued his verbal onslaught throughout the week, no matter how many people looked on.

He, like so many other harassers I encountered over the years, was rather one-dimensional and seemed to have little else to think about.

One day, as he was haranguing me about how women got special privileges and how lazy counterintelligence agents were, I lost my temper and walked away from the conversation. Instead of letting it drop, he followed me into the emergency operations center, running his mouth all the way. As I entered the room, people were already staring since they had heard Darnell hurling insults at me as we approached in the hall. I walked over to the table where I had been working, but he followed. My patience gone, I turned and shouted, "Fuck off, Darnell," and the room burst into applause and laughter. Red-faced, Darnell slithered out of the room.

Darnell's interactions with the agents were contentious as well. He just enjoyed saying "no" for the sake of demonstrating control, and it was impossible for the agents to proceed with their work. In fact, Darnell had become such an obstruction to the investigation that the FBI and EPA agents planned a mutiny. The lead investigators came to me one morning and said, "We need you to help us," Tony, said.

"What can I do?" I asked.

"We want you to take over here. Are you with us?"

"Sure," I said, "but how is that going to happen?"

"Just follow us."

With that, we went into an auditorium where the entire team waited for the morning briefing.

Tony walked to the front with his dark-haired EPA counterpart and held up his hands to quiet the din. "We're pulling a mutiny," he said to the crowd. "Darnell's out and Rosemary's in. Are you with me?"

The applause answered his question. "Okay," he said. "Follow me."

With that, he headed out of the auditorium, followed by the rest. When those agents marched out of the auditorium to confront the assistant special agent in charge and make their demands, it was one of the greatest moments of my life.

Faced with the backlash from the rest of the team, the assistant special agent in charge complied. Later, the United States attorney took me aside and said how sorry he was to see what I had had to endure on the job.

The FBI and EPA occupied Rocky Flats for nine days. When the agents left, they took almost one thousand boxes of evidence, more than 3.5 million pages of documents. A grand jury was impaneled to investigate. After two-and-a-half years of hearing testimony and reviewing evidence, the grand jury was informed that its services were no longer needed because Rockwell International had agreed to plead guilty to ten environmental crimes and pay $18.5 million in fines, a sum that was smaller than what the company had received in performance bonuses over the period of its government contract. The agreement concluded that, despite the environmental crimes, there had been no dangerous contamination and no individuals were to be indicted.

Grand jury members were deeply disturbed by what they saw as little more than a mild slap on the wrist, so they drafted their own report on Rocky Flats and what they believed to be the facts. The judge sealed the report, but someone leaked it to the media, and Rocky Flats became front-page news again. Today, the plant has been given a fresh PR spin and renamed the Rocky Flats Environmental Technology Site. It is scheduled to close in 2006.

After Rocky Flats, Darnell won a spot on the FBI Inspection Staff, making him eligible for promotion to the rank of assistant special agent in charge in the field or a unit chief at headquarters. The assistant special agent in charge who had sat in silence as Darnell harassed me, eventually became an FBI assistant director.

What kept me sane during those years of stress and disappointment was volunteering with nonprofit organizations. In Denver, I volunteered at Ronald McDonald House, and Kendra and I worked with Meals on Wheels. But my favorite organization was the Archdiocese of Denver Colleges for Living, a school that educated mentally challenged adults who were trying to learn practical life skills. Kendra and I volunteered to teach a cooking class, while Chris, a wonderful artist, taught arts and crafts.

I encouraged my squad to get into the act, and many volunteered to take over my obligations when I was traveling. The situation spawned the joke that I was going to be away and one of my squad members would have to donate a kidney in my absence.

Mike and Tracy, a husband-and-wife agent team, had been theater majors in college and both had acted in summer stock. Mike had a wonderful voice and a particularly expressive face, which was great for delivering one-liners. He added humor to the cooking class, even though he typically did more singing than cooking. Our students loved show tunes, and Mike knew the words to them all.

One of the things that made the Colleges for Living so good for me was being around people who'd been taught in special education classes. Every small accomplishment elicited spontaneous applause and words of congratulation from the rest of the students. It was an atmosphere of innocence, human kindness, and love. It healed a week's worth of little wounds and made me appreciate what I had.

One semester, Tracy taught drama, and I served as her assistant. She often took advantage of the opportunity to make me perform outrageous demonstrations, such as walking like an elephant, and would command, "Okay, now raise your trunk, Rosemary," while I mumbled under my breath, "I'll get you for this." But it was guaranteed to make the class laugh, not to mention the fact that it made a great office story the morning after.

When I resigned from the Bureau, one of the hardest things I had to do was leave my Colleges for Living students behind. They had been my touchstone. No matter what was going wrong in my life or how bad my day had been, I could count on warm hugs and sincere smiles from my students. The school accommodated students ranging from those with severe mental retardation to those who held down full-time jobs. They restored my faith in humanity and made me realize there was life outside the Bureau. The school had such a positive atmosphere that the class became my haven, my attitude adjustment miracle. I always ended each evening with my students by saying, "See you next week," and I looked forward to returning.

An awards dinner was held at the end of each semester, during which we handed out certificates of achievement to our students. At the last ceremony I attended, the emcee announced to the students that I was moving back to Washington and encouraged them to say good-bye. I could barely hold back the tears as I handed out certificates and hugged each of them. I'd almost made it through when one cheerful student waved to me and said, "See you next week." I thought my heart would break, but I knew they'd keep on going without me.

I also miss the friendships shared with FBI employees who wanted to excel at their jobs and didn't care that their leader was a woman. My assistant, Marianne, and I became fast friends over the years, and she was very protective of me. Once, when an agent from another squad was in my office and she felt he was being rude to me, she pointedly slammed shut the outer door to my office. She told me later that she didn't want anyone else to hear the way he was talking to me.

Marianne and I both suffered personal tragedies outside the office: children with problems at school, friends who died violent deaths. She was the only person with whom I could let down my guard. I was close to everyone on the squad, as well as those in the resident agencies I supervised, but, around them, I was still an agent with a reasonably tough exterior around them. When I was with Marianne, I was just another woman. Without her friendship, I'd have been lost.

On December 12, 1989, I received a letter from the director of the FBI, along with an incentive award for exceptional management performance. This award was the result of the special agent in charge's recommendation. Finally, I thought, I'd overcome "the woman thing" in the eyes of my rating officials. But just a month later, after a very successful counterintelligence operation, I arranged for letters of commendation for the high-performing agents involved and also for the FBI headquarters supervisor who had done work above and beyond what was expected. I got a call from the headquarters supervisor, who said, "I don't know how to tell you this, but you've got a problem with your special agent in charge. Headquarters put you in for an incentive award, wrote the paper, and all he had to do was say 'yes.' He said 'no.' No one around here has ever heard of that happening."

Instead, on February 14, I received a letter of commendation from the squad and task force:

> Your squad would like to take this opportunity on Valentine's Day to commend you for your outstanding performance as a supervisory Special Agent of the Federal Bureau of Investigation. Your concern, support, and perseverance serve as an inspiration to all who have the pleasure of working for you. You have constantly displayed the highest traits of professionalism and dedication associated with the FBI and you epitomize the FBI's motto: "Fidelity, Bravery, and Integrity."
>
> Thanks for being a great boss lady and more importantly, our pal.
>
> LOVE, The Fighting 5th (or pass the 5th—I'll take the 5th, etc., etc.)

This is the sole FBI commendation that I have framed and display. The rest I keep in a book for my grandchildren.

Chapter 19

HATE COMES IN MANY
FORMS

... at night you feel strange things stirring in the darkness ...
There is a sense of danger ... a queer bristling feeling of uncanny
danger ...

D. H. Lawrence
Letter from Germany, 1924

Although I've investigated some of the deadliest international terrorist groups in the world, it's the homegrown terrorists that I
fear the most. The chronicle of murders and bombings committed by American terrorist groups is long and bloody, Timothy
McVeigh's attack on the Alfred P. Murrah Federal Building in Oklahoma
City being the most notorious. These terrorists range from white
supremacists to neo-Nazis to antitax and other antigovernment groups,
and like foreign terrorists, they have demonstrated an interest in chemical and biological weapons. For example, in 1995, Larry Wayne Harris,
a vocal white supremacist with Aryan Nations connections, was arrested
with three vials of *Yersinia pestis,* the causal agent for bubonic plague or
"The Black Death," in his possession. Bubonic plague is extremely con-
tagious and deadly. Harris, who claimed to be a microbiologist writing
a training manual for the Aryan Nations, had been casually storing the
substance in the glove compartment of his car.

At the time, there was no federal statute criminalizing possession of
Yersinia pestis without a legitimate purpose, but Harris had fraudulently

used a laboratory registration number to order it, and the Bureau was able to prosecute him under the Fraud by Wire statute. To prosecute someone for possession under the Biological Weapons Anti-Terrorism Act of 1989 (Title 18, Section 175), the statute that was used at the time, the government had to prove that a defendant intended to use a substance as a weapon.

The challenge of finding viable statutes under which to prosecute domestic terrorists was one reason I was pleased to be put in charge of the investigation of civil rights violations in Denver. My staff and I were involved in numerous investigations of civil rights violations that were linked with domestic terrorism, mainly by white supremacist groups.

Although they were among the best avenues for prosecution available at the time, civil rights statutes are often a double-edged sword. The statues protect the rights of the victims, but the First Amendment also guarantees freedom of speech. In addition, it is not illegal for a native-born U.S. citizen to be a member of an organization that promotes views that could restrict another person's Constitutional rights. It is illegal, however, to turn those views into actions, and that is what the growing "hate group" population has in mind.

Like most Americans, I find it difficult to accept the idea that hate groups exist at all. When I first arrived in Denver, I didn't want to believe that hate-group activity was anything more than a sick anachronism that was restricted to a miniscule number of people in America. Of course, this was the mid-'80s, and it would be a while before these groups were well known outside the Mountain States.

My office mail was jammed with fliers and letters from anti-Jewish, anti–African American, and antigovernment organizations. Their propaganda was of the most ignorant ilk, definitely not written by deep thinkers or grammar mavens, and this apparent lack of intelligence and/or education caused me to underestimate them for my first few months. I had a lot to learn.

The neo-Nazi Aryan Nation and its scion The Order, also known as the Silent Brotherhood or Brüders Schweigen, were the first groups I encountered. These are just two of the various hate groups that want to take over the U.S. Mountain States and kick out the "mud races," the term they use to describe anyone who is not pure Caucasian. Although the Aryan Nation is a paramilitary neo-Nazi organization, members seem to hate any nonwhite or Jew with equal fervor. For years, members held an annual white supremacist jamboree, known as the Aryan World Conference, in rural Idaho, a festive get-together that attracts Aryan Nation members, Ku Klux Klansmen, tax protesters, militias, skinheads, and assorted hangers-on.

Within the U.S. prison system was the Aryan Brotherhood, a white supremacist group known for trafficking in drugs inside the prisons and controlling ex-con drug rings on the outside. Members are often identified by their tattoos. I spent a less-than-delightful day in a federal prison interviewing an incarcerated Aryan Brotherhood member and photographing his body tattoos for FBI files. He was a chatty white supremacist and volunteered a wealth of information, such as how he maintained his safety in prison by being a "punk," one who trades sexual favors for protection. After sharing that news, he repeatedly asked me for a date, which greatly amused Mike, the agent working with me.

The high point of the interview was when the prisoner unexpectedly dropped his trousers to reveal his tattooed derriere for us to photograph. Mike's voice cracked as he tried to suppress his laughter, directing me to move the light here and there so he could get better pictures. The only way I could maintain my professional persona was to avoid looking Mike in the eye and to talk incessantly, as I do at the gynecologist's office when I pretend I'm not undergoing a pelvic exam but have simply dropped by to discuss current events.

The Aryan Nation was founded by Nazi-admirer Rev. Richard Butler in the mid-1970s. Butler called himself "reverend" because he shepherded the Church of Jesus Christ Christian, one of the "Christian Identity" churches that justifies hate by twisting Scripture. This was also a convenient ploy under the law because the Constitution protects religious practice; and until the 2002 loosening of the Attorney General Guidelines that govern investigative practices, it was difficult for the FBI to mount investigations involving religious organizations. Butler has interpreted Scripture to support his view that God intended for the white race to rule and all other races to serve, with the Jews being "the spawn of Satan."

Established in 1983, The Order is composed mostly of Aryan Nation members, and its guide to revolution is *The Turner Diaries,* a dark fantasy about an activist-built truck bomb that blows up a Washington federal building killing hundreds of people. This book was a favorite read of Oklahoma City bomber Timothy McVeigh. He later turned that twisted story into reality by constructing his own 4,800-pound bomb from a rented Ryder truck, fertilizer, and fuel. The explosion destroyed the nine-story Murrah Federal Building, and murdered 168 men, women, and children.

The Order robbed banks to fund its activities, set off bombs, and killed in support of its goals. Its leader was Robert J. Mathews, who held off two hundred law enforcement officers for more than thirty-six hours at Whidbey Island, Washington, in December 1984. He burned to death when tear gas ignited the trailer in which he was holed up.

The most famous murder attributed to members of the Aryan Nation is probably that of Radio KOA talk-show host Alan Berg, the self-proclaimed "Wild Man of the Airwaves." A former lawyer and a pioneer of shock radio, Berg managed to insult and enrage his audience on every subject—from sex and race to religion and gun control. His shtick was to provoke his listeners, especially members of the white supremacists groups, who phoned in to argue with him on the air. Tired of Berg's anti-Aryan comments, Order members Carroll Pierce and David Lane used automatic weapons to gun down the talk-show host in the driveway of his Denver home on June 18, 1984. They later robbed an armored car in another state, and were eventually caught and convicted of both crimes. The FBI tried the pair under civil rights statutes and proved in court that they had deprived Berg of his civil rights when they killed him because he was Jewish.

The agents investigating the Berg case were assigned to my squad, although the Berg case itself was not. However, as the civil rights supervisor, my name had been in the newspaper in connection with various civil rights cases, and as far as the public knew, I was the agent in charge. The night before the Berg murder trial was scheduled to start, my house was spray-painted with white supremacist graffiti. Oddly, the City of Denver quickly ticketed me for putting up an "unauthorized sign," and authorities would not listen to my protests that the "signs" were actually the result of vandalism and not some decoration I had put up. Instead, the city gave me ninety days to repaint or be fined.

Then there were the skinheads. Even at my son's high school, these trendy dressers were gaining prominence. They traveled in packs, looking for people to hurt or property to destroy. They set themselves apart with their shaven heads, jeans, white T-shirts, Doc Marten shoes, and identical tattoos. Their public activities increased during the summer when warmer weather permitted them to loiter outdoors, and their numbers were growing.

According to a November 23, 1997 *Rocky Mountain News* article, in 1985, Denver police had identified thirty skinheads, but by 1991, there were four hundred. In 1992,

> Denver became the site of the worst Martin Luther King Day violence in the nation. A court-sanctioned Ku Klux Klan rally on the Capitol's west steps ended with police trying to sneak 125 white supremacists through an underground tunnel to buses.
>
> Counter-demonstrators figured out the escape route in time to pelt the bus with snowballs and bottles. Then they turned their rage on police, resulting in an hour-long tear gas-laced street battle . . .

By November 1997, Matthaus Reinhart Jaehnig, a twenty-year-old Denver skinhead, had already racked up seven arrests: weapons, drug charges, menacing, and vehicular assault. On the afternoon of November 12, Jaehnig shot and killed Denver police officer Bruce VanderJagt with a semiautomatic rifle as VanderJagt pursued him in connection with a stolen vehicle. Within hours of VanderJagt's murder, the

Denver SWAT team found Jaehnig dead. He'd shot himself in the head with the gun he'd taken from the dying officer. Later, someone threw a dead pig on the lawn in front of the District 3 police station. Officer VanderJagt's name was carved into the dead pig's side.

During the same two-week period, white supremacists in Denver shot Oumar Dia, an immigrant from West Africa, who was waiting for a bus. Nathan Thill, a skinhead with Aryan Nation connections, not only killed Dia, but also shot Jeannie Vanvelkinburgh, a white nurse, who tried to aid the injured Dia. The bullet paralyzed her from the waist down.

Thill, then nineteen-years old, confessed to the two shootings during a television interview, calling himself a "Nazi warrior" fighting a race war against minorities in the United States. Eventually, Thill was sentenced to life plus thirty-two years in prison, where he remains today.

Denver is not the only place that has experienced hate-motivated attacks, and the crimes continue across the country, the U.S. government being a common target. Domestic hate and antigovernment group members have attempted to use deadly chemical compounds and biological toxins in attacks against the government. In March 1995, Douglas Baker and Leroy Wheeler, members of the Patriots Council, a Minnesota antitax militia, were convicted of conspiring to kill a U.S. marshal with ricin, a castor-bean derivative that is fatal if applied to human skin or ingested through the respiratory system. Produced as a white powder, ricin is not easily recognizable, and, unlike anthrax, which can be treated with antibiotics, it has no known antidote. In fact, ricin is approximately six thousand times more toxic than cyanide and is the third most toxic substance in the world, behind plutonium and botulism. Bulgarian secret agents used ricin to kill defector Georgi Markov in London in 1978 when they stabbed him in the leg with a ricin-coated umbrella tip.

Baker and Wheeler had planned to combine ricin with the solvent, dimethyl sulfoxide, which would carry the ricin into the victim's body with a mere touch, and they intended to spread this deadly mixture on public door handles. Interestingly, the procedure for use of ricin and dimethyl sulfoxide can also be found in the *al Qaeda Jihad Training Manual* that was seized from a computer in London and entered as evidence in a trial in New York. Although both would be loath to admit it, al Qaeda and white supremacists have a lot in common. Al Qaeda is nothing more than a hate group that rejects all who do not follow its particular brand of Islam.

In addition to their interest in ricin, Baker and Wheeler also schemed to blow up federal buildings, but they were captured before they could carry out any of those crimes.

In 1997, FBI agents arrested Thomas Leahy, white supremacist from Wisconsin, for possession of ricin for use as a weapon. Agents also seized solutions of nicotine and dimethyl sulfoxide, which Leahy had combined in a spray bottle. In its pure form, nicotine is considered one of the most toxic of all poisons, a fatal dose being 40 mg. When mixed with dimethyl sulfoxide, it is rapidly absorbed through the skin, moving as rapidly—and fatally—into a person's nervous system as if it has been injected. White supremacists have also attempted to acquire anthrax, which at one time could be purchased fairly easily via mail order.

Terrorism is about hate and intimidation, and groups that espouse hate can be found in every state in this nation. White supremacy is nothing more than terrorism, and it is a sad, but enduring part of United States history.

Chapter 20
THE KINDNESS OF STRANGERS

But they who give straight judgements to strangers and to those of
the land and do not transgress what is just, for them the city flour-
ishes and its people prosper.

Hesiod
Eighth century B.C.

I n Denver, I met new people and made good friends, something that
had been sorely lacking in most of my other assignments. It was
there that I finally experienced acceptance—not from the FBI—but
from officers of other law enforcement agencies. Working closely with
those officers gave me the opportunity to see what it was like on the
inside of other police organizations. It made me realize that the prejudice I was experiencing on the job was unique to the FBI and not just
the way women in law enforcement were routinely treated.

As commander of the Denver Joint Terrorist Task Force, the Secret Service invited me to participate in presidential and vice presidential protective duties. President George Bush was in office and, because he had a son
in Denver, he visited there frequently. Working around First Lady Barbara
Bush made a big impression on me. When our assignment was completed
one day, she took time to shake our hands and say "thank you." I provided
protection for various dignitaries over the years, but she was the only one
who openly acknowledged that my colleagues and I were committed to
giving our lives for hers if necessary, and that this warranted her gratitude.

One of the first nights I was in Denver, I attended a retirement party for a Secret Service agent. When I was introduced to their special agent in charge, he shook my hand and said he'd heard of me from their headquarters. Someone from the Secret Service in Washington had called him to say that their director had awarded me a letter of appreciation for my work with the Secret Service while I was in the Terrorism Section at FBI headquarters. This was in sharp contrast to my own special agent in charge who had called my future employees together before I arrived in Denver and announced that I was not qualified for the job but was being forced on him because I was a woman. Later in the meeting, he admitted to the group that he actually had no knowledge about my qualifications because he hadn't bothered to read my résumé.

Officers of the various police jurisdictions in the Denver area also helped with protective duties. One of the best known was Detective Sgt. Bill Carter of the Denver Police Department, who was a master at controlling situations before they escalated into violence. Fondly known as "The Hefty Bag Man," Carter was an imposing figure. This Vietnam veteran of the 101st Airborne was well over six feet tall and more than 250 pounds, with a full beard, longish hair, and a disarming smile. It was rumored that the Hefty Bag factory made his police uniforms, but I never actually saw him in uniform.

One day Carter and I were working a protective detail for President and Mrs. Bush and had been warned in the pre-brief that protesters might try to disrupt the event. The president's speech was to be held in a gymnasium at the University of Denver. As we scanned the crowd, a couple of skinheads swaggered in, trying to look tough. A Secret Service agent and I were near the podium where the president was to speak, but Carter was nearest the skinheads. We radioed Carter to find out what was happening and then watched as he sauntered up behind the pair.

As Carter walked up behind them, I noted that he was about a foot taller than either of the muscular, young toughs and had easily a hundred pounds on them. He rested his hands on their shoulders, and they tried unsuccessfully to jerk away. When they turned and saw Carter towering over them, their cockiness melted. Visibly deflated, their shoulders sinking and their heads bowed docilely, they were escorted out of the gym by a smiling Carter, his long arms still encircling their shoulders.

Carter had the ability to intimidate, but he also had a winning way with people. If he walked into a group of strangers, they tended to accept him. Once, an informant told him that a group of demonstrators planned to get arrested during a protest march by causing property damage. When Carter arrived on the scene, the group was singing a '60s folk song to rally their supporters. Carter walked into the group, linked arms with the surprised demonstrators, and joined in the song. His presence made them reconsider breaking the law. They just stood there with him and sang.

Lieutenant Dan Rueben, Carter's boss, was another interesting man. A law school graduate, he preferred skiing in Colorado to practicing law in his native New York City, so he became the supervisor of the Denver Police Department's Intelligence Unit. We worked together many nights searching for skinheads suspected of crimes, including the night that Carter was seriously wounded in an attempt to arrest a skinhead suspected of murder.

That night, we chased down a skinhead who matched the description of our suspect. Bill Matens, an FBI bomb technician, drove our car across the median in the street. It momentarily took flight and narrowly avoided oncoming traffic. Fortunately, we landed wheels-down and came to a halt on the sidewalk in front of the suspect. Dan ran up from a side street as Matens and I burst from the car, adrenaline pumping. When you've just completed a high-speed maneuver and barely avoided flipping your car, it's natural to be excited. I was ready to grab the skinhead and throw him across the hood of the car, but Dan began talking to the guy in a smooth, reassuring voice, and soon the youth was cooperating with us. Dan's winning way even calmed me. This was a demonstration that the best, most effective police officers are the ones who have the gift of speaking softly, calming those who might commit violent acts, and preventing tense situations from escalating. After listening to Dan, I realized that the man we had in custody was not the person we were looking for and that he was absolutely terrified of us.

The day that Carter was injured was one of the most frightening of my career. Matens and I were at our office when a call came in from an informant, a native Spanish speaker. He was so excited that he lost his English skills and kept saying Detective Carter was "on the floor" and couldn't "get up." While we were trying to figure out what that meant, we heard the "officer-down" call on the police scanner.

Matens and I ran to an unmarked car and drove "red-light-and-siren" to the location. The bubble light, which was supposed to stick to the dash of our car, didn't. Matens and I kept yelling and slapping each other's hands away from the light because we each thought we could repair it en route. In truth, we were terrified for our friend. For years, it had been ingrained in us that we couldn't show emotion, so we found it more acceptable to drive down the street acting like two of the Three Stooges than to admit our personal fears.

By the time we reached the scene, Denver officers armed with shotguns were clearing the area. We were certain Carter was dead and we were already mourning inside ourselves, but, being cops, we just couldn't acknowledge our fear to each other. When one of the officers told us that Carter had been taken to the hospital, we headed over at breakneck speed and squabbled all the way. By the time we arrived, we were so pumped that neither of us could speak in a normal tone of voice. We badged our way through throngs of officers and found Carter standing by the nurses' station, his right arm in a sling. Lieutenant Ruben was at his side, keeping the investigation going, fielding a myriad of questions over the police radio and dealing with press calls at the same time. I volunteered to stay with Carter so Dan could do his job.

Carter had been chasing Maxwell Thomas, a skinhead who'd shot a gay man, then torched the victim's car with the body inside. During the chase, Carter slipped and fell on his right arm, and his elbow was fragmented. Doctors would try to rebuild the joint, but they'd warned he might never be able to use his right hand again. That would mean the end of his law enforcement career.

As we sat waiting for his wife, I noticed that Carter looked pale and damp as if he were going into shock. I urged him to lie down on a gurney—knowing I wouldn't be able to pick him up if he collapsed in front of me—but he refused. He told me that in Vietnam it was the guys who passed out and went into shock who died, and he wasn't going to do that.

Carter's wife, Jan, arrived, and we waited out his surgery together. She told me that this very day was Carter's twentieth anniversary in the police department, and that it was the first time he'd ever been taken to a hospital. He'd been involved in eight fatal shootings and walked away from each of them without a scratch. One of those incidents was at such close range that Carter and the criminal were hitting each other with their free hands while firing their weapons. Over the years, Jan had come to believe that, despite her husband's line of work, nothing terrible could happen to him. This experience had shattered more than Carter's elbow. It destroyed the fragile psychological zone of safety Jan had built around her husband and his job. Any feelings of security she'd had were gone for good.

I shared with Jan some stories about her husband's affection for practical jokes, particularly the ones he'd played on me. Once he wrote me a faux letter from the Humane Society, concerning my fur coat. It read,

> Madam:
>
> Per your request, our agency has researched the problem of your fur "garment" and determined that the Schnauzer has never been considered an endangered or threatened species.
>
> Also, in light of the fact that the pelts in question were harvested in the grille-work of a speeding Yugo, no shame should attach to the social use of your critter coat; provided, however, that pains are taken to tastefully conceal the tread marks.

Surgeons put pins in Carter's arm, but they didn't hold and had to be replaced later. He recovered after months of physical therapy and just gutting through the pain, and he remained on duty until he was able to retire. Maxwell Thomas got seventy-three years.

Chapter 21
PASSING INSPECTION

Back in the week prior to September 11th, I gave a power point [*sic*] ethics presentation twice to personnel in our Division as part of the "Back to Basics" training which the FBI's prior Director mandated for every field division in the wake of the newly discovered "OKBOMB" documents. One of the frames of the ethics presentation said, "DO NOT: Puff, Shade, Tailor, Firm up, Stretch, Massage, or Tidy up statements of fact." Another frame, entitled "Misplaced Loyalties," stated, "As employees of the FBI, we must be aware that our highest loyalty is to the United States Constitution. We should never sacrifice the truth in order to obtain a desired result (e.g. conviction of a defendant) or to avoid personal or institutional embarrassment." To be honest, I didn't think a whole lot about the slide show at the time I was giving it, but since September 11th, I've been forced to do a lot of thinking about this.

Statement of Coleen M. Rowley
FBI Special Agent and Minneapolis Chief Division Counsel before the
Senate Committee on the Judiciary "Oversight Hearing
on Counterterrorism"
June 6, 2002

After taking over my duties in Denver, I was selected to become an inspector's aide in place. The FBI Inspection Staff is composed of aides, who are GM-14s and GM-15s, and inspectors, who are comparable in rank to field special agents in charge. The staff is responsible for evaluating programs, personnel, and budgets throughout all field offices and FBI headquarters divisions. It's a grueling assignment that entails a minimum of fourteen-hour days, seven days a week on every inspection. It's also a serious job since the careers of special agents can be made or broken by the written reports that Inspection submits to headquarters. In fact, if an inspector's aide discovers criminal wrongdoing at any FBI office, the aide reads the person under investigation his or her rights.

Generally, the FBI Inspection Staff was the epitome of professionalism. A notable exception occurred during my mandatory training, which was held at FBI headquarters. At the end of the inspection course, all new aides gathered in an auditorium to hear the chief inspector's instructions on how we were to behave on inspections. He informed us we were never to address an inspector by name if he were in the company of a woman, because he may not have given her his true name. He also said that inspectors are "invisible" when away from home, so no one was to repeat stories about anything they saw after business hours on an inspection trip. This outrageous speech, transparently designed to justify philandering, went on and on, and many people in the room, including some of the men, were disgusted by the tone of duplicity and deceit that these instructions set. I took the inspector's words as a warning that I could become the target of one of these inspectors sooner or later.

The inspection trips began, and I remained reclusive after hours. I rarely went for a drink with the guys after a day on the job; when I did, I made sure I was with men or women I could trust. During one inspection, I'd gone to the hotel bar with another woman on the staff. We chatted a while and then returned to our rooms. My phone rang all night, but I didn't answer it. I knew it meant trouble. My friend answered hers and found that it was an agent who had been sent to procure women for the chief inspector. The man invited her to the bar for a drink, but she said she couldn't make it because she'd just taken a shower and her hair was wet. He then asked where I was, because the chief inspector had indicated an interest in me. Flustered, but wanting to protect me, she said I'd just taken a shower and my hair was wet, too. The man hung up. When she told me this story the next day, we laughed at what those would-be Casanovas must have thought.

This sort of blatant behavior was shocking, but more shocking still was the atmosphere that made these men feel so protected in their actions. Their sense of privilege and entitlement was engendered by FBI culture and the prevalence of harassment that is so commonplace in the Bureau. The chief inspector himself had set the tone during training at FBI headquarters.

Being away from home on inspection was part of the cascade of events that led to my decision to leave the Bureau. While I was away from my office, Frank, another Denver supervisor, requested more manpower for his squad. Since there was no one available to join his group, Frank evaluated my agents' caseloads, then told the executives that one particular agent was under-assigned and should be transferred immediately to his command. Although it's unprecedented for one supervisor to evaluate the agents under a peer's supervision, office management accepted Frank's claim and transferred my agent to Frank's group before I returned. In reality, Inspection had always found my agents to be over-assigned, but not Frank's. The agent in question was not consulted about his transfer, and he was furious. I learned of the transfer through the grapevine, confronted management, and won the agent back.

Ten days later, a second file review appeared on my desk. Frank was at it again. He'd claimed another agent from my program was under-assigned and had requested that the agent be transferred to his supervision. This time I took the documentation to the special agent in charge. He said he was unaware of Frank's efforts at personnel theft and vowed he'd take care of it. Apparently he did, because I never heard another word from Frank.

As if this wasn't enough, I was sexually accosted by Darnell, who had been hostile and demeaning to me at Rocky Flats. He also took advantage of his inspection trips to belittle me to others. In fact, I received calls from agents across the country saying that Darnell had plopped down in their offices uninvited and begun to criticize me. Since Darnell was obsessed with the idea that women in the FBI received special privileges and never pulled their weight, I was surprised when he came to my room one night at a supervisors' off-site conference.

The special agent in charge had assigned me to the hospitality suite. This room was larger than the ones reserved for the rest of our group. Unfortunately, there was a hitch. It had been decided that others participating in the conference could drop by my room when they wanted a drink, since it was the only room that had a bar. Darnell dropped by and said he wanted a drink, and I let him in, but moments after he arrived, he tried to grab me and give me a kiss. Disgusted, I threw him out. His uncouth behavior was nothing more than an attempt to exert physical power over me, to gain control and demonstrate his imagined superiority.

It wasn't only the men in management who didn't like the idea of a woman serving as a supervisory special agent. A woman, an assistant office service manager, came to me after I'd been in Denver a few months and apologized for not briefing me about the proper handling of office administrative matters. For months, she confessed, she had been holding up priority outgoing communications and sending them back to me in the routine mail with notes like, "You can't do it this way," but without hinting at what was wrong or how to make corrections. I'd have to track her down to get the paperwork moving again. Deadlines were missed, and much time was wasted in the process. She knew I would be criticized at headquarters for lateness, a transgression for which I could actually be censured in certain cases. Now, she admitted that she'd done this because I was a woman, but after she realized I "wasn't so bad," she decided to apologize and help me as she had done for previous (male) supervisors. Basically, she now decided she would do her job.

One would think that at least the FBI Inspection Staff would be able to enforce reasonable behavior, but that was not my experience. At the end of my second inspection as a squad supervisor, one of the inspectors took me aside and said that personnel throughout the office had reported that management had created a hostile work environment for me and those under my supervision. He asked whether he should proceed with an Equal Employment Opportunity (EEO) investigation. We talked about what that type of investigation might do to my career in the Bureau, and I hesitated. We both knew that, as the next career step for me was as an assistant special agent in charge, I'd never be able to get a special agent in charge to accept me if an EEO investigation were launched. At that time, EEO complaints were nearly as bad for the victims as rape cases: Even if a woman won, she was a loser for the rest of her career. Despite what I'd been through in the past, I didn't want to suffer anymore and, frankly, I didn't believe anything constructive would be done on my behalf. So, I said "no thanks" to the idea of an investigation. The inspector was acting in my best interests, but I was looking at reality as I knew it in the FBI, not as it might be in an ideal world.

In retrospect, I ask myself: If agents from various squads had volunteered information about what was happening, why didn't the inspectors see my situation as a systemic management problem and investigate it based upon that? Why did they put me in the position of having to complain? After all, when law enforcement officers come upon a crime in progress, they're supposed to take action.

It's not as if there were no rules or training for EEO matters. While I was in Denver, EEO "sensitivity" training was mandated from headquarters; however, the contractor who was hired to facilitate the sessions ran from the room crying after a couple of days of being heckled and thwarted by the men in the Denver office. She was so upset that she refused to come back. It was another waste of taxpayer money.

Chapter 22

KNOWING WHEN TO LEAVE

To every thing there is a season, and a time to every purpose under
the heaven.

Ecclesiastes 3:1
The Thompson Chain Reference Bible
4th Improved Edition

On January 19, 1990, while traveling on an inspection team
assignment in Honolulu, Guam, and Saipan, I heard that my
former partner, Doug Abram, had been killed in the line of
duty. Leading a SWAT team, Doug was executing a search warrant on
James Price for weapons and drugs in St. Louis, Missouri. As the agents
broke through a door and dove from bright sunlight into darkness, Price
fired a wadcutter round that hit Doug between his eyes and embedded
in his brain. Wadcutters are practice rounds that do not mushroom in
the body like combat rounds. Had it hit him anywhere else, Doug might
have survived. Seconds later, the SWAT team fired on Price and shot
him through the heart, killing him instantly. Doug was transported to a
hospital, but died on full life support in an intensive care unit.

The inspection team agents I was traveling with had no idea I knew
Doug, much less worked as his partner, and as we drove to the office
together, they mentioned rather casually that he'd been killed. I was dev-
astated. That night we had a command appearance at the home of the special agent in charge. I spent most of the evening crying in the bathroom.

Though it would be six months before I resigned, Doug's death signaled the end of my FBI career. The loss of such a decent man caused me to question whether a life in law enforcement was worth the price. For the first time, I admitted to myself that I wasn't bulletproof and that there was a real possibility my children could lose the only parent they had.

At that point, I began to question why I was still at the same job after years of frustration and unrelenting disappointment. Why was I risking my life to put offenders through a criminal justice system that changed nothing and did little for victims? I was tired of seeing prisoners released from jail after serving short sentences, especially the recidivists who immediately sought new victims. I no longer felt my work made a difference, nor that I was contributing to positive change. And of course, my work environment continued to reinforce my ongoing feeling of dissatisfaction.

The day I resigned, I surrendered my badge, credentials, weapon, and Kevlar vest. The final insult came when I discovered I would receive no interest on the pension money that had been withdrawn from each paycheck over the previous thirteen years. Indeed, it was noted in an administrative manual that, if an agent resigned before serving twenty years, accrued interest remained with the Bureau's retirement program. So I walked away with exactly the amount I had put into the fund, not a penny more. When I left the FBI, I wrote on the resignation form that I was leaving because of "treatment of women in the Bureau." The assistant special agent in charge (second in command of the office) called me in and warned me that "others" could find out what I wrote, and when I applied for future jobs, my potential employer might learn how I felt. He claimed I would hurt my chances of finding future employment. I felt like a woman being told she should be ashamed that she'd been raped and shouldn't press charges, but I wouldn't change the statement. When I received my separation papers from the FBI, the official reason recorded for separation was "to take a job in private industry." This was a blatant cover-up to keep EEO statistics low. If the complaint doesn't exist on paper, it doesn't exist.

People from various squads and agencies attended my going away party, but Frank was the sole supervisor from my office who bothered to come. The evening included the gift of an original poem from Bill

Carter, which he entitled "To Rosie on the Wall," in honor of the "Rosie is a bitch" graffiti that had greeted me on my arrival.

TO ROSIE ON THE WALL

Rosie was an S-S-A
A diamond in the rough
In a coat of finest Airedale,
Or other road-killed stuff.
All eyes would turn to her in awe
As she strode upon the scene
With a manicured grasp of field command
That would turn George Patton green.
The K.G.B. and Hezbollah
Would panic and retreat,
And klansmen run away in herds
At the sound of her Gucci-clad feet.
Now it's time to wish our Rosie well
She's moving on, you see
To put her expertise to work
For private industry.
But even though our Rosie's moved
Two thousand miles away
We'll have a small reminder
to recall our S-S-A.
For, you see, a kindly wino
Has had the wherewithal
To emblazon "Rosie is a bitch"
On the bricks of the alley wall.
So out-of-sight's not out-of-mind,
Be it winter, spring or fall,
We can always see our Rosie
On the bricks of the alley wall.
                    Hefty-Bag Man

• • •

After the party was over, I went out for a nightcap with an Aurora police officer, Tim, and his wife. After visiting a local club, we decided to call it a night. When we walked out into the parking lot, a huge biker-type character was sitting in his car and yelling at a woman parked nearby. Although he obviously knew the woman, we advised her to leave, which she did.

Now, the thug directed his anger at us as he stepped from his car. About six foot two and 250 pounds, he was clad in black leathers that showed off his tattoos to their best advantage. His long, greasy hair was pulled back in a ponytail. Tim held up his badge and warned the man to move on. Meanwhile, I rummaged through my purse for my badge, but to no avail. Since it was my last night on duty, I'd dropped it in the bottom of my cavernous bag. As I fumbled around, I said, "FBI, just get back in the car."

The man began spewing threats and curse words, and started to move toward Tim. I dropped the purse and stuck my right hand, fingers extended, hard and deep into his pendulous gut, which closed around my wrist like a massive glob of bread dough. With a panicked look on his face, the huge man scurried back to his car and drove away. No doubt, he thought I was crazy.

Tim and I were laughing and slapping each other on the back, when we noticed his wife crouching behind the rear fender of a nearby auto. For the first time, it occurred to me that some people might not find my job the least bit attractive. That night at home, I paced my kitchen, chastising myself for risking a fistfight my last night on duty. Life in the Bureau had turned reality upside-down for me. Years of daily exposure to the toughness, crudeness, and excessively macho mentality of the FBI trained me to expect that type of behavior from all men. After I left the Bureau, I realized how skewed my perceptions had become when a former United States national science advisor pulled out a chair for me at a meeting, and my first thought was that he was trying to make me fall on the floor.

I look back on my special agent days with pride and sadness, and I've often wished there was something I could do to contribute to positive change in the Bureau. I miss the friends I made but I don't miss the battles required just to make it through a day.

Dietrich Bonhoeffer is my hero. A Lutheran pastor in Nazi Germany, he not only led the anti-Nazi Confessing Church, he used his ability to travel abroad as a pastor to pass messages to Allied intelligence about the resistance movement within the German officer corps. When this group carried out an attempt to kill Hitler in March of 1943, Bonhoeffer was arrested by the Gestapo. He was hanged in a Bavarian concentration camp in 1945, but during his imprisonment, he wrote prolifically about his beliefs and his life. How I wish I had the strength to maintain his serene manner of thought and expression.

In his *Letters from Prison,* Pastor Bonhoeffer wrote:

> When you've deliberately suppressed every desire for so long, it may have one of two bad results: either it burns you up inside, or it all gets so bottled up that one day there is a terrific explosion. It is, of course, conceivable that one may become completely selfless, and I know better than anyone else that that hasn't happened to me.

While I in no way compare my years in the FBI to Pastor Bonhoeffer's struggle against the Nazis, what I experienced was persistent and pervasive. It engulfed my way of life and burned me up inside. I was unable to rise above it or to become a selfless fighter against the system's flaws. My primary career goal became nothing more than day-to-day survival. I broke some ground, but it nearly broke me too, and I never stopped having to prove myself, trying to fit in, and seeking approval in that never-ending game. My good work was an also-ran in the scheme of how I was treated. It didn't matter who accepted me on the job, if one new man were added to the equation, I was back to being a rookie. All I can say is, I stuck it out for almost thirteen years and fought a good fight, but what a waste of taxpayer money there was.

It would be too easy, if not flippant, to sum up the years that followed by saying "it all worked out," but in truth, it did. After resigning from the Bureau, I returned to Washington, D.C., and became a program manager in a small consulting firm, which later merged with one of the top ten defense contractors.

Christopher became a noncommissioned officer in the U.S. Army Rangers. He's married and has made me a grandmother. Kendra works for another top-ten defense contractor. She, too, is happily married. And, finally, I am happily married to a computer scientist who worked on the Celera Genomics algorithm team that sequenced the human genome.

Yes, folks, there is life after the Bureau, and it is good.

PART II

Chapter 23
THE FORMATIVE YEARS

When a reporter from a newspaper here in Maryland asked to talk to me, he said he had heard that I was writing another book . . . what about? . . . I gave him the title and the names of Sacco and Vanzetti. There was a wavering pause . . . then "Well I don't really know anything about them . . . for me it's just history."
It is my conviction that when events are forgotten, buried in the cellar of the page—they are no longer even history.

Katherine Anne Porter
The Never-Ending Wrong
1977

The complexity of FBI culture developed over time, and the context of history is an important key to understanding the Bureau that serves the United States today. I realized that the historical context of the FBI I knew had become buried when a reader for a literary agency commented on a piece of fiction I'd written about a woman who was an agent in the 1990s. This is what she read:

All the agents had their feet up on desks and cups of coffee in their hands. It was a form of rebellion, because J. Edgar Hoover would not allow FBI agents to drink coffee—not in the squad room, not anywhere. No one knew why, but challenging the Director meant sure and severe consequences, so it became a fact of Bureau life. It is said that agents bolted from restaurants and hid in the men's room when he walked in, so he wouldn't see that they had ordered coffee. These days, coffee is almost obligatory in squad rooms, demonstrating that modern FBI agents are wild and crazy guys who aren't afraid of any man who wore pink lace.

Next to the line that mentioned Hoover, she penned: "You can't introduce a new character this late in the story."

I was shocked that a college-educated reader either didn't recognize who J. Edgar Hoover was nor that he had been long dead by the '90s.

Without a doubt, Hoover and the historical events that influenced his actions are germane to any analysis of the FBI system. Hoover's personality and beliefs helped mold the Bureau into an organization that has been at times heroic, and at other times, has strong-armed with total disregard for individual rights. Meanwhile, the context of history has been the key to whether the FBI's methods are accepted—even encouraged—by the public, or not.

The fledgling Bureau was shaped by the public's fear that the American way of life could be obliterated on its own soil. The Bureau was established in a period when public opinion was similar to what has been seen since the morning of September 11, 2001. It was a time when war and anarchy threatened to blow the country apart, and it is important to consider this context to understand the evolution of the FBI.

John Edgar Hoover was born on January 1, 1895, to a middle-class family in Washington, D.C. The United States was still growing. Alaska, Arizona, Hawaii, Montana, New Mexico, Oklahoma, and Utah were not yet states, and anarchists were wreaking havoc around the world. In 1881, an anarchist's bomb disguised as an Easter cake had killed Czar Alexander II of Russia and twenty-one bystanders. That act had hurled Russia into a period of disorder, poverty, and violence. In 1894, another anarchist had fatally stabbed French president Marie-François-Sadi Carnot. In 1889, a French-born Italian anarchist drove a sharpened file into the heart of Empress Elizabeth of Austria, wife of Franz Josef. She wasn't the killer's first choice for an assassination-victim, but she was the highest-ranking person who crossed his path on the day he chose to act. In 1900, an Italian-American anarchist from New Jersey murdered Humbert I, the king of Italy, and on September 6, 1901, Polish/Russian-American anarchist Leon Franz Czolgosz shot President William McKinley as he walked through the Pan-American Exposition in Buffalo, New York. The president died a week later from his wounds, and authorities suspected that an anarchist conspiracy was behind his murder. Chicago police immediately arrested Emma Goldman, an immigrant from Lithuania, one of the most outspoken anarchists of the time. Czolgosz claimed to have been inspired by Goldman's speeches, but Goldman was released due to a lack of evidence that her words had incited him to murder. The anarchist movement had become such an issue in America that the government inserted provisions into the Immigration Act of March 3, 1903, to exclude aliens who were "anarchists, or persons who believe in, or advocate, the overthrow by force or violence the government of the United States, or of all government, or of all forms of law, or the assassination of public officials."

It was in this turn-of-the-century, immigrant-fearing society that Hoover grew to manhood. The anarchist movement and Red Scares (the decades-long waves of American fear that anarchists, socialists, and communists would rise up and overthrow the U.S. government) gave birth to Hoover's unquestioned power, and that omnipotence shaped the attitude of every agent who came after him. Four historical events—the Haymarket bombing, World War I, the bombings that led to the Palmer Raids, and the Sacco and Vanzetti murder trial—are examples of the environment in which Hoover was raised and the Bureau was formed.

CASE 1: THE HAYMARKET BOMBING

In the 1870s, the United States was suffering a severe economic depression and political upheaval. The Industrial Revolution had created strata of the fabulously rich and the hopelessly poor, the latter of whom were relegated to the slums of major cities, such as New York and Chicago. American factory workers were little better off than slaves as they toiled in dangerous conditions with no power to make demands for a better work environment or reasonable hours. To make matters worse, even the bad jobs were scarce: of the 45 million people who comprised the 1877 U.S. population, nearly 3 million were jobless and 15 million were living at the poverty level.

And yet, new immigrants streamed into American ports, fleeing even worse conditions abroad and bringing with them dreams for a new way of life. Exploitative labor conditions were a common rallying point for many of the new arrivals, and the anarchists, socialists, and communists among them wanted to change the plight of the working class, even if the change necessitated violence. The goals of anarchists differed from the desires of socialists and communists, who wanted to reform government. Anarchists believed that any form of government was inherently bad and that, when freed from the yoke of law, people would naturally form the optimal society.

Anarchist philosophy was propagated by nineteenth-century French writer Pierre-Joseph Proudhon, who defined anarchy as "the absence of a master, of a sovereign." This idea took hold in Europe and quickly spread to America as immigrants sought the quality of life they could never hope to attain in their homelands. Russian, German, and Italian immigrant anarchists rallied American workers to strike for better labor conditions and better lives. It was a call to arms, not a call to the ballot box, with Chicago, Cleveland, and New York being the most prominent centers of rebellion.

In the 1880s, the United States experienced waves of violent labor strikes and demonstrations, some of which attracted thousands of workers. Anarchist rhetoric was violent, with dynamite touted as the great equalizer. In fact, in the popular press, anarchists were caricatured with bombs in their hands.

The City of Chicago reacted brutally to the labor strikes. With the full support of influential citizens, Chicago police swooped down on striking workers—including women and children—beating them with clubs and sometimes firing into the crowds. In this shoot-first-ask-questions-later period of American history, the wealthy populace encouraged the government's violent reaction and stood its ground against the laborers' demands for better working conditions and an eight-hour workday. In Chicago, a citizens' association purchased two Gatling guns—hand-cranked machine guns that could fire six hundred rounds per minute—for local police to use against demonstrators. Some newspapers advocated using grenades to clear the crowds, and it was during this period that armories were established in the center of U.S. cities so that federal troops would be available when needed on the home front.

The scene was set for the Haymarket bombing when, on May 1, 1886, workers across the United States struck for eight-hour workdays. Two days later, police dispersed strikers at Chicago's McCormick Reaper Works, killing several in the process. On May 4, police arrived to break up a workers' meeting near Haymarket Square when, suddenly, an unidentified person threw a bomb. The police immediately began firing their guns, and between the bomb and the shooting, one officer was killed at the scene, and seven others died later as a result of injuries. Sixty other police officers were wounded. The number of civilians wounded or killed has never been confirmed, since many of the injured participants hid rather than risk arrest while seeking medical care.

The next day, police rounded up an unconfirmed number of workers, conducted warrantless searches and arrests, and held suspects incommunicado for days. There was no regard for probable cause; instead, police actions were based upon suspected association with the anarchist cause or even association with those merely suspected of being anarchists.

Before the month was over, a grand jury had indicted thirty-one people. Of these, defendants Samuel Fielden, Michael Schwab, August Spies, Albert Parsons, Louis Lingg, Adolph Fischer, Oscar W. Neebe, and George Engel were convicted of murder. On August 19, Neebe was sentenced to fifteen years in prison, and the others were sentenced to death by hanging. The Illinois Supreme Court upheld the rulings and verdict, and, on November 2, 1887, the U.S. Supreme Court denied the defendants' appeal. Eight days later, Governor Oglesby commuted Fielden's and Schwab's sentences to life imprisonment, and, on the following day, Spies, Fischer, Parsons, and Engel were hanged. Prior to the hanging, Lingg committed suicide in his cell by biting down on a dynamite cap.

But the story didn't end there. In 1893, the governor of Illinois pardoned the men who remained in prison. By this time, it was clear that numerous abuses of the legal system had been committed and lack of evidence had been clearly established.

The Haymarket incident marked the beginning of the first Red Scare, the national fear of communism that led to the McCarthy hearings and persisted until the end of the cold war. Even many years later, this fear was strong enough to drive the United States' incursions into the war in Vietnam.

The Bureau that Hoover created was specifically charged with guarding the United States from what was seen as a pervasive threat. As his Bureau evolved, there were public cries for restricting immigration and deporting undesirables, and the majority of citizens quietly accepted this disregard for due process. The country's way of life and cherished freedoms seemed to depend upon the FBI's war against the Red Menace, and in times when the public feared annihilation of its way of life, the cost of saving the free world was not to be weighed against rights of the individual.

CASE 2: WORLD WAR I

World War I erupted in Europe in 1914 after Gavrilo Princep assassinated Archduke Franz Ferdinand in Sarajevo. The United States remained neutral, even after 1915 when the *Lusitania,* a Cunard cruise liner traveling from New York City to Liverpool, was torpedoed without warning by a German U-boat, and more than 120 American passengers died. In 1916, when it became obvious that German submarine warfare would not cease, President Woodrow Wilson began strengthening U.S. military forces, but Wilson would not commit the country to war. A British intercept of a German message that encouraged Mexico and Japan to attack the U.S. finally pushed the United States to declare war against Germany on April 6, 1917.

That same year, Hoover received a master's degree in law from George Washington University, passed the bar, and was admitted to practice before the Supreme Court. He'd attended night classes to earn his law degree while he worked in the ordering and cataloging departments at the Library of Congress.

During the national military call-up, Hoover registered for the draft, but he never served in the military. Instead, he landed a job as a clerk in the Department of Justice's files division, where he worked as a permit officer, processing applications from aliens who wanted to live in parts of the United States that were officially restricted for security reasons, such as areas around military installations or munitions plants.

Due to the war, President Wilson revived the July 6, 1798, Act Respecting Alien Enemies and called for the registration of aliens living in designated areas. In essence, the act states that in time of war, the president can declare that alien enemies are to be apprehended and deported, and that their property can be confiscated.

The influence of the more recent Act Respecting Alien Enemies is apparent in the Uniting and Strengthening America by Providing Appropriate Tools Required to Intercept and Obstruct Terrorism Act (USA PATRIOT Act). Passed after September 11, 2001, to expand law enforcement powers in the war against terrorism, the USA PATRIOT Act hits immigrants hard. As was seen in the widespread arrests and detentions after September 11, the USA PATRIOT Act allows the federal government to detain and deport non-U.S. citizens suspected of lending support, including financial support, to organizations deemed terrorist. Right or wrong, the USA PATRIOT Act promotes a mass roundup mentality that, according to an April 2003 Department of Justice report, has already resulted in detentions that are reminiscent of those of the anarchist era. This is because the guidelines for processing illegal aliens taken into custody under this law had not been worked out at the time it was employed, and the only policy the government had formulated was to hold illegal aliens until cleared of terrorism, whether they had been arrested in connection with terrorism or not.

In July 1917, as Europe was at war, Hoover moved to the War

Emergency Division and the Alien Enemy Bureau. Historians disagree as to whether he was, at the time, an attorney or a special agent of the Bureau of Investigation (BOI). The FBI's official biography glosses over specifics, saying, "Hoover entered on duty with the Department of Justice on July 26, 1917, and rose quickly in government service." In either case, his career took off just as the Bolsheviks were seizing power in Russia and American anarchist Emma Goldman was in trouble again, this time convicted of obstructing the U.S. draft. Hoover was put in charge of the department's General Intelligence Division (GID), "where his job was investigating suspected anarchists and communists." In November 1918, he became an assistant to the attorney general.

The wartime BOI augmented its forces with a group of citizen volunteers known as the American Protective League. Although it sounds like a ludicrous plan at this point in time, the Bureau gave 260,000 citizens badges that identified them as Justice Department auxiliaries and empowered them to investigate whomever they wished to call subversive or disloyal.

In its 1977 report, the Select Committee to Study Governmental Operations with Respect to Intelligence Activities and the Rights of Americans recounted the history of the American Protective League and its various activities:

> Repressive practices during World War I included the formation of a volunteer auxiliary force, known as the American Protective League, which assisted the Justice Department and military intelligence in the investigation of "un American activities" and in the mass round-up of 50,000 persons to discover draft evaders. These so-called "slacker raids" of 1918 involved warrantless arrests without sufficient probable cause to believe that a crime had been or was about to be committed (FBI intelligence Division memorandum, "An Analysis of FBI Domestic Security intelligence Investigations," 10/28/75.)
>
> The American Protective League also contributed to the

pressures which resulted in nearly 2,000 prosecutions for disloyal utterances and activities during World War I, a policy described by John Lord O'Brien, Attorney General Gregory's Special Assistant, as one of "wholesale repression and restraint of public opinion."

CASE 3: THE PALMER RAIDS

Even after World War I, anarchists remained a top priority for the United States government. This is evident in Attorney General A. Mitchel Palmer's comments when William J. Flynn was named director of the BOI in 1919, a year of tremendous social conflict that included massive strikes, the passage of the Woman's Suffrage and Prohibition Constitutional amendments, and a race riot in Chicago. The attorney general described Flynn as "the leading, organizing detective of America . . . Flynn is an anarchist chaser . . . the greatest anarchist expert in the United States."

In June 1919, a bomb exploded at Attorney General Palmer's Washington, D.C., house, and other bombs exploded at the homes of government officials in eight major U.S. cities. Palmer saw this attack as one more piece of evidence that foreign agents were planning to overthrow the government. On January 2 and 6, 1920, massive raids by law enforcement officials in several cities resulted in the arrests of an estimated six to ten thousand aliens, suspected communists and anarchists. Known as the "Palmer Raids," these cases were the ones on which young J. Edgar Hoover, then head of the Anti-Radical Division at the Department of Justice, cut his investigative teeth. Despite the bombs and subsequent raids, no evidence of a widespread revolution was ever uncovered, and most of the Palmer Raids' arrestees were eventually released. However, Emma Goldman, always in the middle of a scrap, was deported to Russia, along with 247 others.

So what did Hoover do to distinguish himself during the Palmer Raids? He made lists, extensive lists of people and the names of their associates. This cataloguing, harassing, and disregard for civil rights would surface again in the FBI's investigative support of the House

Un-American Activities Committee, which was formed in 1938 and remained in existence until 1975, and in the handling of cases against Vietnam-era radicals, such as the Weather Underground and the Black Panthers.

Hoover was proud of his role in the Palmer Raids and dedicated his life to fighting communism. He used his personal views on the communist threat to expand the Bureau's mandate and manpower. No matter how oppressive Hoover seems in retrospect—and he often was just that—he knew that public support was paramount to his success, and he knew how to garner it.

CASE 4: SACCO AND VANZETTI

Nicola Sacco made shoes, and Bartolomeo Vanzetti sold fish. Together, they were accused of shooting a paymaster and a guard during the April 15, 1920, robbery of a shoe factory in Braintree, Massachusetts. Sacco was charged with firing the gun, and Vanzetti was named as one of four accomplices. None of the others was tried, but after an eighteen-month trial, Sacco and Vanzetti were found guilty.

There was conflicting witness testimony. Both men were armed at the time of arrest and both lied during questioning; yet, both had alibis. It was proven that the prosecution altered certain witness testimony, and the judge made prejudicial statements outside of the courtroom, such as, "Did you see what I did with those anarchistic bastards the other day?" Today's defense attorneys and judges would not let such discrepancies pass without notice, but in that post-World War I era, when the nation feared anarchism, superficial evidence was sufficient for convictions and death sentences. Sacco and Vanzetti were anarchists, that much was proven. But the validity of the remaining evidence presented by the prosecution remains a subject of much debate.

In 1924, Hoover became the fifth director of the BOI. On August 23, 1927, Sacco and Vanzetti were electrocuted, while the world watched and protested. Over the years, the two anarchists had become powerful symbols for laborers, radicals, and immigrants. Their plight attracted international attention, and demonstrations protesting their unfair treatment were held in Paris, London, Buenos Aires, and other major cities.

In 1932, the BOI absorbed the Bureau of Prohibition and was renamed the Division of Investigation. In 1935, the Division of Investigation became the Federal Bureau of Investigation. All told, Hoover would be the head of the old and the new Bureaus for forty-eight years.

Chapter 24

CRUCIBLES

The broad mass of a nation . . . will more easily fall victim to a big lie than a small one.

Adolph Hitler
Mein Kampf

Steel is made by heating iron at a high temperature to remove impurities, and a crucible is a container in which this process takes place. Colloquially, a crucible is a severe trial or test. Arthur Miller's famous Broadway play, *The Crucible,* is the story of New England Puritans and accusations of witchcraft. When he wrote the play, Miller was not particularly interested in witches per se as much as in the House Un-American Activities Committee (HUAC). Between 1947 and 1954, the HUAC suppressed artists and ideas—ideas that are protected by the First Amendment to the Constitution.

While many of his contemporaries crumbled from fear and accused friends, acquaintances, coworkers, and even people they'd never met of being communists, or associating with communists, Miller refused to name names before the committee and was convicted of contempt of Congress. He risked prison and the loss of his livelihood by standing up to the committee. Miller's conviction was overturned in 1958, but others were less fortunate and either served time in jail or found themselves blacklisted from their professions.

History repeats itself, and what happened in the investigation of antigovernment groups, such as the Prairie Fire Organizing Committee and the Black Panther Party, was the culmination of a decades-long chain of historic events that began during the BOI's anarchist-hunting days and continued through Watergate and the '70s. One hallmark of these investigations was the FBI's COINTELPRO, short for counterintelligence program. COINTELPRO was a program of covert dirty tricks, which operated out of the Domestic Intelligence Division at FBI headquarters. Its targets were U.S. citizens, and its goal was to disrupt and neutralize activities of certain groups and individuals, including activities protected by the First Amendment.

> The techniques were adopted wholesale from wartime counter-intelligence, and ranged from the trivial (mailing reprints of *Reader's Digest* articles to college administrators) to the degrading (sending anonymous poison-pen letters intended to break up marriages) and the dangerous (encouraging gang warfare and falsely labeling members of a violent group as police informers).

COINTELPRO was put into action in 1956 and continued until 1971. The program provided a means to maneuver around U.S. Supreme Court rulings that reaffirmed the First Amendment rights of dissident groups and limited the government's ability to work against them. *Brandenberg v. Ohio*, 395 U.S. 444 (1969), which struck down the conviction of a Ku Klux Klan member, remains the standard for judging freedom of speech today. In this landmark ruling, the Supreme Court held that the government is not permitted to "forbid or proscribe advocacy of the use of force or law violation except where such advocacy is directed toward inciting or producing imminent lawless action and is likely to incite or produce such action." In other words, speech is protected unless it is intended to incite violence and unless the incitement is likely to succeed. There is a vast gray area in applying this concept, but it is safe to say an individual could be prosecuted for planning to carry out specific acts, such as bombing a government building or assassinating the president, and also for encouraging others to do so.

The stated purpose of COINTELPRO was to protect national security by impeding the growth of dangerous groups but, in practice, the program also targeted people and organizations that did not engage in or promote violence. "The unexpressed major premise of the program was that a law enforcement agency has the duty to do whatever is necessary to combat perceived threats to the existing social and political order."

Five groups were identified by the Bureau as key targets: the "Communist Party, USA" (1956–71); the "Socialist Workers Party" (1961–69); the "White Hate Group" (1964–71); the "Black Nationalist Hate Group" (1967–71); and the "New Left" (1968–71). These groups were broadly defined, which gave the FBI quite a bit of latitude in choosing whom to investigate. Cases were opened for the flimsiest of reasons. For example, two students became COINTELPRO targets because "they defended the use of the classic four-letter-word" during a free speech demonstration. Among the reasons the FBI investigated Martin Luther King Jr. was that he might possibly advocate violence at some point in the future.

> In short, the programs were to prevent violence indirectly, rather than directly, by preventing possibly violent citizens from joining or continuing to associate with possibly violent groups.

Concurrent with COINTELPRO, the FBI and other agencies were conducting illegal wiretaps and break-ins, which were often referred to as "black bag jobs." During World War II, President Roosevelt gave the FBI the power to wiretap individuals who were suspected of being involved in subversive activities. All wiretapping activities were to be overseen by the attorney general, and the president instructed that such wiretaps be limited "insofar as possible to aliens." It was the fact that wiretapping and COINTELPRO activities had spun out of control that caused Attorney General Edward H. Levi to introduce the 1976

Attorney General Guidelines Governing FBI Investigations. It also spurred Congress to pass the Foreign Intelligence Surveillance Act of 1978, which regulates wiretaps and searches for intelligence purposes.

The Bureau tends to receive wide-ranging intelligence and counterintelligence jurisdiction during times of war. Hoover's account of a 1936 meeting with President Roosevelt was that the president asked him to provide " 'a broad picture' of the impact of Communism and Fascism on American life." Hoover described his mandate as including pure intelligence collection and "preventive intelligence" concerning acts of espionage or sabotage.

FBI headquarters sent out vague instructions about gathering "general preventive intelligence" on "potential" espionage or sabotage.

> In 1939, for instance, field offices were told to investigate persons of German, Italian, and Communist "sympathies" and any other persons "whose interests may be directed primarily to the interest of some other nation than the United States." FBI offices were directed to report the names of members of German and Italian societies, "whether they be of a fraternal character or of some other nature," and members of any other groups "which might have pronounced Nationalistic tendencies." The Bureau sought lists of subscribers and officers of German, Italian, and Communist foreign language newspapers, as well as of other newspapers with "notorious Nationalistic sympathies." The FBI also made confidential inquiries regarding "various so-called radical and fascist organizations" to identify their "leading personnel, purposes and aims, and the part they are likely to play at a time of national crisis."

The USA PATRIOT Act reflects the spirit of a country at war. The act was specifically designed to supplement law enforcement's ability to collect information and share it among themselves and intelligence agencies. It obliterated the strict prohibitions against the CIA participating in law enforcement activities concerning "United States Persons," which include U.S. citizens and permanent resident aliens. In fact, the National Security Act of 1947, which established the CIA, specifically prohibited the CIA from exercising "domestic law enforcement powers." Finally, Executive Order 12333 delineates each federal agency's responsibilities in the intelligence community. It specifies that CIA's responsibility is foreign intelligence collection and assigns counterintelligence collection responsibilities on U.S. Persons to the FBI. The USA PATRIOT Act requires that, if a law enforcement officer comes across information of intelligence value, he or she is required by law to report it to the intelligence community.

To facilitate investigations, the act eases previously strict limitations on wiretaps, Internet surveillance, and search authority. For example, Foreign Intelligence Surveillance Court warrants were formerly issued for the "primary purpose" of intelligence collection. The language inserted by the act now permits wiretaps, surveillance, and searches when there is a "significant foreign intelligence purpose."

While the act eases the collection of information and increases the opportunity for information sharing among the many agencies involved in the war on terrorism, it has codified activities that became disallowed in the 1970s and has substantially reduced the checks and balances designed to protect an individual's civil liberties. For instance, business records under the act include "any tangible things (including books, records, papers, documents or other items) for an investigation to protect against international terrorism or clandestine intelligence activities." To obtain business records of a United States Person (citizen or permanent resident alien) under the act, the investigator must "certify that information is relevant to an ongoing investigation to protect against international terrorism or clandestine intelligence activities, provided that such investigation of a United States Person is not conducted solely upon the basis of activities protected by the First Amendment to the Constitution." The past requirement was the Foreign Intelligence Surveillance Act's demand for "specific and articulable facts giving reason to believe" that the person for whom the records are sought is an "agent of a foreign power." While this was not tantamount to a demonstration of probable cause, it required an investigator to produce some significant facts.

The USA PATRIOT Act brings back the old HUAC-imposed guilt by association. Returning to the business of investigating people's associations and their expression of ideas is chilling in light of the stories of oppression and suffering caused by the now-defunct House Un-American Activities Committee and COINTELPRO. Membership in or monetary support of an organization that has been labeled "terrorist" by the U.S. government is a deportable offense. It also is possible for noncitizens to be detained or deported for supporting organizations that are not officially designated as "terrorist" for as long as that organization engages in violent activity. While this may seem appropriate in the immediate aftermath of September 11, it is important to note that many groups that have committed terrorist acts serve the dual purpose of providing social services in some countries, especially in the Middle East. For example, as reported in a 1996 *New York Times* article, the Israelis estimated that about 95 percent of Hamas's "$70 million a year goes into such charities as hospitals, clinics and schools, with only a small portion siphoned off to pay for weapons and military operations." The report also pointed out that Hamas uses some of the charitable funds to support families of suicide bombers, which has proven a viable recruitment tactic.

Considering this complex web of activities, it is reasonable that there are people out there who support organizations for reasons that have no connection to terrorism. Furthermore, the act's loose definition of terrorism could be extended to cover almost any violent situation, such as destruction of property that occurs during a protest demonstration.

I appreciate the fact that the USA PATRIOT Act makes it easier to investigate suspected criminals, but I find the trend toward the discredited activities of the past to be troubling. In fact, in 2003, the Justice Department's Office of the Inspector General reviewed complaints about the treatment of aliens in the wake of the September 11 attacks. The Inspector General's Office found that the Immigration and Naturalization Service (INS) had detained 762 aliens in connection with the attacks. Twenty-four were already in INS custody prior to September 11, on immigration violations. The rest were arrested between September 11, 2001, and August 6, 2002, as a direct result of FBI investigations. All of them became part of the "INS Custody List," which, according to Department of Justice policy, meant that the detainees were to be held until the FBI could clear them of connections to terrorism. This is a policy of guilty until proven innocent.

After a while, the media began to report the detainees' complaints, such as that they had not been informed of the charges against them, that they had been denied access to attorneys or suffered verbal and physical abuse in custody. After lawsuits were filed, the Department of Justice decided to look into the charges. Their report found a disturbing bureaucratic logjam. While the detainees were all illegal aliens, most of whom had overstayed their visas, they were detained for an inordinate amount of time.

The Department of Justice report said:

> The FBI cleared less than 3 percent of the 762 September 11 detainees within three weeks of their arrest. The average length of time from arrest of a September 11 detainee to clearance by FBI headquarters was 80 days, and the median was 69 days. Further, we found that more than a quarter of the 762 detainees' clearance investigations took longer than 3 months.

The reality is that the FBI was overwhelmed with thousands of investigative leads, and was simply unable to carry out within a reasonable timeframe the investigations that were necessary to disprove more than seven hundred aliens' connection with terrorist groups. To make matters worse, by the end of October 2001, the Bureau decided that all clearance reports had to be approved by FBI headquarters, which created another bottleneck. Meanwhile, the INS was under orders not to release anyone who had not been cleared by the FBI.

Here is a sad example of what happened:

A Muslim man in his 40s, who was a citizen of [deleted], was arrested after an acquaintance wrote a letter to law enforcement officers stating that the man had made anti-American statements. The statements, as reported in the letter, were very general and did not involve threats of violence or suggest any direct connection to terrorism. Nonetheless, the lead was assigned to a special agent with the JTTF [Joint Terrorism Task Force] and resulted in the man's arrest for overstaying his visa. Because he had been arrested on a PENTTBOM [September 11 attacks] lead, he automatically was placed in the FBI New York's "special interest" category.

Within a week, the New York FBI Field Office conducted a detailed interview of the detainee. By mid-November 2001, the Field Office concluded that the detainee was of no interest. However, FBI headquarters did not request a CIA name check until December 7, 2001. In addition, FBI Headquarters failed to include the INS Form I-213 with its request to the CIA, even though the FBI Field Office's records reflected that the FBI had a copy of the detainee's Form I-213 in its file. A CIA response to the FBI's request, dated late February 2002, indicated that the detainee's case was one of those "pending 213s from 12/7." The response also indicated that the CIA found "no identifying information" about the detainee in its databases. FBI Headquarters issued the detainee a clearance letter the next day. Thus, it appears that this alien, who was cleared by the New York FBI Field Office by mid-November 2001, was not cleared by FBI Headquarters until late February 2002 due to an administrative oversight.

This example is too reminiscent of the American Protective League for comfort.

What is more, there are troublesome facets of the USA PATRIOT Act that seem to obliterate Constitutional protections that are the tradition of American law. In particular, are the requests for information that a judge is compelled to grant based upon the testimony of law enforcement that the information is "relevant to an ongoing criminal investigation." For example, trap-and-trace and pen register orders require that telephone companies hand over numbers dialed to and from a particular phone, along with related information, such as the period of time the line was in use. While the calls may originate from an alien, the law does nothing to protect U.S. citizens whose numbers may be captured in the records, and the basis for collecting them is weak in comparison to other statutes' requirements. Also, compelling the judge to grant the order takes away the protection of judicial review that has been an important part of legal checks and balances in this country.

Until the USA PATRIOT Act, there was also a strict prohibition on sharing information from grand jury proceedings. Disclosers of grand jury information could be charged with contempt of court, except in the very few circumstances outlined in Rule 6(e) of the Rules of Federal Criminal Procedure.

Most of us have come to believe that our educational, medical, financial, mental health, student, and travel records are confidential, unless subpoenaed. Now the FBI can certify in court that the records may be relevant to an intelligence investigation, and they must be turned over.

All of this greatly expands the FBI's ability to gather information. But in hindsight, wasn't the real problem on September 11, 2001, that the FBI and the rest of the intelligence community couldn't process the massive amounts of information they already had gathered? In the end, will this potential onslaught of new information help in the fight against terrorism, or bury the agencies deeper in an overwhelming mountain of data—much of it worthless—that they are no more able to process than they were before September 11, 2001?

Chapter 25
MOST UNWANTED

No State shall make or enforce any law which shall abridge the privileges or immunities of citizens of the United States; nor shall any
State deprive any person of life, liberty, or property, without due
process of law; nor deny to any person within its jurisdiction the
equal protection of the law.

Fourteenth Amendment, Sec. 1.
Constitution of the United States

When I was offered an opportunity to leave the FBI and join a defense-contracting firm in the Washington, D.C., area, I was intrigued and complimented. It was a great offer with plenty of potential, but I wavered because government service was important to me. The decision was made easier when a junior agent from a squad located on the floor above mine rushed to my office door. He was a GS-10 and I a GM-14, comparable to the military ranks of lieutenant and lieutenant colonel.

"Rosemary," he called, both hands on the doorsill and leaning his body into my office as if he were doing a push-up. "You won't believe what's going on upstairs."

I turned my chair toward him, encouraged by his breathless smile. His face was slightly flushed because he had run down a flight of stairs. "This must be a good one," I said.

"Oh, man," he chuckled, "when you walked through the squad room a few minutes ago, your nipples were erect. Now the guys are so excited that none of them can think!"

I stared at him for a minute, so shocked I couldn't speak, then I drew my sweater over my blouse, got up, and closed the door in his face. I sank back in my chair, feeling as if I'd been kicked in the gut. This was not the first time I'd felt the sting of a fellow agent's leering gaze or abusive words. In the past, things like this had sparked my spirit, and I'd gone through the chain of command, fighting as the system would allow. But on that day, I knew that the thirteen years I'd fought were all I was going to fight. I felt hopeless, humiliated, and profoundly sad. That encounter, combined with hundreds of similar intrusions that had gone before, was the push I'd needed. I turned to my computer and typed out my letter of resignation, closing a chapter on my life that had been filled with high expectations and intense disappointment. I moved on to a thriving career, and the FBI lost a highly commended agent who would take hundreds of thousands of dollars in training and years of experience to replace.

At the time I had accepted my appointment to the academy, there had been about ten thousand men and sixty-eight women in the agent workforce. Since I had been the ninety-sixth woman hired, it had appeared that the women who'd come before me had not had much career longevity.

Today's FBI agents are well paid. The starting pay cited on the FBI Web site as of May 2003 is $43,705 while training at the academy and $53,743 to $58,335 upon graduation. With time-in-grade promotions (meaning if one stays on duty, one automatically receives the promotion) through GS-13 within five years, the total grows to a minimum of $76,564, without considering locality or other pay enhancements. Also, the job carries a certain amount of prestige and mystique, and the casework can be fascinating. From the outside, it would seem inexplicable that the Bureau has had problems retaining personnel; but there are compelling reasons why well-qualified candidates choose to take their talents elsewhere:

In 1993, special agent Suzane J. Doucette sued the FBI because she had endured continuing sexual harassment from the men in her office, including supervisory personnel. Doucette claimed she was repeatedly called "derogatory, sexist names, such as 'PMS' and 'bitch'" and was told to "dress in a more feminine manner." She also said there were sexually explicit posters and calendars displayed around the office. More shocking was that the special agent in charge had told her he'd get her the office transfer she wanted if she would have sex with him. She further charged that he had put her in a choke hold and touched her "in ways that are very sensitive." The accused special agent in charge called her story "garbage."

The Bureau exonerated him in its internal inquiry, but paid Doucette and her attorneys approximately $300,000 to settle. Not long after that, two additional sexual harassment cases were settled out of court for $192,000 and $155,000. In 1995, a group of female agents went public with their plans to file a class-action suit if negotiations with the Bureau could not resolve widespread bias and discrimination. They said that women were often assigned to lower prestige jobs, passed over for promotion, and denied assignments in the career-enhancing divisions that handle violent and organized crimes.

In 1988, the FBI lost a lawsuit to 311 Hispanic agents who proved that they were not given promotions at the same rate as white men and that they received more dangerous, less desirable assignments. Only one Hispanic headed an FBI office at the time of the suit, yet the complainants were able to show examples of white males becoming special agents in charge with as few as nine years on duty. The court held that Hispanic agents had been discriminated against because they did not receive assignments that offered promotion potential, but were relegated to translating wire taps, a job that can be handled by nonagent translator personnel. Three-fourths of the Bureau's Hispanic agents joined the suit. The court awarded class participants up to $50,000 each in pay and retirement benefits.

Another tragic example is the case of special agent Donald Rochon, an African American who was awarded $1 million in his suit against the FBI. The problems began in 1983, while Rochon was assigned to the

FBI's Omaha field division. Among the denigrating "jokes" perpetrated by his fellow agents were pasting an ape's head over his son's photograph and placing invitations to office functions in his mailbox that read "Don't come." Not only did his supervisors fail to take action to protect Rochon, they belittled his feelings about his coworkers' behavior. One supervisor called the harassment "healthy" and a sign of "esprit de corps."

Even after Rochon complained about the incidents and was transferred to the FBI's Chicago office in 1984, harassment by white agents continued. Soon after the transfer, he began receiving obscene calls and death threats. He also received a bill for a life insurance policy that had been taken out in his name, and a photograph of a mutilated black man with a detailed threat of sexual assaults on Mrs. Rochon, who is white. Chicago agents passed it off as hazing. One agent summed it up as: "These guys like to goof around."

Donald Rochon filed his lawsuit in 1985, and in 1990, after settling with him, the FBI disciplined eleven Caucasian agents and supervisors for harassment or failure to respond to Rochon's complaints. The punishments ranged from mandatory counseling, oral reprimands, and written censure to one twenty-one-day suspension without pay. I would have fired the lot of them and sought prosecution for the threats of violence to Rochon and his wife, but I was never in a position that was powerful enough to allow me do so.

With a severe case of discrimination such as Rochon's receiving national media attention, you'd expect the Bureau to do everything in its powers to make sure that no additional cases of discrimination against African Americans were brewing in the ranks. Not so. In 1991, a group of 250 African-American agents alleged that they, too, suffered discrimination in job assignments and promotions. The following year, they settled without filing suit, because the Bureau promised to review their claims and to promote several African Americans. To the Bureau's shame, a federal mediator had to be appointed in 2001—nine years later—to ensure "a new process for handling complaints about promotions, performance evaluations and disciplinary proceedings." Then just over a year later, on September 26, 2002, one Hispanic and three African-American agents in the New York office filed a discrimination suit against their supervisors. In a letter to Director Robert Mueller and several lawmakers, the agents outlined their complaints. They said that photos of their faces were posted on their squad's "Wall of Shame," an area reserved for gang members and wanted criminals. The pictures had been cut from a photograph of the squad taken at the Fresh Kills Landfill on Staten Island, where, only a few days after September 11, they had sifted through debris from the World Trade Center site to collect body parts and other evidence.

Under their faces were cartooned bodies wearing warm-up suits and gold medallions. The caption read: "whiners." According to their attorney, the agents had gone through the administrative complaint process, "a system that minority agents have frequently said was slow, often arbitrary and a forum that seldom reached conclusions that minorities regarded as just."

It disgusts me that anyone could conceive of using a photograph taken during such a traumatic assignment as the September 11 recovery efforts to harass these agents. It is even more shocking to think that someone felt perfectly comfortable posting these offensive materials in the middle of the New York FBI office. The defaced photos demonstrate a complete lack of respect for fellow agents, as well as for the victims of the terrorist attacks.

Management controls on harassment—both sexual and racial—have been conspicuously lacking in the Bureau, even though all the right rules are on the books. The FBI Inspection Division reviews all FBI investigative and administrative programs. Made up of headquarters and field supervisors, the members of the Inspection Division are comparable to inspectors general, internal affairs (which it shares with the FBI Office of Professional Responsibility) or auditors in other government agencies. I'm familiar with instances when even members of the inspection team saw "hazing" as fun. During one Washington field office inspection, a group of male agents cut nipple photos out of an adult magazine and glued them onto a female agent's bulletproof vest. They hung the vest so the back faced her, and she unwittingly handed it to the inspector during a personal property check. The pranksters and the inspector thought this joke was hilarious and perfectly acceptable.

While it is true that the Caucasian male agents often endured practical jokes, they tended to be shenanigans of a different sort. It was common to hear people scream and curse in the Bureau garage because the last person to use the car had flipped on the siren after turning off the engine. The siren doesn't work when the motor isn't running, but it will startle the bejeebers out of you when you turn the key.

Coworkers broke into locked desks to play practical jokes or to forage for food. The man who sat next to me in one office was a bomb tech who kept jars of peanuts in his desk. He noticed his jars were emptying faster than he was eating peanuts, and he set a trap by putting a special chemical around the rim of the jar, then returning it to his desk. When an unsuspecting peanut thief twisted the lid, it popped loudly and shot sparks and smoke from under the rim. These jokes were "gotchas" among comrades, unlike the gender-based or racially motivated jokes that were intended to humiliate and isolate the person on the receiving end.

From the taxpayer's standpoint, discrimination and harassment waste money and take time away from casework, which is a real problem in the overworked Bureau. But these offenses also bring up a humanitarian issue. The harm that a victim suffers often extends beyond the job to the victim's psyche. I know it did mine. I also know that not every law enforcement agency functions in this manner. I never experienced prejudice or harassment when working with officers from other agencies, and there is simply no excuse for it in the FBI.

Many of the attitudes that pass from generation to generation of agents begin at the academy. The academy is the first place to influence the way new agents think and behave. Indoctrination into the "Bureau way," both official and subtle, began in the academy. "It's the Bureau way" or "It's always been done that way" is fraught with subtle messages: "Don't question authority," "The bureau never has to explain anything to anybody," "Your job is to do what I say." By the end of our academy training, we knew that FBI agents were to be unquestionably in charge of all situations and that they were never to explain anything to anyone outside the Bureau.

The Bureau is legendary for many things—including resistance to change. The hiring of women is a case in point. There were several women who were agents in the old BOI, one of whom did not resign until 1928, four years after J. Edgar Hoover was named director. However, from that time until July 17, 1972, the FBI hired no women as agents. It took a 1969 presidential order, a 1971 U.S. Supreme Court ruling that hiring policies should be the same for men and women, and the Equal Employment Opportunity Act, signed by Richard Nixon in 1972, to force the FBI to offer women the same opportunity to become special agents as was offered to men. Acting Director L. Patrick Gray III lifted the hiring prohibition in the wake of the federal legislation and in the midst of a class-action suit sponsored by the American Civil Liberties Union. The first two women hired were an ex-Marine Corps first lieutenant and a former nun who had been working as an FBI clerk.

Long after women had become commonplace in other government and law enforcement agencies, the Bureau continued to send subtle and not-so-subtle messages of institutional intolerance. For example, while I was assigned to the Washington field office from 1980–84, the Bureau still hand-stamped all physical forms "Mr." This presented problems at Bethesda Naval Hospital where the special agents went for annual Bureau physicals. The medical labs were in a central area flanked by two hallways: one for men and one for women. I had to wait on the women's side, shivering in a flimsy hospital gown, until the staff called me for my blood work. Since my form was marked "Mr.," the nurses often went to the men's hall to find "Mr. Rosemary," who of course wasn't there. Why, if women were first hired as agents in 1972, did they go to the trouble of hand-marking all agent forms male more than a decade later?

When I resigned from the FBI, a high-ranking official confided to me that he really didn't know how to handle harassment complaints. After all, he said, it wasn't really a crime. In his opinion, harassment was more like a behavior problem that mature adults ought to be able to resolve between themselves. His response was a typical example of the FBI rewriting of reality. While it is not uncommon for organizations to hush up cases of sexual harassment and other types of discrimination, it is extraordinary that senior officials in a law enforcement agency would disregard this and other illegal behaviors. That attitude also helped create an environment where agents could act outside the law with impunity. It is no surprise that some agents felt free to commit espionage, kidnapping, theft, or even murder. The irony is that the trained investigators of the very agency that honed psychological profiling to an art accepted, rather than suspected, aberrant behavior, as long as it occurred inside their own organization.

The FBI's historic response to serious internal problems has been to suppress the victims, but that tactic doesn't work any longer. It is time for the Bureau to reform—not reorganize—the hostile work environment that has been hidden behind its towering walls of silence.

Chapter 26
THREE WHO LOST
THEIR WAY

During our review of FBI security programs, we found significant deficiencies in Bureau policy and practice. Those deficiencies flow from a pervasive inattention to security, which has been at best a low priority. In the Bureau, security is often viewed as an impediment to operations, and security responsibilities are seen as an impediment to career advancement.

> **U.S. Department of Justice**
> *A Review of FBI Security Programs*
> **Commission for Review of FBI Security Programs**
> **March 31, 2002**

When someone asks me how it is possible that spies can function within the FBI and not be noticed, I have to say that the foundation is laid in the advice I received from my colleagues in my first months on the job:

- Don't ever rat out a buddy.
- When a fellow agent is screwed by the Bureau, which means censured and "put on the bricks," also known as "leave without pay," you will contribute $20 to help bail him out, no matter what the reason for censure.
- Never ever forget that headquarters will screw you at the drop of a hat.

- Keep a low profile. The less you do, the less chance you have of making a mistake.
- Don't associate with agents who don't toe the Bureau line, meaning agents who are "different" in any way.
- And by all means, if you make a mistake, cover up, cover up, cover up. Or wait. Perhaps no one will find out.

In short, it is not acceptable in FBI culture for one agent to "get another agent in trouble" by reporting a problem. My peers made it clear that, if an agent does get into trouble, it's not his fault, so everyone has to excuse it—even things like having a wreck while driving drunk in a government car. (I was actually asked to contribute $20 to a guy who did that. I refused.) Thus, the system that was designed to ensure a public image of perfection actually perpetuates problems. Once you're in, you're in, and the chances of getting fired for anything are remote. One of the most damaging outcomes of this is that agents do not recognize potential problems—for the Bureau and the nation—in their own ranks.

The FBI has an interesting history of insider turncoats, most of them long-tenured, experienced agents, and all but the first were supervisors or higher. I'll talk about three of them here—Robert Hanssen gets his own chapter.

The Bureau's first convicted spy was Richard W. Miller, a twenty-year, not-so-special agent. Miller had a string of disciplinary actions in his personnel folder before he was transferred to a counterintelligence squad in the Los Angeles field office and given the task of interviewing Soviet immigrants. His entree into espionage was a phone call from a Russian woman, Svetlana Ogorodnikova, who said she wanted to meet with him. Miller was a married man and the father of eight children, yet his get-togethers with Ogorodnikova quickly blossomed into sexual liaisons and betrayal.

There had been overt signs of trouble with Miller for some time. He had received several "fat man letters," as the agents called them: official notification from FBI headquarters that he had to lose weight to avoid censure and eventual loss of pay. In the health-conscious, athletic culture of the Bureau, this was very unusual.

Miller's coworkers accused him of selling Amway products over the phone from his FBI desk, and he persistently failed to keep his cases current. But, instead of requiring him to bring his performance up to standards or dismissing him from service for failing to do his job, FBI officials transferred him to a squad that handled national security matters, and there he stayed until his arrest on October 2, 1984.

As with any organization, there are stringent policies on the books instructing managers to counsel and discipline low performers, but they are not followed consistently. In the Bureau, there was a saying that poor performers, like Miller, should be assigned to the "rubber gun squads" where they can't hurt anyone. "Rubber gun squads" were investigative teams that don't make many arrests. Instead, their work includes such duties as preemployment security background investigations, counterintelligence, and counterterrorism.

Miller was proficient at avoiding work. During the investigation that followed his arrest, he admitted he sometimes hung out for hours at a 7-Eleven store where he could eat free donuts and read comic books. He skimmed money from an informant file, stole money from his relatives, and illegally used Bureau resources to conduct research for a private investigator who paid him for the information. In 1984, he was excommunicated from the Mormon Church for adultery.

Miller's defense against the spy charges was that he was conducting his own secret investigation of Ogorodnikova, and that he had passed her classified government information in an effort to win her trust. Unquestionably, Miller knew that any contact with certain foreign nationals had to be reported to the Bureau immediately, not months down the road, and certainly not after you're under investiation for espionage. When FBI agents searched Miller's apartment, they found mounds of classified documents that he'd removed from the office, a problem that might have been avoided if even a minimal security system had been in place. Miller was no master spy, and the fact that such a bumbler could repeatedly take classified documents from the office is as much a comment on the FBI's lack of security as it is on Miller himself.

Before Miller's trial began, Ogorodnikova and her husband were tried on charges of conspiring with Miller to obtain classified documents for the Soviets. After two months in the courtroom, the pair pleaded guilty in exchange for an eighteen-year sentence for Ogorodnikova and eight years behind bars for her spouse. Later, Miller was convicted on six counts of espionage and received a twenty-year sentence, which was reduced to thirteen. Eventually, P. Bryce Christensen, the man who supervised the lying, spying Miller on a day-to-day basis received a promotion to special agent in charge of the Salt Lake Office.

The second FBI spy, supervisory special agent Earl Pitts, was not an unsuccessful ne'er-do-well. According to the affidavit for his arrest, he was sworn in as an agent on September 18, 1983. He was an attorney when he entered on duty as an agent, and his first assignment after new agents' training was the Alexandria field division, where he worked general criminal matters until his January 1987 transfer to a foreign counterintelligence squad in New York City. There, Pitts investigated KGB officials assigned to the Soviet Mission to the United Nations. In August 1989, he was promoted to supervisory special agent in the Document Classification Unit, which is part of Records Management at FBI headquarters, and later, he moved to the Security Programs Section, where he supervised personnel investigations. Next, he became an attorney in FBI headquarters' Legal Counsel Division. Finally, in January 1995, Pitts transferred to the FBI Academy's famed Behavioral Science Unit, where his duties included conducting security briefings for FBI personnel.

According to a joint press release of the FBI and United States Attorney's Office at the time of Pitts's 1996 arrest:

> Pitts had access to "a wide range of sensitive and highly classified operations" that included "recruitment operations involving Russian intelligence officers, double agent operations, operations targeting Russian intelligence officers, true identities of human assets, operations against Russian illegals, defector sources, surveillance schedules of known meet sites, internal policies, documents, and procedures concerning surveillance of Russian intelligence officers, and the identification, targeting,

and reporting on known and suspected KGB intelligence officers in the New York area."

Pitts claimed his treachery was driven by indignities he suffered on the job, as well as anger over what he considered a meager salary. He wanted to get back at the Bureau and confessed, "I realized at the time that the way to hurt the FBI was to screw around with its secrets." So his response was to contact the Soviets in 1987, and for less than $250,000, betray his country until his arrest nine years later.

While the atmosphere in the Bureau in no way excuses espionage, it is well documented that the desire to exact revenge for things that happened in the workplace is a major motivating factor for traitors worldwide. And, as Will Rogers said: "When you give a lesson in meanness to a critter or a person, don't be surprised if they learn their lesson."

Though Pitts cited money as part of the reason he committed espionage, he certainly sold out cheaply. Less than a quarter of a million dollars over nine years doesn't seem like much when compared to the $2.7 million that CIA traitor Aldrich Ames and his wife made in the same timeframe. Like Pitts, Ames felt he wasn't given the respect and recognition he deserved. Considered the most damaging mole in CIA history, Ames's thirty-one-year career as a CIA officer culminated in his 1994 arrest after he had sold the Soviets information about more than one hundred covert operations and at least thirty recruitments, some of whom were also disclosed by FBI agent Robert Hanssen, and ten of whom were executed by the Soviets.

What motivates people to commit espionage is complex and fascinating from an investigator's point of view. One rule is hard and fast: Happy people don't commit espionage. There is always something dark and twisted in their psyches. For example, after his arrest, Pitts's wife discovered that he had an expensive secret sex life that included adult toys and prostitutes. He later told her he felt a strong need to humiliate himself as a form of self-punishment for his dealings with the Soviets.

In a 1998 CNN interview, Aldrich Ames called his own acts banal and greedy. He said that, at the time of his crimes, he had decided that the loss of "so many CIA agents . . . would not compromise significant national defense, political, diplomatic interests." He used this rationalization to assuage his conscience while he made "some quick and easy money, at very low risk and doing very little damage."

Earl Pitts cut off contact with the Russians after 1992, but unfortunately for him, his former Soviet handler, Aleksandr Karpov, became a cooperating witness for the FBI. In 1995, Karpov helped the FBI conduct a sting against Pitts that resulted in his arrest. The Bureau also learned of Pitts's involvement from his wife, Mary Colombaro Pitts, who confided her suspicions about her husband's activities to the FBI's Fredericksburg Resident Agency on August 29, 1995. In 1997, Pitts pleaded guilty and is now serving a twenty-seven-year sentence.

In April 2003, another case surfaced when retired supervisory special agent James J. Smith was arrested. In May 2003, Smith was indicted on six counts of fraud by wire and removal of national defense information through gross negligence. Also indicted was Katrina Leung, a naturalized U.S. citizen who has been described in news reports as a "socialite and political activist." Code-named "Parlor Maid," Leung served as Smith's longtime asset (informant), providing him with information about intelligence activities picked up from her contacts in the Peoples Republic of China (PRC). It is alleged that Leung, over the course of eighteen years, also worked for the PRC, passing them classified information about U.S. security investigations and operations, as well as the identities of U.S. intelligence officers. She obtained some of the information she passed to the Chinese from Smith, who removed classified documents from the Los Angeles FBI office and took them to her house. There, Leung allegedly swiped them from his briefcase, copied them, and then transmitted the copies to PRC intelligence officers.

Over nearly two decades, Leung collected $1.7 million from the FBI for the information she provided about the PRC. During that same period, she had a decades-long romantic relationship with the married Smith, plus another with a San Francisco supervisory special agent. News sources have identified the second agent as William Cleveland Jr., who resigned his position as chief of security for Lawrence Livermore

Laboratories concurrently with Smith's arrest. (Cleveland was not charged in connection with the case.) But what did Smith, and more importantly, the rest of the FBI know about Leung's alleged double life? And for how long?

Back in 1991, the San Francisco agent recognized Leung's voice on a wiretap and realized that she was cooperating with the PRC. He reported this to Smith and FBI headquarters. Headquarters called Smith to Washington and confronted him but left it to Smith as to how he would handle the problem. Smith in turn confronted Leung then sent reports to FBI headquarters, assuring them that Leung was reliable because, among other reasons, she had passed a polygraph. In reality, she'd refused to be tested. Apparently, that's where the headquarters inquiry stopped, at least for the next decade. It would have been easy for headquarters to verify whether the polygraph was conducted. All they had to do was ask for a copy of the polygrapher's report.

Did other agents know of Smith's relationship with his asset? Smith flaunted his personal relationship with Leung. They appeared together in public, and she even attended his retirement party and videotaped the event for posterity.

While Smith and Cleveland were both well-respected agents, one of the security breakdowns that allowed this problem to occur is the casual acceptance of extramarital affairs by many people in the Bureau. Highly cleared personnel in the Department of Defense and elsewhere know that they can lose their clearances for such improprieties. In the locker-room atmosphere of the FBI, it would have never crossed anyone's mind that extramarital affairs might be a security vulnerability.

Recognizing potential spies in the ranks—and then taking action to prevent possible espionage and crime—are two of the most important issues that the Bureau must address as it moves its focus to reform its system. Another is ensuring that the day-to-day work environment is set up to protect top-secret information.

Security was seriously ailing when I was an agent. As a supervisory special agent, I was in charge of security for the Denver field division, which was, at the time, the thirteenth largest office in the Bureau. Its territory encompasses the states of Colorado and Wyoming. My position as security program manager was completely devoid of power. It took me two years to get a key to my own office so, throughout that period, I was unable to lock it. It took me an equal amount of time to get cabinets for storing classified documents, even though suitable containers had been declared surplus and discarded in the interim while my classified files lay around the office unsecured. I wrote a number of memoranda to the special agent in charge to obtain a safe, but the response came back that other supervisors didn't have them. It was as if I was asking for some special privilege, and, as I pointed out in the memos, I was the only supervisor who stored classified documents, aside from the special agent in charge and assistant special agent in charge. It was irresponsible not to store these documents properly.

The James J. Smith indictment describes proper storage with a quote from the FBI's Foreign Counterintelligence Manual:

> Section 1-5.2—Storage of "Secret" and "Confidential" Material —Whenever "Secret" and "Confidential" material is not under the direct supervision of authorized persons . . . it must be stored in specific types of cabinets according to the Code of Federal Regulations [CFR] . . .

The floor of an office that could not be locked because I couldn't get a key, does not fit the description of "proper storage" described in the CFR. Since I had in my possession classified documents from most offices in the Bureau and from FBI headquarters, I reported the condition to anyone at headquarters who would listen. As no help was forthcoming, I guess they saw it as meddling in the private business of the special agent in charge of the Denver Field Division. I don't know, but I do know that Denver was not the only place where things like this happened. Among the Webster-led Commission for the Review of FBI Security Program's findings was that:

> In November 2000, three months before his arrest, [Robert]

Hanssen gave the Russians "the largest package [of documents he] ever produced," between 500 and 1,000 sheets of photo-copied material. He downloaded to disks from the FBI's Auto-mated Case Support system a great deal of the information he divulged in this final period . . .

Hanssen obviously had no problem copying up to one thousand pages of classified materials right there in the FBI office. In addition, he com-mented on the ease of stealing from the FBI Automated Case Support system:

Any clerk in the Bureau could come up with stuff on that system. It was pathetic . . . It's criminal what's laid out. What I did is criminal, but it's criminal negligence . . . what they've done on that system.

How, one would ask, could Bureau management feel comfortable per-petuating an atmosphere totally lacking in security? The answer begins in the academy where we learned that real agents worked criminal vio-lations and wimps worked counterintelligence, so whatever happens in counterintelligence is not worth notice.

Still, I thought surely the Bureau would put an immediate halt to the security problems once they were publicly identified after the Hanssen arrest. Imagine my horror when I read the Department of Justice Office of Inspector General's August 2003 report, *A Review of the FBI's Perfor-mance in Deterring, Detecting, and Investigating the Espionage Activities of Robert Philip Hanssen,* and saw the following recommendations:

Recommendation No. 14: Detecting Improper Computer Usage and Enforcing "Need to Know"
The FBI should implement measures to improve computer security, including (a) an audit program to detect and give notice of unauthorized access to sensitive cases on a real-time basis; (b) an audit program designed to detect whether

employees or contractors are using the FBI's computer systems to determine whether they are under investigation; (c) procedures designed to enforce the "need to know" principle in the context of computer usage; and (d) a program designed to ensure that restricted information cannot be improperly accessed through the use of security overrides or other means.

Recommendation No. 15: Tracking Classified Information

The FBI should create and implement a program enabling it to account for and track hard copy documents and electronic media containing sensitive information. This program should also be designed to prevent the unauthorized removal of sensitive information from FBI facilities, either through the use of technology that "tags" classified documents and computer media or through other means. The FBI should likewise develop a program to prevent the improper copying of classified information.

In any other classified government setting, these recommendations have been standard operating procedures for decades. Audit trails on computer usage and restricted access are common practice, even in nonclassified business. Not being able to track loss of hard-copy classified documents, a deficiency pointed out in Recommendation 15, was among the reasons that not having proper storage for my documents in Denver was so unnerving for me. Of course being a part of blatant noncompliance with federal regulations was bothersome, too. Too bad it didn't bother my management.

Chapter 27
MASTER SPY? I THINK NOT.

During his 25 years with the FBI, Hanssen was a mediocre agent who exhibited strong technical abilities but had weak managerial and interpersonal skills. Despite his failings as a supervisor, Hanssen was on the FBI's promotional track for much of his FBI career, and he generally received average to favorable performance evaluations. While Hanssen's day-to-day behavior did not suggest that he was engaged in espionage, he continually demonstrated an unwillingness to properly handle classified information. His indiscretions and security violations were largely ignored and wholly undocumented, however, and he was allowed to remain in positions offering him broad access to highly sensitive counterintelligence information. Ultimately, Hanssen's inability to effectively interact with subordinates and colleagues derailed his FBI career.

U.S. Department of Justice Office of the Inspector General
A Review of the FBI's Performance in Deterring, Detecting, and Investigating the Espionage Activities of Robert Philip Hanssen
August 2003

When Senior Executive Service (SES)–ranked supervisory special agent Robert Hanssen was arrested in July 2001, he officially became the highest-ranking FBI agent ever accused of spying. He pleaded guilty to fifteen criminal counts, including thirteen of espionage and one of attempted espionage. In

NO BACKUP

exchange, he got to keep his life, and his wife Bonnie got to keep a portion of his FBI retirement benefits, which amounted to about $39,000 a year.

The son of a police officer, Hanssen grew up in Chicago and became a police officer himself prior to joining the Bureau in 1976. Over the years, he held a number of responsible positions in the FBI, including counterintelligence squad supervisor in New York, inspector's aide, and GM-15 unit chief in counterintelligence at headquarters.

So why in 1979, three years after taking the oath of office, did Hanssen take a document containing information about the Bureau's penetration of a Soviet residential complex into the offices of "a company in New York run by an officer in the Soviet military intelligence service?" Why did he embark upon the path of betrayal that would cost him his family and land him in jail for life?

Hanssen has made many excuses. He has claimed that he was frustrated in his career, but he only gave it three years before he first committed espionage. In 1981—after five years on duty—he was promoted to supervisor, a fast rate of promotion. He has also peddled the story that he had been fascinated with '40s-era British spy Kim Philby, who was posted to the British embassy in Washington and was the top liaison officer between the British and American intelligence agencies, including the FBI. When Philby defected to Moscow, he became a consultant to the KGB who treated him as the *über*-spy, a way in which Hanssen would like to be viewed. Hanssen's claim that his interest in Philby was sparked when he read Philby's book, *My Silent War,* at the tender age of fourteen makes good copy, but, if you do the math, it can't be true: Hanssen was born on April 18, 1944; Philby fled to Moscow in January 1963 when Hanssen was eighteen, and *My Silent War* was published in 1968, when Hanssen was already in his twenties.

I think the real answer is threefold—ego, revenge, and money—but that he valued the money most in the sense that it validated his worth, rather than as something to improve his lifestyle. Hanssen was paid in cash and diamonds, and, in his plea bargain, he forfeited $1.4 million dollars that he'd collected from the Soviets and Russians. Some of the

210

money he received over the years has never been accounted for. But money and diamonds don't fully explain his actions. If it only took money and jewels to get people to commit espionage, U.S. intelligence officers would have an easy job. It is more likely that the root of Hanssen's problem was a messianic complex coupled with a sense of rejection he'd carried since childhood. This situation was exacerbated and perpetuated by the FBI's schoolyard culture that ridiculed him and nicknamed him "Dr. Death," due to his dark-suited, morose nature that to some seemed appropriate to an undertaker.

A CIA officer once told me that the perfect spy is the man who couldn't get a waiter's attention in a fine French restaurant. Hanssen was that nondescript kind of guy. He and I worked at FBI headquarters at the same time but never on the same cases. I was in operations, and he worked in analysis and liaison, the perfect job for a spy, since it gave him access to a wide variety of classified documents. Because it doesn't involve kicking in doors, however, most agents consider liaison and analytical jobs to be unglamorous, but these positions allowed Hanssen to do what he wanted without attracting undue attention. In fact, according to the August 2003, U.S. Department of Justice Office of the Inspector General's review of the FBI's performance in handling the Hanssen affair:

> Hanssen's work responsibilities at OFM consumed no more than a few hours a day, and he was wholly unsupervised by either State Department or FBI personnel. The job carried no significant operational or managerial responsibilities, and once Hanssen was at OFM, FBI management largely forgot about him. No one checked on him or his work—or even ensured that he was at work. No performance evaluations concerning Hanssen were completed during the entire six years that he served at OFM.

Hanssen's crimes were very damaging to the United States. During his FBI career, he passed twenty-six diskettes and approximately six thousand pages of classified documents to the Soviets and Russians. Among other intelligence facts, he revealed how the U.S. would retaliate against a nuclear attack and handed over information on top-secret communications intelligence, as well as early warning and defense systems, all of which could affect our ability to defend against attack, including terrorist attacks.

According to the March 31, 2002 report of the U.S. Department of Justice's Commission for Review of FBI Security Programs, led by Judge William Webster, Hanssen revealed the names of several Soviets who had been recruited by the FBI. Some of them died as a result of his revelations. In the period spanning 1985–87 alone, he

> surrendered a "complete compendium of double-agent operations." . . . Hanssen also disclosed the Director of Central Intelligence Congressional Budget Justifications for several fiscal years, the FBI's technical penetration of a Soviet establishment, U.S. penetration of Soviet satellite transmissions, U.S. attempts to recruit Soviet intelligence officers, a limitation in NSA's ability to read Soviet communications, detailed evaluations of FBI double-agent operations, and other extraordinarily sensitive intelligence operations. For instance, Hanssen revealed that U.S. State Department diplomat, Felix Bloch, was under investigation for espionage on behalf of the Soviet Union. Bloch's Soviet handlers warned him about the investigation, and he was able to avoid prosecution.

The media has portrayed Hanssen as a master spy whose cleverness allowed him to evade detection while he worked clandestinely in the midst of the nation's counterintelligence professionals. Again, it makes good copy, but many of the things he did were quite blatant. Examples from the OIG review of the Hanssen case include the facts that, Hanssen

> (1) set up an FBI camera on a drop site he used for exchanges with the GRU [Soviet/Russian military intelligence] during his

first period of espionage; (2) used an FBI telephone line and answering machine for communications with the KGB in 1986; (3) deposited much of the KGB's cash directly into a passbook savings account in his name in the late 1980s; (4) suggested to his Russian handlers in 1991 that they attempt to recruit Jack Hoschouer, his best friend; (5) directly approached a GRU officer in 1993 and revealed that he was an FBI agent who had previously committed espionage for the KGB—an approach that led to a diplomatic protest from the Russians and an FBI investigation that could have identified Hanssen as a mole; and (6) searched the FBI's computer system, during his last period of espionage, for references to his own name, address, and drop and signal sites—conduct that would have been difficult to explain if the FBI had utilized the computer system's audit feature.

The 1993 approach to the GRU officer provides insight into Hanssen's state of mind. He told Judge Webster's commission that one of the reasons he made the approach was to find out why the Russians continued to run agents whom Hanssen had previously identified as doubles. It is as if he thought he was so important that he should control the Russians' operational decisions and he risked this insecure meeting and diplomatic protest to make them explain.

By 1993, there were longstanding indicators of a mole in the Bureau, and specifically in connection with double agent operations. For example, Judge Webster's review of FBI security programs cited the following:

An internal FBI report issued in this period [1985–87] noted serious compromises and disruptions in the Bureau's recruitment, recruitment-in-place, and double agent operations. The report raised the possibility that the KGB had "somehow acquired inside or advance knowledge of [Bureau] operations."

According to the OIG report:

> After learning that its two most important KGB assets had been
> arrested, the FBI formed a six-person task force to determine
> how they had been compromised and whether an FBI mole was
> responsible. In the course of its review, the Task Force discov-
> ered that because of poor document controls and violations of
> the "need to know" principle it was impossible to determine
> who within the FBI had had access to the Motorin and Mar-
> tynov cases. Accordingly, no FBI employee with knowledge of
> these assets was investigated. Nonetheless, in September 1987
> the Task Force issued a final report stating that there was no evi-
> dence of a Soviet spy in the FBI. The Task Force, however, did
> not resolve how the assets had been compromised.

Had the Bureau decided to pursue an investigation, would there have
been any reason to believe that the Bureau might have uncovered
Hanssen? By 1993, Hanssen had displayed plenty of indicators that
should have raised suspicions, but it would not have been discovered
through analysis, because incidents connected with Hanssen had not
been documented. The following is a chronology that hits the high
points:

In 1987, Hanssen was assigned to the Soviet Analytical Unit, where
he received "very favorable performance evaluations, though his supervisor regarded him as " 'the strangest person' he had ever worked with in
the FBI—a kind of cipher who was rigid, dour, and a religious zealot."
The OIG report on the FBI's handling of the Hanssen investigation
states that, despite the good performance appraisals:

> Shortly after his return to the Unit, Hanssen committed a
> serious security breach by disclosing sensitive information to a
> Soviet defector he was debriefing. Hanssen's colleagues recog-
> nized that he could not be trusted with highly sensitive infor-
> mation and informally attempted to restrict his access.

Although this security breach was reported to an FBI supervisor, it was not documented, and no formal action was taken against Hanssen, whose access to sensitive information remained largely unchecked.

In 1990—the year Hanssen was assigned to the Inspection Staff, a necessary box to check for promotion—his brother-in-law FBI agent Mark Wauk attempted to file a report, in the Chicago office, that Hanssen was hiding thousands of dollars in his house and spending beyond his means. Here was Hanssen with large amounts of cash that his own family couldn't explain, which is a classic indicator of criminal activity, and yet

> the supervisor readily dismissed Wauck's concerns, in part because there was no policy or procedure mandating that he pass the information on for analysis and possible investigation. This incident highlights deficiencies in the FBI's protocol for the receipt and investigation of derogatory information about an agent. There was no standard procedure for reporting and collecting such information, nor was there a central repository at the FBI responsible for collecting this information.

In 1992, as chief of the National Security Threat List Unit at FBI headquarters, Hanssen was considered a low performer. The field offices complained because he "rejected an inordinately high percentage of their proposals for investigations." Also, it was during this assignment that Hanssen hacked into his counterintelligence colleagues' and supervisors' classified hard drives. Attempting to preempt discovery, he reported what he had done, but said he had been conducting a security test. Hacking a federal computer is a federal felony under Title 18 Section 1830, but did the Bureau see it that way? According to the OIG report, "No one questioned his breach of computer security."

Hanssen followed the computer intrusion with yet another security breach when he was told not to give British Intelligence information about a highly sensitive FBI investigation, but did anyway. Also in 1993—the same year the Bureau received the protest from Russia about an FBI agent approaching one of their embassy staff with a proposition about committing espionage—when a woman left a meeting at FBI headquarters, Hanssen grabbed her and tried to drag her back into the meeting. He was suspended for five days for that incident. Though not directly a result of these incidents, Hanssen, along with a number of other supervisors, was sent back to the field as part of the FBI headquarters mandate to downsize. This was not a demotion, and in 1995, he won the position of senior FBI liaison representative to the Department of State's Office of Foreign Missions, where he stayed until January 2001 totally without supervision, surfing the FBI Automated Case System, the repository of FBI case files.

According to the Webster report, while he was at the Department of State,

> Hanssen installed unauthorized software on his office computers, an action counter to Bureau regulations. While he was serving as FBI liaison to the State Department, a password-breaking program was discovered on his hard drive. When questioned about this at the time, Hanssen explained that he had to re-configure his FBI computer system at [the Department of] State to install a color printer, but that he could not do so without the password of a systems administrator, who was not often available. Consequently, Hanssen said, he broke the administrator's password and solved the problem. Hanssen was not disciplined for this conduct.

What is more: "As with Hanssen's other security violations, nothing about the matter was recorded in either his personnel or security file."

Even a novice information security person would recognize that Hanssen's attempt to gain system administrator privileges, which would provide unimpeded access to private areas throughout the entire Department of State system, was a hacker crime. The fact that the break-ins were never investigated as criminal activity is a glaring example of how FBI culture protects higher-ups. I also believe that the unwritten rule of "don't rat out a buddy" covered for Hanssen and enabled his game of spying.

The OIG report says: "Hanssen's personality traits set him apart from his FBI colleagues. He had poor interpersonal skills and a dour demeanor, and was an awkward and uncommunicative loner who conveyed a sense of intellectual superiority that alienated many of his co-workers."

Hanssen seemed to take hiring women as FBI agents as a personal injustice, and he used this anger to rationalize why he hadn't excelled in his career in the ways he had hoped. He spoke vehemently about his prejudice. Unfortunately, this view was so widespread among his and my contemporaries, that his fixation wasn't seen as a sign of danger.

In 1997, Earl Pitts told FBI debriefers that he believed there was another spy in the FBI because the Russians and Soviets had not taken advantage of Pitts's access to information. He correctly reasoned that they must be getting it elsewhere, and he reported

> that he did not know of other spies with certainty, but he had heard that Hanssen had hacked into an FBI computer. The Bureau did not follow up on this information because it was already known.

In 1999, a senior investigator at the FBI, Thomas Kimmel, informed then-FBI director Louis Freeh that there appeared to be a mole in the Bureau's ranks, but Freeh didn't believe it. He surmised instead that there was a spy in the CIA and told Kimmel to focus on that agency instead.

Kimmel's story may be a factor of yet another quirk of FBI culture. Kimmel was an organized crime investigator, and there has long been a rivalry between those who investigate criminal cases and those who investigate counterintelligence matters, with those who conduct violent crime investigations looking down on those who conduct counterintelligence investigations and vice versa. This is yet another attitude that is difficult to understand, since all FBI investigations concern violations of federal statutes. Perhaps Kimmel's logic was rejected because he wasn't one of the homeboys, another example of the harm that one part of the Bureau looking down on the other can do.

Finally, on January 13, 2001, Hanssen was promoted to the Senior Executive Service (SES) and "assigned to a newly created position in the Information Resources Division at FBI headquarters. This new job allowed the FBI to monitor Hanssen's activities without tipping him off to the fact that he was under investigation." His career ended in a Northern Virginia public park, after he left a black plastic garbage bag full of top-secret documents for his Russian handlers to pick up, and as he faced the arresting agents, he asked, "What took you so long?"

Here's a clue from the OIG report:

Between 1987 and 1991, the FBI suffered continuing losses of Soviet human assets and technical operations that it could not explain. During this period, the FBI conducted two analytical studies that considered the penetration issue, but neither study led the FBI to investigate the possibility of an FBI mole. The first study was a two-year effort aimed at resolving historical allegations of an FBI penetration. The project proceeded chronologically, and by late 1988 the team had analyzed leads only from the 1950s and 1960s. In an interim report, the team concluded that two penetrations of the FBI existed before 1964, but the team never reached the time period relevant to the FBI's more recent and unprecedented losses. The project was abandoned in the summer of 1989.

The second study systematically examined more than 50 FBI operations that had been compromised since 1986, including human assets, technical operations, double agent programs, and recruitment operations. The final report, issued in November 1988, described the continuing, across-the-board problems within the FBI's Soviet operations, but was equivocal with respect to the possibility of an FBI mole. The report suggested that a CIA penetration was a more likely explanation for the FBI's losses. We now know that Hanssen compromised most of the significant operations discussed in the report.

Chapter 28

LACK OF CANDOR

I think there is a cultural problem here in not taking seriously the very clear and explicit commands that were given in a very important case.

Director Louis Freeh
May 17, 2001, Testimony before a Senate Appropriations
Subcommittee concerning the FBI's failure to produce
documents in the Oklahoma City bombing case

The FBI's unwritten code of silence has done more than permit spies to operate among the nation's most elite law enforcement agency. It also has been behind some of the FBI's biggest debacles, such as the incident at Ruby Ridge, which occurred in northern Idaho in August 1992. It all started when U.S. marshals attempted to arrest white supremacist Randy Weaver for failing to appear in court on weapons charges. A shootout ensued between two marshals and Weaver's fourteen-year-old son and ended when the boy and one of the marshals were killed. What followed was a weeklong standoff between Weaver and federal agents, and it ended when an FBI agent shot and killed Weaver's wife, Vicky.

The incident led to an intensive internal review of the FBI, with Attorney General Janet Reno creating a Justice Department task force to investigate the events at Ruby Ridge. In 1994, the task force issued a report charging that the FBI's Hostage Rescue Team overreacted to the threat of violence by instituting a policy that any armed adult be shot on sight, an edict that violated both FBI guidelines and Fourth Amendment restrictions on police power. As a result, the FBI disciplined twelve agents and employees.

In the investigations and prosecution that followed the Ruby Ridge shooting, inspector E. Michael Kahoe was convicted of having destroyed the FBI after-action report rather than giving Randy Weaver's defense attorneys access to it as required by law. While Kahoe was sentenced to two years in a federal prison and ordered to pay $4,000 in fines, supervisory special agent Gale Evans, former chief of the violent crimes unit, got off with administrative sanction for obeying Kahoe's order to destroy his copies of the report.

Meanwhile, the FBI Hostage Rescue Team sharpshooter Lon Horiuchi and Eugene Glenn, the special agent in charge of managing the Ruby Ridge situation on the ground, were in the hot seat. The question was whether Larry Potts, then-assistant director of FBI headquarters' Criminal Division, had verbally approved the special rules of engagement. In the end, the sharpshooter, who had followed those rules of engagement, was cleared of criminal charges, because the bullet that killed Vicki Weaver had first struck Kevin L. Harris, an armed man at the Weaver compound.

While the FBI sharpshooter fought manslaughter charges, brought by the State of Idaho, Potts was promoted to deputy director, second in charge of the FBI and the highest-ranking career agent position. After two months in that job, during which time his conduct regarding Ruby Ridge was examined, Potts was demoted to assistant director of the FBI Training Division, the third level under the director and head of the FBI Academy. Following the Ruby Ridge tragedy, but before the Department of Justice report was released, Kahoe was promoted to special agent in charge of the Jacksonville, Florida, field office.

After being censured over the rules of engagement, Glenn testified before Congress that Potts had verbally approved the rules and that the assistant director of Criminal Division, Danny Coulson, once the commander of the Hostage Rescue Team, had reminded Glenn to obey them. Other agents also gave sworn statements that Potts had approved a "shoot on sight" order against any armed adult around the Weaver's house. However, Director Freeh swept this away in promoting Potts, because he said Potts had had a stellar track record prior to Ruby Ridge. This is where the system broke down: Freeh could not see that the public's trust had been broken by Potts's involvement, and he viewed Potts's promotion to the number two man in the FBI as an internal matter. He thought that such an egregious act that resulted in a death and attempts to prosecute the agents who followed instructions, should have no repercussions on a manager who was directly involved in the incident. Promoting a man who was facing such serious charges once again reinforced the system that says there is no behavior that can't be accepted if you are in favor with the right people.

The denouement of the Potts saga was an FBI Academy training course, entitled "New Agent Curriculum and Training Conference," which was hastily thrown together to coincide with Potts's October 9, 1997, retirement party. On October 2, special agents in charge were notified that the course would be held at Quantico and that space would be limited to twenty-five special agents in charge, who would be selected on a first-come, first-serve basis. Oddly, the notice contained neither a description nor a schedule for the conference. The assistant director in charge of the academy initiated the course, giving the course instructor only three days to prepare for the conference. The alleged course, held on October 10 lasted ninety minutes, including lunch.

Two accusations were later investigated by the FBI and eventually by the General Accounting Office (GAO): that the training session was merely a ruse to get the government to pay for special agents in charge to travel to the Washington, D.C. area to attend the Potts retirement dinner, and that disciplinary actions in the FBI were different for SES personnel—government executives ranked above the pay scale by which all other career federal employees are paid—and for lower-ranking employees.

Since all the people involved in the conference-cum-retirement party were in the Senior Executive Service ranks, the responsibility fell to the

SES board to investigate and submit recommendations for disciplinary actions to the deputy director of the FBI, Potts's former post. The SES board, investigating its own, recommended

> that three special agents in charge be issued letters of censure for inappropriate travel and that the Training Division's Section Chief receive a 15-day suspension for neglecting his duty by failing to exercise proper administrative oversight of the October 10, 1997, conference.

In January 1999, the deputy director adopted the SES board's recommendations for the three special agents in charge, one of whom had actually retired before he received his letter of censure. However, the deputy director declined to suspend the section chief, because he found such a measure to be "unnecessarily harsh."

Next came a review by the FBI's Law Enforcement Ethics Unit to determine whether a double standard existed within the FBI for disciplining SES and non-SES employees. The conclusion: there was indeed a double standard. The Law Enforcement Ethics Unit cited examples of various disciplinary actions, including those resulting from the Potts retirement dinner. The study stated:

> "A fair and reasonable reading of the final OPR [Office of Professional Responsibility] report clearly shows both voucher fraud and lack of candor on the part of several SACs." In response to the study, on August 15, 2000, former FBI Director Freeh announced the creation of a single disciplinary system for all FBI employees to replace the two separate disciplinary systems for SES and non-SES employees.

Voucher fraud and lack of candor? What a euphemism! Lack of candor on your taxes, for example, may equal jail time. These are crimes, not administrative foul-ups. In fact, Title 18 subsection 1001, known in the FBI as "lying to an FBI agent," is one of the charges against Martha

Stewart. Aside from that, the bogus conference originated in the FBI's Training Division, the same group that trains all FBI personnel and sets the tone for every agent's ethical outlook and behavior.

One voice that cried out against the double standards in discipline was supervisory special agent John Roberts, who works in the FBI's Office of Professional Responsibility, the office that investigates allegations of FBI employee wrongdoing and levies punishments. In a 2002 *60 Minutes* interview, Roberts, a twenty-year bureau veteran, said he was "threatened, intimidated and humiliated for exposing what he said has become a pattern of misconduct at the highest levels of the FBI."

After the *60 Minutes* show aired, Roberts's boss, assistant director Robert Jordan, called together Roberts's colleagues, including Roberts's wife, who was Jordan's secretary, and read sarcastically from the transcript. He then told the assembly that Roberts "had betrayed everyone at the FBI."

The Department of Justice's Office of the Inspector General (OIG) investigated Roberts's claims of harassment and concluded that Jordan had not intended to threaten or harass Roberts for statements made on *60 Minutes*. They concluded that it was not improper for Jordan to discuss the *60 Minutes* transcript at an all-employees meeting, but that Jordan "exhibited poor judgment in several respects." Jordan scheduled the all-employee meeting in which he discussed the *60 Minutes* broadcast at a time when he knew Roberts was on sick leave, actually moving it from its scheduled day. (Due to the advice of another employee, Roberts was informed in time to allow him to participate via a speakerphone.) OIP also found that Jordan should have consulted legal counsel before the meeting and questioned "the appropriateness of Jordan's statement at the meeting that 'he who creates ambiguity shall have that ambiguity resolved against him.'" OIP found it "even more troubling" that Jordan did not respond to a question suggesting that Roberts be removed from OPR. "Finally, we believe Jordan's selection of another Unit Chief to be the Acting DAD [deputy assistant director], including the timing of it and the way it was handled, left the appearance of retaliation against Roberts for his statements on *60 Minutes*."

For the newly appointed assistant director for the Office of Professional Responsibility—the very executive who oversees employee misconduct investigations and punishments for the entire FBI—to set that kind of tone was more than "lack of judgment." He should have been removed from the position.

Roberts's troubles began when he concluded, from the internal investigation of FBI actions at Ruby Ridge, that six senior FBI officials had "lied or committed misconduct in their handling of the case." None of the six was ever disciplined. All were promoted, and some were given bonuses. One example he cited was Van Harp, who was promoted to special agent in charge of the Washington field office even after Roberts found that he had "altered a report to cover up serious wrongdoing." Harp was promoted and received a $22,000 bonus while he was under investigation. The subsequent Department of Justice report said "the FBI's handling of the incident was rife with misconduct, obstruction, and was, at best, grossly deficient and, at worst, intentionally slanted to protect the FBI and senior FBI officials."

Roberts testified to his findings before Congress, pointing out that the problem is more than unfairness to individuals, the greater problem is: " . . . if the rank and file of any law enforcement organization believe their executive management condones or approves of misconduct, that is a precursor for corruption."

There was more lack of candor concerning the use of pyrotechnics during the Branch Davidian siege near Waco, Texas.

It all started on Sunday, February 28, 1993, when agents of the Bureau of Alcohol, Tobacco, and Firearms (ATF), dressed in SWAT uniforms, went to the Branch Davidian's Mount Carmel compound near Waco, Texas, to arrest cult leader David Koresh on illegal firearms and explosives charges. Gunfire erupted. Who fired first is still in dispute, but when the first round of fighting ended, four ATF agents were dead and sixteen others were wounded. The FBI joined in the fray of this televised media event, but Koresh and his group of followers held off authorities for fifty-one days. Several children were released over the period of negotiations, but meanwhile, the FBI moved armored vehicles onto the compound property.

Early on Monday, April 19, FBI agents notified Koresh and the Davidians that they were about to fire tear gas into the compound, but instead of giving up as the FBI hoped, the Davidians begin shooting and the FBI responded with CS gas, a combination of methylene chloride and orthochlorobenzylidenemalononitrile.

For several hours, the gas assault continued, and then the FBI's armored vehicles begin smashing holes in the cult's building in order to insert gas directly into it. At about noon, multiple fires started inside the Davidian complex. Within minutes, the wooden buildings were engulfed in flames, and Koresh and more than eighty followers were killed. A controversy would ensue over the FBI's use of CS canisters at the Branch Davidian compound, and this incident would later become Timothy McVeigh's stated reason for bombing the Murrah Federal Building in Oklahoma City.

I'm not going to argue whether the action was prudent or not, but I do not doubt that the decision to use CS gas to end the Branch Davidian standoff was made in hopes of saving lives. The idea was to get the occupants of the building to come outside, and CS will usually do that. It is an irritant gas that has been proven reasonably safe for use on humans. It causes highly uncomfortable results, such as burning sensations, coughing, profuse mucous, and eye irritation. It has also been known to produce nausea, vomiting, and elevated blood pressure. I know its effects well because, aside from the obligatory gas room exercise that every new agent class at the FBI Academy endures, I got a personal demonstration of what CS can do when it comes in contact with skin and mucous membranes: An instructor painted some on my lower eyelashes in an FBI Academy class and it splattered into the sclera (white part) of one eye. The burning sensation was so painful that I ran out of the classroom and rubbed snow on my face until the tearing calmed down. It left a small streak of chemical burn on my cheek for a day or so, but my vision was not permanently impaired.

After reading the governmental reports on the Waco incident, I believe that the fire was started by Branch Davidians, and again, I won't argue whether the FBI's actions were right or wrong. I'm more interested in the systemic foul-up that followed, causing officials of the FBI to insist for six years that no pyrotechnic devices were used, even though FBI agents testified to the contrary immediately after the siege. Special counsel John C. Danforth stated in his preliminary report on the events surrounding the Branch Davidian standoff:

> The only antidote to this public distrust is government open-ness and candor. Instead, and tragically, just the opposite occurred after Waco. Although the government did nothing evil on April 19, 1993, its failure to fully and openly disclose to the American public all that it did has fueled speculation that it actually committed bad acts on that day. Even in their dealings with this investigation, some government officials have strug-gled to keep a close hold on information. More important, the government did not disclose to the public its use of pyrotechnic devices at Waco until August 1999—six years after the fact. This nondisclosure is especially puzzling because the use of these pyrotechnics had nothing to do with the fire. They were used four hours before the fire began, 75 feet from the Branch Davidian residence, and in a manner that could cause no harm. Yet the failure to disclose this information, more than anything else, is responsible for the loss of the public faith in the govern-ment's actions at Waco, and it led directly to this investigation. The natural public reaction was that, if the government lied about one thing, it lied about everything.
>
> The issues that remain open in this investigation concern the reasons why the government did not disclose this information. We have not found evidence of a massive government con-spiracy. The team of agents who fired the pyrotechnics told the truth about it from the very beginning. Many government offi-cials, including the Attorney General and the Director of the FBI, did not know that pyrotechnics had been used at all.

Unfortunately, a few individuals within the Department of Justice and the FBI, including a few attorneys, had this information and did not tell.

When the agents at the scene told the truth, why didn't those who took their testimony tell the FBI director and the attorney general? Supervisory special agent Dick Rogers, the Hostage Rescue Team leader at Waco, told prosecutors in the after-action interviews that, hours before the fire, military pyrotechnic rounds were fired at a concrete construction pit that was located about seventy-five feet from the house. The agent who fired the rounds also reported it. Yet, according to Danforth's final report:

> HRT commander Rogers did, however, sit silently behind Attorney General Reno when she testified to Congress in April 1993 that she had sought and received assurances that the gas and its means of delivery would be non-pyrotechnic. Rogers claims that he was not paying attention and did not even hear her when she made this statement . . . . Similarly, Rogers attended the 1993 testimony of FBI Director Sessions, and did not correct misimpressions left by Sessions' statement that the FBI had chosen CS gas because it could be delivered without pyrotechnics. Rogers' failure to correct the misleading implications of the testimony of Attorney General Reno and Director Sessions was a significant omission that contributed to the public perception of a cover-up and that permitted a false impression to persist for several years. Rogers attended the congressional hearings precisely to ensure that Congress was provided with accurate information. Instead, in the terms of the Attorney General's Order to the Special Counsel, Rogers "allowed others to make . . . misleading statements."

I have helped prepare Department of Justice executives for congressional testimony, and that preparation included a thorough discussion of anticipated questions, as well as a review of the details of the case. I cannot fathom why Rogers or others did not brief the attorney general and the director about the use of the military rounds before their testimony. And I surely don't understand how an agent, who had the privilege of accompanying heads of agencies to testify before Congress, would not pay attention during the testimony.

I have wondered about the motives for omitting such key information, and the only answer I can come up with is that it was part of a chain reaction sparked by Rogers's fear and his hope that if he didn't call attention to the error, the problem would somehow just fade away.

Attorney General Reno and then-Director Freeh were given assurances in the planning sessions that no pyrotechnics would be used, and they stated that publicly in response to early questions. While the military rounds that were fired into the concrete construction pit are not officially classed as incendiary, they can cause fires. However, this is an argument of semantics. Those who knew the answers were afraid to correct the already public statements of the director and attorney general.

In 1994, Freeh developed the "bright line" policy to ensure proper conduct by FBI agents, and the creation of this policy was a clear statement about what Freeh experienced as an FBI agent and supervisor before he became the director. He knew the agency from the inside out, and he knew what behaviors were rampant in the "family." He also understood how much this aberrant behavior impacts the work of the agency. This is Freeh's "bright line" policy in his own words:

> In 1994, I created the "bright line" policy, designed to enhance the integrity and independence of the FBI. The "bright line" puts all employees on notice as to what is expected of them.
>
> The FBI must constantly strive to be a positive force in our society. How the FBI is viewed by Americans—and how FBI employees view themselves—is a crucial factor to succeeding in our many difficult missions.
>
> In addition, FBI employees must uphold and revere core values that include integrity, reliability, and trustworthiness.

Any employee whose conduct is at odds with those core values forfeits his or her right to FBI employment.

While this list is not all-inclusive, there are clear examples of behavior for which employees can expect to be dismissed. They include:

- Lying under oath.
- Failure to cooperate during an administrative inquiry when required to do so by law or regulation.
- Voucher fraud.
- Theft or other unauthorized taking, using or diversion of government funds or property.
- Material falsification of investigative activity and/or reporting.
- Falsification of documentation relating to the disbursement/expenditure of government funds.
- Unauthorized disclosure of classified, sensitive, Grand Jury, or Title III material.

At the same time, there is firm discipline for lesser incidents of misconduct.

I have always summed up the "bright line" concept in clear, simple terms:

I believe in the basic truth that lying, cheating, or stealing is wholly inconsistent with everything the FBI stands for and cannot be tolerated.

After creating the original "bright line," I later developed other important "bright lines" regarding employee conduct—one covering sexual harassment and the other alcohol abuse.

Regarding sexual harassment, it is my belief that there is no place in the work environment for discrimination or harassment of any nature. Such conduct will simply not be tolerated in the FBI under any circumstances. Every employee is held to this standard.

Clear procedures have been created to process complaints

and FBI management officials will promptly investigate such incidents. Disciplinary action will be taken against such misconduct, and the discipline can range from an oral reprimand to dismissal. FBI employees are assured they can seek redress without fear of reprisal from anyone.

Alcohol abuse is also a serious problem that must be met in two ways—FBI-sponsored treatment programs to aid those who abuse alcohol and discipline for those who violate FBI regulations.

FBI policy forbids use of alcohol for employees while on duty. Since Special Agents must be available for duty on a 24-hour basis, they must take affirmative steps to make certain they are fit for duty at all times. There is severe administrative action for alcohol-related misconduct. I take a particularly serious view of those who drive while under the influence of alcohol or while intoxicated, whether on or off-duty, and termination of employment may result.

These were the issues that Director Freeh knew had to be addressed to heal this patently dysfunctional organization. Imagine how pervasive the problems must have been for a man like Freeh to make this list of do's and don'ts. He was a successful agent who had left the Bureau for twelve years, then had a chance to come back and bring about change. He had had twelve years to think about what issues to address in the "bright line" list. The fact that he needed to delineate the "bright line" at all is evidence that the FBI workplace was not the professional atmosphere one would expect. Unfortunately, what Director Freeh couldn't do was bring about the cultural revolution that might have made his policies an enforcable reality.

Chapter 29

THE THIN LINE BETWEEN COPS AND CRIMINALS

[I swear that] I will support and defend the Constitution of the United States against all enemies, foreign and domestic; that I will bear true faith and allegiance to the same; that I take this obligation freely, without any mental reservation or purpose of evasion; and that I will well and faithfully discharge the duties of the office on which I am about to enter. So help me God.

FBI Special Agent Oath of Office

The Bureau has never given a warm reception to its whistle-blowers, even when they are reporting criminal activity. Take the case of FBI Minneapolis field division special agent Jane Turner, who was assigned the task of investigating thefts from the wreckage of the World Trade Center. Turner testified before the Senate Judiciary Committee in October 2002 that a crystal globe had been stolen by the Minneapolis FBI Evidence Response Team and given to a secretary in the Minneapolis office as a souvenir. Turner reported the theft to prosecutors and to her supervisor, but their response was that the theft "wasn't a big deal." After two weeks, when she found that nothing had been done, the twenty-four-year FBI veteran confiscated the evidence and sent it to the Department of Justice Office of Inspector General. Three weeks after that, she received a performance rating of "unacceptable." Turner stated that the rating was the result of her decision to notify the Department of Justice about the theft, an act her supervisor called "tarnishing the FBI's reputation."

In an April 29, 2003, interview with Lisa Myers of NBC News, Turner said that, as of that date, there had been no actions taken against the person who stole the globe, but that she had been notified she was being fired and had been asked to turn in her badge and gun.

This was not Turner's first accusation of FBI unfairness. In August 2001, Turner filed a sex discrimination suit, alleging that she was unfairly passed over for promotion on two occasions. She also claimed that she had suffered discrimination while assigned to Minot, North Dakota, in 1987, and that when she transferred to Minneapolis in 2000, her desk was isolated from the other agents, who were warned to avoid her.

Turner's record is in sharp contrast to that of special agent Halbert Gary Harlow, who served as a firearms instructor at the FBI Academy from 1980 to 1991. On December 13, 1996, his house burned down shortly after it had been searched by FBI agents. Later in court, Harlow admitted that he'd stolen 100,000 to 200,000 rounds of ammunition, as well as handguns, shotguns, holsters, stun grenades, tear gas canisters, and night-vision goggles during the eleven years he worked at the academy. There are fifty .38 rounds per box. That adds up to two to four thousand boxes, or approximately a box a day, plus all the other stolen armaments. Weren't these items ever inventoried? Didn't anyone notice Harlow carting off multiple rounds and weapons? And why was he able to load that much merchandise into his car without anyone questioning his motives?

As it turns out, Harlow's wife had mentioned the arsenal of weapons in their house when, a few days before his arrest, she filed assault and battery charges, stating that he had thrown her on the bed and pounded her face, broken her nose, chipped her tooth, and injured one of her eyes. This was not the first time he'd been accused of violence. During Harlow's trial for theft of government property and falsely claiming he had conducted background interviews, an FBI specialist on criminal behavior testified that Harlow had been investigated in the '80s for trying to run his ex-wife and her boyfriend off the road. The FBI expert also testified that Harlow had a fascination with violence and had falsely claimed to be a government assassin during the Vietnam War. From 1994–95, he was assigned to background investigations for the Clinton White House. Finally, in December 1996, the FBI fired him—not for theft, attempted murder or assault, but for filing false interviews on background investigations that he claimed to have conducted.

The FBI agents' unspoken code of silence helped cover up corruption in the FBI crime lab for several years. During my career in the Bureau, I was in awe of the lab's outstanding accomplishments. Imagine my shock when I learned that lab officials had been accused of shoddy work, including falsifying findings in big-name cases, such as the Oklahoma City bombing, the 1993 World Trade Center car-bombing, the Unabomber prosecution, and the O. J. Simpson murder trial. While many of his allegations were eventually proven, Dr. Frederic Whitehurst, the lab whistleblower, was mandated to undergo psychiatric evaluation and treatment and was suspended without pay from his position as special agent/FBI explosives expert as a result of his unwelcome disclosures.

In the end, the Department of Justice found that certain important allegations made by Whitehurst were true. In January 1995, a Bureau unit chief reported that, of forty-eight FBI cases studied, thirteen of the related lab reports had been "significantly altered," although lying on a government form is a felony.

Investigators also found that some of the lab's personnel, examiners, and managers did not have the necessary scientific background that would qualify them to testify as experts in court and that there were serious gaps in management oversight, including failure to investigate credible allegations. The errors were made public in a report that was released in response to a lawsuit filed by the National Association of Criminal Defense Lawyers. These revelations resulted in a number of petitions to the court for new hearings on old cases.

One would think the FBI laboratory would rush to clean up such an embarrassing problem. Instead, in April 2003, FBI lab technician Jacquelyn Blake resigned while she was under investigation for failing to follow required scientific procedures over a two-year period when analyzing 103 DNA samples. A second lab employee was indicted for false testimony. At least, this time, FBI management didn't mandate anyone to undergo psychiatric counseling for reporting the situation.

Psychiatric evaluations have been ordered for Bureau whistleblowers, but what about evaluating FBI agents with a penchant for violence? A special agent in Kentucky, Mark Putnam, had an affair with a female informant. On June 8, 1989, he flew into a rage and choked the pregnant informant to death as they argued over financial support for her unborn child. The first FBI agent to go to prison for murder, Putnam received a sixteen-year sentence but was released on parole after ten years. FBI officials had failed to recognize his potential for violence, as well as his inappropriate relationship with an informant. Had they done so, it might have prevented two deaths.

Since the James J. Smith espionage case broke, there has been a well-publicized move to ensure that FBI assets/informants are handled according to the book. Was this 1989 murder not enough to start a crackdown? Or was it just a guy having an affair that got out of hand?

A more well-known example of misbehavior associated with informant handling involves organized crime in the Boston area. In May 2002, retired special agent John Connolly was convicted of racketeering, accepting bribes, and lying to the FBI. He was acquitted of obstruction of justice. Testifying against him with the promise of immunity from prosecution was his former supervisor John Morris, who admitted taking bribes from James "Whitey" Bulger and Stephen "the Rifleman" Flemmi.

Connolly had been charged with racketeering conspiracy, racketeering, conspiracy to obstruct justice, obstruction of justice, and making a false statement. At the same time, Stephen Flemmi was charged with conspiracy to obstruct justice and obstruction of justice. The indictment alleged that Connolly and Flemmi

—protected and (in Flemmi's case) participated in a criminal enterprise, engaged in murder, bribery, extortion, loan sharking and illegal gambling in the greater Boston, Massachusetts area. The charges relate to activities alleged to have occurred both during and after the time CONNOLLY served as an FBI Agent and involve his interaction with James J. ("Whitey") Bulger and FLEMMI both during and after they were being used by the FBI as informants.

Connolly and Bulger grew up in the same neighborhood but took distinctly different career paths, at least in the beginning. Bulger went into crime at an early age, was fearless when dealing with his enemies and generous to the Irish citizens of South Boston. Connolly joined the FBI and made his name by handling highly placed organized crime informants, such as Bulger and Flemmi.

Informant-handling is always problematic because, to catch criminals, you need to find someone who associates with them. Criminal-informants are often a bit shady themselves. There's really no way around it, but what is acceptable is a matter of degree. The problem in the Connolly case is that, while Bulger passed along valuable information about rival mobsters, he continued to commit crimes as dire as murder while he was on the FBI payroll.

Presented as part of Connolly's defense, was a 1983 FBI training video on handling criminal informants that featured Connolly teaching informant-handling at the FBI Academy. In the video, he warned FBI agent trainees not to get too close to their informants. "You can get friendly with them and you can like them, but you can never forget who you work for and that you're an FBI agent." Yet, Connolly and Bulger were reportedly friends and even owned luxury condos in the same building.

In 1995, just before Bulger was to be indicted on multiple charges, including murder, he disappeared from sight. Today he is on the FBI's list of Ten Most Wanted Fugitives, and there is a $1 million reward for his capture. According to the wanted poster:

James J. Bulger is being sought for his role in numerous

murders committed from the early 1970s through the mid-1980s in connection with his leadership of an organized crime group that allegedly controlled extortion, drug deals, and other illegal activities in the Boston, Massachusetts, area. He has a violent temper and is known to carry a knife at all times.

There have been several reports that Bulger is hiding out in Ireland, while John Connolly, the once-respected FBI agent, serves time in federal prison.

Chapter 30

NO JUSTICE FROM JUSTICE

The FBI maintains over six billion pages of paper records and a similar number of automated records. It is a mountain growing bigger with each passing day. We are investigators focused on preventing terrorism and solving the most sophisticated crimes. Perhaps that is why the seemingly mundane tasks of proper records creation, maintenance, dissemination and retrieval have not received the appropriate level of senior management attention.

Statement for the Record of Louis J. Freeh, Director Federal Bureau
of Investigation on FBI File Management before the House
Appropriations Subcommittee May 16, 2001

I f I look at the FBI through the eyes of screenwriters and novelists, I see far more comedy than drama, especially when it comes to information systems. While I was on the inside, I often wondered why the FBI lagged so far behind the rest of the free world in the area of technology. At the time, I was in operations and was not privy to how the Bureau's technology decisions were made. All I knew was that FBI communications didn't work well.

I recall an instance in 1990, when I was working undercover. I had a bag full of cash, and my assignment was to carry it into an alley where a second undercover agent and a police officer were to buy illegal arms from a white supremacist. My job should have been simple, but there was a hitch. I had not been able to pick up transmissions from the undercover agent's body wire, and so neither my backup nor I had a clue about what was going on. We didn't know if the agent and the officer were okay, so we decided that I would drive in and check out the situation. And how did I confirm this plan with the rest of the backup team? We all drove to a parking lot, got out of our cars, and talked face to face because our FBI radios didn't work. In the end we figured that, if things went bad in the alley, I could honk my car horn to alert the backup, a low-tech, but effective way to call for help. Fortunately, like my first extortion drop back in 1978, no one died because of poor communications. The arrest was swift and mishap-free.

The FBI computer systems worked no better than the radios. As agent-turned-spy Robert Hanssen has pointed out, computer systems in the Bureau were a liability. The FBI has hired only the best companies to develop its information systems. So why have these leading companies, which could develop effective systems for the Department of Defense and others, not succeed at the FBI? In its December 2002 report, the U.S. Department of Justice's Office of the Inspector General said: "We concluded that the FBI has not effectively managed its IT investments because it has not fully implemented the management processes associated with successful IT investments."

When I left the Bureau to join a private firm and became a consultant to the government, I dealt mainly in information systems. It was a job I held for nearly ten years. During that period, I worked on contracts for the Joint Chiefs of Staff at the Pentagon, the Defense Information Systems Agency, the United States Transportation Command, and the Secretary of Defense for C3I (Command, Control and Communications), as well as for agencies of the Departments of Treasury and Justice. From 1997–99, I was a member of the President's National Security Telecommunications Advisory Committee (NSTAC), Electronic Commerce/Cyber Crime Working Group under President Clinton. Established by Executive Order 12382, the NSTAC was created to provide the president with industry-based advice and expertise on implementing a national security and emergency preparedness communications policy. A major function of the

NSTAC is to conduct continuing risk assessments of communications throughout the nation's vital infrastructures.

I was neither inexperienced nor unknown in the information technology world, and I was pleased to land a spot as a program manager on an FBI contract. At last, I thought, I can help the operational agents get the systems they need to provide for their safety. The fact that I was the company's fifth person in less than two years to hold this position was a clue as to how difficult a customer the Bureau would be, but I'd fought that system before and was confident I could succeed this time. Besides, FBI contracting comes out of headquarters, where I'd had some of the greatest successes in my FBI career. I did not anticipate resistance.

True to the Hoover ideal that all agents be capable of doing all things, the Bureau did not think it necessary to assign a software, network, or any other kind of engineer to deal with information technology contractors. Instead, my team was assigned a GM-15 FBI agent with no experience in communications systems and insufficient training in government contracting. He, in turn, was directly supervised by a deputy assistant director.

In our first official meeting, the agent took me aside. "When they started working on the system," he began, "there were a bunch of ragheads sitting in here. I had to get rid of them."

He was referring to several computer scientists who practiced the Sikh religion. They had been working in the adjoining project area, and he was bragging about having them relocated. Immediately, I knew I'd descended into that Bureau hell where racial slurs were de rigueur, and no one would take offense at religious slurs.

What he wanted from my company were extremely costly security measures, including new construction that had neither been specified, nor costed into our contract.

During the months that followed, I began to understand why such a straightforward project had stalled and why four very competent project managers had resigned before me. The FBI asked for several major changes a month, which is the best way to ensure that an engineering project will never move forward.

Before a government contract is let, the contracting agency decides what it wants, and contractors submit proposals detailing how they'll accomplish the work and how much the project will cost the government. It's not uncommon to make changes along the way in software and system development when better options or new requirements come up. When that happens, however, another written agreement is issued, which carefully lays out the revised plan, the manpower needed, and the new costs. This is known in federal contracting as a "contract change." The contractor may or may not receive additional money or time to accomplish the new task, but the change is mutually agreed upon and written into the contract.

The system we were developing was not a difficult concept, but since the FBI manager was a nonengineer who picked up most of his knowledge from reading computer magazines, he frequently wanted to change the system based upon the latest magazine articles and news items, whether the changes made sense or not. He could not comprehend that changing one part of the system would impact the entire system and possibly precipitate a cascade of expensive, time-consuming revisions. The ultimate result was a fragmented approach that produced tangents rather than completed tasks.

If I said, "We can do this, but we either have to add manpower or stop doing something else," I was told, "Just do it." Things got particularly frosty when I refused to work beyond contract parameters and demanded the written contract changes that federal regulations require. What I never would have guessed was that contracting laws were irrelevant in Bureauland. I was actually told, "We're paying you so much that you owe us some free things." Gifts to the government from contractors, which is the true definition of "free things" in this context, are illegal. In fact, "free things" fall into the category of gifts to the government, but the Bureau's contracting officer didn't care.

During the decade I spent in government contracting, no other agency even hinted at "free things." In addition, I was asked only by the FBI to have my engineering staff fix employees' personally owned computers, which was definitely not part of the contract. It was sickening to hear these requests coming from an organization whose mandate is to enforce the law.

Another hindrance was the fact that the FBI didn't focus on moving the project ahead. Instead, the focus was on minutia and window dressings that a nonengineer could understand. I attended one technical meeting, along with about twenty agents, the lowest ranking of whom was a GM-15. We spent almost two hours watching an even higher-ranking official sit with a graphic artist trying to decide what colors the logo should be. The other agents were there to help determine what content would be available to system users, but we never got beyond discussing what color the logo should be.

In general, software and network engineers suffered severely from the FBI caste system. The prevailing attitude was that "they may have M.S. and Ph.D. degrees, but since they are not agents, their opinions and suggestions can be ignored. Only an agent can understand FBI operations." This approach disregarded the fact that the agent may not have the necessary technical background or an understanding of engineering to get the job done. But that was judged unimportant. The reality of FBI culture is that agent trumps nonagent in every situation, whether it makes sense or not.

While working on another project to revamp operational communications systems, I discovered that any new ideas my team presented were viewed as criticism, almost as if we were accusing the designer of the decades-old system of making mistakes and indicting the current manager for perpetuating them. This was another cultural problem in the FBI. When something went wrong, it was more important to lay blame and mete out punishment than to analyze the situation and determine whether there was an institutional policy or practice that should be modified. The blame-laying was a warning to all: no one should ever try anything similar again. Thus, responses to new ideas often were met with: "It didn't work in 1950 and it won't work now." As a result, institutional change rarely occurred. This persisted throughout my career as an agent and as an outside contractor; thus I am convinced, based upon all my experience and observation, that reform in the Bureau will remain problematic. As Hugh Heclo points out in his *A Government of Strangers: Executive Politics in Washington,* the natural tendency for the permanent staff of a government organization is to struggle to maintain "the integrity of government programs and organization."

Undoubtedly, there have been some improvements since my 1999 experience, but an April 2003 Institute of Electrical and Electronics Engineers *Spectrum* article leads me to believe progress is excruciatingly slow. The article recounts a November 2002 speech that William Hooton, the assistant director of the FBI's Records Management Division, presented before the Association for Information and Image Management in Washington, D.C. Hooton said that the Bureau assisted D.C. police during the fall 2002 serial sniper attacks by setting up a hotline to receive tips from the public. Those who answered the phones reported calls on handwritten forms that were driven to FBI headquarters every hour. At FBI headquarters, the handwritten forms were scanned and "the digital images fed into a bureau-wide database." The fact that handwritten notes scanned as images are not electronically searchable may help explain why the Bureau did not connect eyewitness reports placing New Jersey license plates at several crime scenes until late in the investigation.

And what has happened with shoring up the gaping holes in FBI computer security that permitted Robert Hanssen to pilfer classified information with impunity? The Department of Justice Office of the Inspector General's report, *A Review of the FBI's Performance in Deterring, Detecting, and Investigating the Espionage Activities of Robert Philip Hanssen,* made some frightening comments on the state of FBI computer security as of August 2003. Concerning the Automated Case System, which Hanssen used to collect information on intelligence cases and to track any investigation he wanted:

Today, more than two years after Hanssen's arrest, the ACS system remains insecure and vulnerable to misuse. The current audit program relies on case agent review rather than third-party auditing. Moreover, the program has only retroactive effect; case agents do not receive real-time notice when someone seeks unauthorized access to their cases. The "need to know" principle is not adequately applied in the computer context within the Counterintelligence Division; all Headquarters Counterintelligence Division agents have access to all cases in the Division whether or not their section or unit is connected to the case.

And most shocking of all:

Finally, the system's susceptibility to human error has not been remedied. In response to the OIG's findings regarding the ACS system, the FBI reported in July 2003 that "attempting technical changes to improve ACS security would not be a smart business decision" in light of plans to implement a new automated case system known as the Virtual Case File (VCF). The FBI stated that the first delivery of VCF is scheduled for December 2003.

All I can say is, "huh?"

Chapter 31

WHY THE FBI CAN'T PLAY
WELL WITH OTHERS

We have had access issues in a number of agencies over the years.
However, across law enforcement-related agencies, FBI access issues
have been the most sustained and intractable.

GAO's Work at the FBI: Success to Data, Documents, and Personnel
The Government Accounting Office
June 20, 2001

O ne of the most acute complaints about the Bureau is that
headquarters' bureaucracy may have hindered the discovery of
the September 11 terrorist plot weeks before it was carried
out. The FBI's inability to share information and work with others is an
historic and pervasive problem on many levels. First, there are internal
problems between headquarters and the field, large and small offices, as
well as agents and clerks that bog down investigations and prevent cultural change. Then there are difficulties working with other agencies;
and finally, there has been a refusal to share information with the Government Accounting Office, which inhibits oversight. This has affected
the way the Bureau conducted investigations, such as the Robert
Hanssen espionage case, as well as the way in which it has set up some
of the internal components that were intended to protect the country
against terrorism.

On May 21, 2002, special agent Coleen Rowley, the principal legal
advisor for the Bureau's Minneapolis field office, wrote a thirteen-page

letter to Director Mueller and members of Congress outlining her accusations that FBI headquarters had thwarted her office's attempts to obtain a search warrant for Zacarias Moussaoui's computer and personal effects. She added that FBI public disclosures about what the FBI knew before September 11 were misleading. Now known as "the twentieth hijacker," Moussaoui was detained on August 16, 2001, and charged with overstaying his visa, but he refused to give the FBI agents consent to search his computer, so FBI Minneapolis needed a warrant. Rowley said that headquarters had hindered the field investigation of Moussaoui, and perhaps prevented discovery of the September 11 conspiracy before it occurred, by changing the information that Minneapolis had submitted in support of the warrant.

According to French Intelligence, Moussaoui is a French Moroccan with ties to al Qaeda and Osama bin Laden. He arrived in the U.S. in February 2001 and began taking flying lessons in Norman, Oklahoma. After washing out at flight school, he moved to a suburb of Minneapolis, where he paid thousands of dollars to practice in flight simulators designed for use by commercial pilots. When Moussaoui insisted on learning to fly a 747, even though he lacked the skills needed to fly smaller aircraft, his flight instructors became suspicious and phoned the FBI.

Rowley wrote in her letter that Minneapolis had identified two potential criminal violations: "Title 18 United States Code Section 2332b (Acts of terrorism transcending national boundaries, which, notably, includes 'creating a substantial risk of serious bodily injury to any other person by destroying or damaging any structure, conveyance, or other real or personal property within the United States or by attempting or conspiring to destroy or damage any structure, conveyance, or other real or personal property within the United States') and Section 32 (Destruction of aircraft or aircraft facilities)." While FBI headquarters found the evidence presented for the pre-September 11 search warrant to be insufficient, on September 11, they sought a warrant based upon probable cause that Moussaoui had committed a violation of Section 32.1 [Conspiracy to commit destruction of aircraft or aircraft facilities]. The only difference in the information presented was that the terrorist attacks had already occurred. There was nothing tying Moussaoui more strongly to the event than there had been the day before.

Rowley went on to say that her charges were not mere "20-20 hindsight."

> Also intertwined with my reluctance in this case to accept the "20-20 hindsight" rationale is firsthand knowledge that I have of statements made on September 11th, after the first attacks on the World Trade Center had already occurred, made telephonically by the FBI Supervisory Special Agent (SSA) who was the one most involved in the Moussaoui matter and who, up to that point, seemed to have been consistently, almost deliberately thwarting the Minneapolis FBI agents' efforts (see number 5). Even after the attacks had begun, the SSA in question was still attempting to block the search of Moussaoui's computer, characterizing the World Trade Center attacks as a mere coincidence with Minneapolis' prior suspicions about Moussaoui.

Among the evidence that agents found during the search were computer discs containing details of how to dump pesticides from a small plane. Moussaoui has since been indicted for conspiracy to commit acts of terrorism transcending national boundaries, conspiracy to commit aircraft piracy, conspiracy to destroy aircraft, conspiracy to use weapons of mass destruction, conspiracy to murder United States employees, and conspiracy to destroy property.

The potential problem I see at work here is the fact that Minneapolis is not a big FBI office, and there is a mentality in the Bureau that large offices, such as Washington, New York, San Francisco, and Los Angeles, have the "real" cases and experience in the Bureau. When Phoenix and Oklahoma City, two smaller offices, warned of terrorist connections to flight schools across the United States long before September 11, they were virtually ignored.

The premise that no one in the smaller offices knows what's going on in the world is ridiculous on the face of it and merely an arti-fact of cultural arrogance. I worked in large and small offices where I dealt with agents who were equally as knowledgeable as those in large metropolitan areas. I found significant cases of all types in the smaller offices I inspected. Furthermore, it is obvious that organiza-tions like al Qaeda know that the heartland of America is a good place to hide.

Another example of the FBI's lack of cooperation, which came to the public's attention in the timeframe of the September 11 attacks, is inability to cooperate with outside agencies. A November 9, 2001, *New York Times* article entitled "Experts See F.B.I. Missteps Hampering Anthrax Inquiry," recounted testimony from experts, who said the FBI may have lost important pieces of evidence needed to solve the post–September 11 anthrax crimes because it lacked scientific knowl-edge of what is important in tracking a strain of anthrax back to its source. After being interviewed by the FBI, laboratory officials asked whether they should destroy their anthrax stores. Since the FBI did not understand how valuable the materials would be for identifying the strain from which the anthrax used in the attacks came, the Bureau let the labs make their own decisions. As a result, the labs destroyed the samples, obliterating the ability to study them should the need arise. In addition, at the time of the November testimony almost two months after the attack, the FBI had not sent agents to all the labs known to hold anthrax stores.

Bureau officials stated that they'd been "forced" to turn to outside experts for help, as if they were admitting a defeat. The fact that experts weren't consulted from the beginning of the investigation is a clue that the system's arrogant "we-can-do-it-all" attitude inhibited the investiga-tion. While I have seen agents start from zero knowledge and come up with impressive, even brilliant results, all FBI agents cannot do all things. This ideal may have inspired some individuals to excel when the Bureau was a nascent organization with limited jurisdiction and per-sonnel numbering in the hundreds, but it does not work now. Times change and threats change. The only way the Bureau can keep up is to fundamentally change the way it does business.

Because the Bureau now has greater responsibility protecting the U.S. from terrorist attacks, it is useful to look at how business was conducted in an FBI-controlled organization set up to do just that. The Bureau opened the National Infrastructure Protection Center (NIPC) in 1998. The NIPC was conceptualized in President Clinton's Presidential Decision Directive (PDD) 63 as a national center for gathering information about threats to the nation's critical infrastructure, as well as for issuing warnings and coordinating responses to attacks, with a special emphasis on cyber threats. The critical infrastructures are the various support systems the U.S. needs to survive; specifically, "telecommunications, energy, banking and finance, transportation, water systems and emergency services, both governmental and private," Each of these functions is a likely target of terrorist attacks or in the event of war.

Before it was absorbed into the Department of Homeland Security, the NIPC functioned within the FBI as a domestic and international task force with full-time representatives from twelve agencies, who coordinated with officials throughout the government. The majority of the representatives were from the FBI and Department of Defense, but there were also government representatives from the United Kingdom, Canada, and Australia.

The General Accounting Office (GAO) conducts continuing analyses of all governmental organizations, and a common theme that ran through its 2001 GAO analysis of the FBI-controlled NIPC was a lack of coordination between the FBI and other agencies. And while the GAO said the NIPC had "provided valuable support and coordination related to investigating and otherwise responding to attacks on computers," three years after the NIPC was founded, its analytical and information-sharing capabilities "needed to protect the nation's critical infrastructures had not yet been achieved, and the NIPC had developed only limited warning capabilities."

There are cultural problems that have inhibited the development of strong analytical support in the FBI. Analysts are nonagent personnel, and no matter what their qualifications, analysts and other clerks are treated as second-class citizens in the Bureau. Analysts are hired because they offer a depth of knowledge in some specialty. They should be respected professionals whose opinions are valued, but that was not the case in the FBI I knew.

The NIPC did not take advantage of subject matter expertise in identifying the key assets that should be protected in the event of a terrorist attack. According to the GAO, despite the fact that FBI agents are not trained to analyze the industries that keep this country running, the FBI did not coordinate with the "entities that own and control the assets." The resulting problem is that

> the key assets recorded may not be the ones that infrastructure owners consider to be the most important. Further, the Key Asset Initiative was not being coordinated with other similar federal efforts at the Departments of Defense and Commerce.

Another arena in which lack of cooperation has resulted in catastrophic failures is in investigating intelligence losses. The August 2003 Department of Justice Office of Inspector General report on the Bureau's handling of the Robert Hanssen case points out lack of cooperation with CIA:

> The FBI's penetration efforts in the late 1970s and 1980s suffered from a lack of cooperation with the CIA and from inattention on the part of senior management. In 1985 and 1986, the CIA and FBI lost nearly every significant human asset then operating against the Soviet Union. These losses were unprecedented in scope, quantity, significance, and timing, yet the FBI undertook no sustained effort to determine their cause. Senior management was almost entirely unaware of the scope and significance of these losses, and throughout the 1980s the FBI

failed to work cooperatively with the CIA to resolve the cause of these losses or to thoroughly investigate whether an FBI mole could be responsible for these setbacks. We now know that Hanssen compromised many of the assets and operations lost during the mid-1980s.

The OIG report says that the FBI established an internal task force to look into its intelligence losses.

During the Task Force effort [1986–87], the FBI learned that the CIA had likewise suffered catastrophic and unprecedented losses in its Soviet program. Yet, the FBI failed to work cooperatively with the CIA to resolve the cause of these losses.

The same report points out lack of cooperation with the Department of Justice when the FBI pursued the wrong CIA suspect.

Ineffective oversight by FBI management and poor coordination with the Justice Department also contributed to the length of the FBI's investigation of the wrong suspect and the failure to pursue alternative avenues. The FBI managers with supervisory authority over the investigation often deferred to line personnel—even when the managers harbored serious doubts about the progress of the investigation—resulting in a tacit endorsement of erroneous analysis and conclusions. This problem was compounded by the FBI's poor coordination with the Justice Department components responsible for overseeing intelligence investigations—the Office of Intelligence Policy and Review (OIPR) and the Criminal Division's Internal Security Section (ISS).

Even the investigative arm of Congress, the General Accounting Office, has had persistent problems in gaining access to FBI information and personnel. Federal statutes guarantee the GAO access to records of any United States government agency, including "information . . . about the duties, powers, activities, organization, and financial transactions of the agency." But this is what the GAO has experienced when attempting to get the FBI to share information:

> Concern about access to records and people at the FBI is not a new topic for us . . . One of the greatest problems is delay . . . Another problem relates to the quality of documentation the FBI provides . . . While infrequent, in some cases the FBI has denied us access to the information we have requested . . . For example, for our work related to federal teams that respond to chemical, biological, radiological, and nuclear terrorist incidents (requested by Rep. Ike Skelton, the Ranking Minority Member of the House Armed Services Committee), the FBI refused to provide us with information on the missions, budget, and resources of its response teams. The FBI said that providing the information to us would jeopardize the teams' operational security, even though the information was unclassified.
>
> We recognize that the FBI's responsibility to investigate criminal activity carries with it a set of imperatives that limits its discretion to disseminate certain types of information, to protect the rights of the accused and the integrity of the investigative process. We believe, however, that these imperatives do not exempt the FBI from congressional oversight. The FBI can and should provide a much wider range of information about its activities to Congress and to us.
>
> A partially informed Congress cannot provide adequate oversight, balance competing interests fairly, resolve issues effectively, or deliberate soundly.

These are shocking statements coming from the watchdog of Congress. The overall lack of cooperation raises questions about FBI attempts to evade congressional oversight and makes it look like the Bureau has something to hide.

The odd thing is that J. Edgar Hoover created multiple organizations within the FBI that were designed to share information with other agencies. One of the ways he expanded his Bureau was by creating information-sharing services to aid federal, state, and local law enforcement agencies. In 1924, he established the Bureau of Investigation's Identification Division to facilitate the exchange of identification records among state, county, and local police. In 1930, Congress expanded the mandate, and the Identification Division became the clearinghouse for all national crime statistics. Within two years, the Bureau was exchanging fingerprint information with friendly foreign governments and had created a technical laboratory that served U.S. and foreign police agencies. Three years later, the FBI opened a national police-training program that eventually became known as the National Academy. In 1941, the Bureau fielded a Disaster Squad to aid civilian agencies in identifying the victims of an airplane crash in Virginia, and this service is extended to agencies and countries throughout the world today. Then in 1967, the FBI's National Crime Information Center (NCIC) began sharing its electronic database of criminal histories and warrants with law enforcement agencies nationwide.

The discrepancy between setting up organizations to promote sharing—and then not sharing—is rooted in the FBI's pervasive cultural need to control information and everything else. The concept of being in charge, in complete and constant control is the basis of FBI culture. In fact, control is a basic tenet of FBI training. Training for this begins in the academy where control is drilled into every new recruit. My academy classmates and I were taught that when we walked onto a crime scene, we were to take charge immediately. We were to look and act as if we knew what we were doing, and we were to collect information, not give it out.

Control is reinforced from the moment an agent hits the field. Even the newest agent in the field is in charge of his or her own cases, and if other agents assist, the case agent remains in charge without regard to seniority. While this, in and of itself, is not a bad thing, combined with the zero-tolerance-for-mistakes attitude, it promotes an atmosphere where people don't want to ask for help when they should, especially when getting help means giving information to get information, such as was necessary in the investigation of the post–September 11 anthrax attack.

The FBI is the leading agency in investigating many violations of United States law, but the ability to lead implies working well with others. It is time for the FBI to rethink its culture of control and function as a part of the government team.

As it carries out its leadership responsibilities in counterintelligence and counterterrorism, the Bureau would do well to remember Will Rogers's words, "If you're ridin' ahead of the herd, take a look back every now and then to make sure it's still there."

Chapter 32

SCARED OF CHANGES

If the FBI does not adhere to the highest standards of integrity, it will quickly lose the best and brightest of its employees and leaders. In my 21 plus years with the FBI, I have seen tremendous agents and support employees working diligently and selflessly to thwart crimes and protect the country. I don't believe that any computer will ever match the value of human personnel and in this respect, the FBI has always been very lucky in attracting top caliber men and women.

Statement of Coleen M. Rowley
FBI Special Agent and Minneapolis Chief Division Counsel before
the Senate Committee on the Judiciary "Oversight Hearing
on Counterterrorism"
June 6, 2002

F idelity, Bravery, and Integrity is the FBI motto. Bravery abounds in the Bureau, but there is a lack of integrity and fidelity, passed from generation to generation of agents like an inherited disease that has corrupted the system. Hoover often spoke of integrity, then acted without it. He meted out capricious punishments to some employees, yet protected others. He created a system of management that was inconsistent in its treatment of employees, as well as the public, and his definition of fidelity was unquestioned loyalty to himself. In the end, his legacy is an organization where agents demand control of minute details, a stodgy institution that resists change and operates under policies that are inequitably applied. Seventy years after its founding, the system still promotes a workplace environment where harassment and mediocrity thrive, and where some are punished for errors, while major transgressions, such as Robert Hanssen breaking into or putting password cracking software onto others' computers, aren't even made a matter of record.

From my vantage point as a former supervisory special agent and an information technology consultant, I still believe that the Bureau could become the agency we all believed in once upon a time. It will take leaders at the top who are willing to instill cultural change that reaches down to the agent on the street. Without that long reach, the culture will not change.

Among the changes that I recommend are propagating an atmosphere of honesty and respect, continuous process improvement, and honoring the contributions of all employees, whether they are agents or not.

An Atmosphere of Honesty

Having integrity means that other people can consistently trust your word. This is not how FBI employees feel about their employer, nor is it the current public image of the Bureau. Internal policies are not enforced consistently, as demonstrated in the disparate treatment of women and minorities. It is unconscionable that in 2001, a court needed to appoint an arbitrator to ensure that African-American agents be treated fairly in the Bureau or that a senior employee, such as John Roberts, was harassed for pointing out needed change, and the person who did it was merely cited for showing poor judgement. Humiliating employees is not acceptable in the rest of the world and should not be in the FBI.

In addition, internal affairs investigations must be impartial and must be perceived as fair, not capricious. It's time to ensure that the many incidents of senior employees avoiding punishment for misdeeds are not repeated. For years, the internal affairs process at the FBI has been partial to managers and their protégés. The double standard that existed for investigating managers and all others until 2001 has left a strong perception that will take time to overcome. It is important to establish and carry out a scrupulous internal affairs process that does not allow unethical executives to be quietly demoted to slightly lower, yet highly prestigious and influential positions, supposedly as a form of punishment. A glaring example is Larry Potts, who was promoted to deputy director while accused of issuing the "shoot on sight" order that resulted in two deaths at Ruby Ridge in Idaho, then lying about it and letting the field agents take the fall for it. Demoted from deputy director after deception was revealed, Potts was named assistant director of the FBI Academy, where the unethical handling of his controversial case could influence the conduct of new and in-service agents for years to come. People learn from what they see going on around them and all the corporate credos, vision statements, policies, and explanations in the world won't change that.

The current system of FBI self-policing is an incestuous management structure ("you investigate me, I investigate you") that doesn't get the FBI anywhere. Field office and headquarters inspections might be better served coming from the Department of Justice, whose investigators do not investigate their peers and potential supervisors. The present system makes it virtually impossible to avoid conflict of interest among supervisors in the FBI.

Fidelity, bravery, integrity—words for the FBI to live by in dealing with the public and in dealing with its own employees.

CONTINUOUS PROCESS IMPROVEMENT

The anticoagulant heparin was discovered at Johns Hopkins by a doctor who was searching for a drug that would make blood clot. Heparin could be viewed as a mistake, since it actually prevents blood from clotting, but it has been one of the most significant, lifesaving pharmaceutical discoveries in the history of medicine. It is used in dialysis, in preventing deep vein thromboses, and in clearing intravenous lines, among other things.

The FBI should take a cue from science and realize that mistakes can be useful, and that widespread mistakes are probably the fault of the system rather than individuals. Instilling fear and demanding a zero-defect standard will not halt problems, it will only encourage cover-ups. Instead of finger-pointing and punishing when a mistake is made—assuming that is not a criminal act or a breach of the public's trust—the Bureau should use errors to improve the system. A more useful response to such mistakes might be enhanced policy and training that is designed to inform all personnel of the problem and preempt any recurrence.

In the non-Bureau world, there is a trend toward business models that assume every system is inherently flawed and that mistakes will be made. The goal is not to completely avoid mistakes, which discourages action, creativity, and information exchange, but instead to strive for positive change in day-to-day operations. The result is a process of continually assessing, acting on findings, reassessing, improving, and learning. This process is a circle, not a straight line with an endpoint. Adopting the business model used by successful companies throughout the world could help FBI employees overcome the culturally ingrained fear of being singled out for having made a mistake.

Inherent in this process is a willingness to accept positive change. This is the tough part. Despite all the reorganizations that have taken place since September 11, 2001, and despite the calls for change from within and without, I fear there have been nothing but cosmetic changes, affected to please the new director. On August 24, 2003 when *60 Minutes* asked FBI Assistant Director for Counterintelligence and case agent on the Hanssen investigation, David Szady, what the FBI would do differently, in light of the Department of Justice Office of the Inspector General report about the Hanssen investigation, he replied that they would do nothing differently.

Understand that All Employees Can Contribute
Recommendations from nonagent support staff, such as analysts or engineers, should not be seen as of lesser value than an agent's opinion. It is this elitist attitude—similar to the assumption that the FBI must be in charge of all aspects of an investigation—that has kept the Bureau

from developing adequate analytical support and seeking help from outside agencies. This attitude even inhibits the use of contractors, a long-standing, beneficial force-multiplier in the rest of the United States government. It has also seriously impaired the Bureau's ability to develop and maintain technology.

RESPECT FOR INDIVIDUALS

Business management books say that major attributes shared by successful businesses are respect for employees and the attitude that non-management personnel are the heart of operations. I took a management course at the FBI Academy that advised me to take the extra chairs out of our offices so that people would not have a place to sit and "waste our time." To me, this is the ultimate demonstration that a manager does not value employees' opinions and intends to act as dictator.

Also, being open and honest about employees' performance throughout the year is a form of professional respect, and FBI managers should not be kept so busy that they don't have time to discuss with employees what is going well and what is going wrong. Robert Hanssen went for years without a performance review while he was a liaison to the Department of State. Performance feedback is needed to keep good workers motivated and to help poor performers improve.

THE HEADQUARTERS VS. THE FIELD ATTITUDE HAS TO GO

Slow responses from headquarters propagate a "them-against-us" enmity between headquarters and the field, but FBI headquarters is not to blame for all the ills of the Bureau. It provides an overview of fieldwork and centralizes analysis. Headquarters provides liaison with the multitude of other agency headquarters in the D.C. area. And there is a need for legal review and someone to prepare applications and testify in Foreign Intelligence Surveillance Act Court without making the case agent fly in from the field to do it. Without these services, field cases would be stalemated and the nation's interests would not be served. On the other hand, the tradition of iron-fisted control from FBI headquarters is comparable to a multinational company being managed like a small business in which one or two bosses at the corporate office make the bulk of all decisions for thousands of employees. This management style stifles success.

When I was at headquarters, the operational desks were overloaded with cases. No matter how hard the supervisors tried, they couldn't keep up with their mounting workloads, and the field agents often had to wait until a headquarters supervisor got around to responding to requests for approvals on operations. I had approximately one thousand cases under my supervision in counterterrorism, with an analyst assisting me part-time. I couldn't read all the mail I received, much less write responses. I was also responsible for compiling facts for Foreign Intelligence Surveillance Act (FISA) applications and testifying before the FISA court for wiretap orders, not to mention dropping everything to work in the Emergency Operations Center during terrorist attacks. As you might expect, things got buried in the piles of paper on my desk, and field operations under me were slowed.

Every agent begins his or her career as a field agent, so in essence, the field creates headquarters supervisors. As they follow the career path, headquarters supervisors return to field desks, then rotate back to head-quarters. The result is that attitudes learned in the field offices con-tribute to the headquarters culture, and some of the change in culture must be brought about by field agents making the commitment to become good managers.

In Hoover's day, running a good organization meant removing all autonomy from the field and establishing an inflexible system of central control from FBI headquarters, or what Hoover referred to as "the seat of government." Of course, Hoover never changed his management style from the time he became the director in May 1924, when there were only 441 agents on duty, which is about the same number of agents who would be assigned to a midsize field office now. Today, headquarters needs to give the field some latitude to make decisions and trust their judgment, lest we repeat the situation with the Zacarias Moussaoui search warrant.

The same goes for the field, where control-freakishness also abounds.

An example is what my coworkers and I used to call the "Blazing Saddles" arrest. A criminal took a hostage, and the FBI and police SWAT teams surrounded the house where he was hiding out. The FBI supervisor attempted to direct the entire operation from the radio room back in the office rather than relinquish control to the SWAT team commanders on the scene. The hostagetaker came out on the porch with his gun to the hostage's head, then suddenly put the gun to his own head and shouted, "Get back or I'll kill myself." Believe it or not, even though it would have taken mere seconds for the man to adjust his aim and kill the hostage or one of the nearby officers, the FBI supervisor radioed instructions to the SWAT teams to let the hostagetaker move freely but to keep him under surveillance. In the end, the criminal escaped.

FREEDOM TO SPEAK OUT

Approximately eight months after the terrorist attacks of September 11, special agent Coleen Rowley, an attorney with the Bureau's Minneapolis field office, wrote her now-famous letter to Director Mueller explaining how FBI headquarters had ignored her office's concerns about Zacarias Moussaoui.

Ms. Rowley's letter was a bold move. Still years from retirement, she took an incalculable risk in bucking this system that pushes for an employee to resign rather than to take a stand against the Bureau Way. In the ultimate corruption of the meaning of fidelity, speaking out in any way against Bureau processes and personnel has come to represent the supreme disloyalty, and disloyalty is the dirtiest word in the Bureau's vocabulary. In fact, members of the Society of Former Agents of the FBI publicly called her a bigger traitor than Robert Hanssen; and when special agent Janet Turner reported the theft of the crystal globe from Ground Zero, it was she, not the thief who was accused of tarnishing the name of the FBI.

It is said that in Hoover's day there was a plaque in every FBI office featuring the following advice from a 1906 Elbert Hubbard essay:

If you work for a man, in heaven's name work for him; speak well of him and stand by the institution he represents.

Remember—an ounce of loyalty is worth a pound of cleverness.

If you must growl, condemn, and eternally find fault, why—resign your position and when you are on the outside, damn to your heart's content but as long as you are a part of the institution do not condemn it; if you do, the first high wind that comes along will blow you away, and probably you will never know why.

This message permeates FBI culture. Bureau mores permit an employee to voice objections only within the limited set of issues the chain of command is willing to address. It is possible to go to the mat on operational matters and survive, though not always win, as long as the case is presented to the right people in the right way. However, reports about fair treatment, racial discrimination, or corruption are routinely handled with a blame-the-messenger mentality.

Fear of reprisal lasts well beyond on-duty careers, as evidenced by the fact that only a few former agents have dared to write books critical of the agency. A retired agent even warned me that, if I wrote anything derogatory about Hoover, the Society of Former Agents of the FBI would "come after me." To that person, I would say that attempts to improve the Bureau should not be censured. As agents, we swore our loyalty to a nation, not to a man or an agency.

Every agent signs lifelong nondisclosure agreements about Bureau cases and is bound by the espionage statutes not to disclose classified information. When we write about the FBI, for example, we have to send the work through FBI headquarters for prepublication review (which I did) to ensure we've held to our nondisclosure agreements. But there is more to the fear than that. As an article in the FBI's *Law Enforcement Bulletin* pointed out, "In most cases, choosing right over wrong takes courage because people who make ethical choices often subject themselves to social and professional ridicule." In an organization where being accepted by coworkers is an on-the-job necessity, professional ridicule is a serious, and possibly fatal problem.

When FBI Laboratory scientist Dr. Frederic Whitehurst went public with the news that the lab was corrupt and that evidence in hundreds of cases had been mishandled, he was mandated to undergo psychiatric evaluation and treatment and then suspended from the Bureau without pay. That is a clear disincentive against speaking out. The cure for this is real—not nominal—whistleblower protection. I laud Director Mueller for extending that protection to all FBI employees, and I hope it becomes the standard for the Bureau.

ANONYMOUS REPORTING

Historically, the Bureau has suppressed dissenting voices, which means that upper management has not been privy to invaluable information. Layers of management separate dissenters from executive management. Director Freeh had an advisory committee made up of field agents, but that face-to-face confrontation can still inhibit some from expressing their ideas.

Sometimes getting the information is more important than knowing the source of it. Realizing this, the Department of Defense and many corporations encourage employees to report waste, fraud, abuse, and potential security problems through anonymous hotlines. Bureau management could collect needed information without making employees feel that their jobs are in jeopardy. With a competent inspection process in place, these reports could be followed up and the proper actions taken.

REWARDS FOR INNOVATIVE IDEAS

I also suggest that the FBI institute a system of rewards for those who submit viable ideas for process improvement, another simple idea that has served private industry well. However, there should be a mechanism to submit such ideas directly to the level of the director's office without intermediate filters.

TEACH FBI AGENTS WHAT SECURITY IS

When I became a defense-industry consultant, I encountered stringent security rules for the first time. It shocked me, because suddenly I realized that, for the entire time I had been employed by the FBI, I had mishandled documents and national security information out of complete ignorance of security procedures. There was no security training at the academy, and no security culture in the FBI. Instead, as they say in the Bureau: "[the] FBI need to know" means, if the guy's in your carpool, he needs to know.

The August 2003 Department of Justice Office of the Inspector General report on the FBI's handling of the Hanssen affair said:

> we found overarching problems in the FBI's internal security efforts. Most of the deficiencies discussed in our report are of longstanding vintage and reflect the cumulative decisions of many FBI employees, including the Directors and senior managers who failed to remedy serious flaws in the FBI's personnel, document, and information security programs; the Directors and senior managers who failed to devote sufficient resources and attention to the penetration issue in the 1980s and early 1990s, and failed to resolve how important FBI human sources and operations had been compromised; the unwillingness of line personnel working on the espionage investigation of the CIA suspect to reconsider initial conclusions and judgments in the face of investigative failures, and senior managers' failure to insist that they be revisited; the failure of senior managers to ensure that accurate information was supplied to the Justice Department concerning the investigation of the CIA suspect; the supervisors and colleagues who ignored Hanssen's pattern of security violations and his obvious lack of suitability for handling sensitive information; and the managers who provided such lax supervision of Hanssen that he was able to spend much of his time on nonwork related matters, or worse, committing espionage. These were widespread failings. We believe that what is needed at the FBI is a wholesale change in mindset and approach to internal security.

Sadly, it has been all too easy for someone like Hanssen to get away with selling government secrets because his colleagues ignored the telltale behavioral cues. Consider this finding from Judge Webster's 2002 commission, which reviewed FBI security programs:

> Before leaving material at drops for his handlers, Hanssen would scan the Bureau's systems to see whether the FBI had identified the locations as drop sites. He would also run his name in the systems to determine whether he was a subject of an investigation.

In the early '80s, years before I met Hanssen, I knew he was searching for his own name in the Bureau's indices, and we weren't even assigned to the same office. I heard about this strange behavior from my supervisor in the Washington field office. When I asked him why any agent would do such a thing, he waved me off, saying that Hanssen just wanted to know if there was information about him in FBI records. This remark came from an experienced counterintelligence supervisor, who apparently saw nothing odd about Hanssen exceeding his authorization for use of FBI databases. It never occurred to me that there might be anything about me in FBI operational files. The obvious question is: why would there be? It's odd that a senior counterintelligence supervisor didn't find Hanssen's behavior to be a problem, but as I've said before: Virtually no behavior from an FBI agent peer was considered unacceptable.

Everyone in the security and counterintelligence business knows that the biggest security threat to an organization is the insider. That's why intelligence agencies prefer to recruit an insider rather than infiltrate, and that is why the FBI should pay attention to how agents behave. Insiders are also the biggest threat to information systems. Just as insiders are more likely to damage the system—either on purpose, by mistake, or from lack of training—insiders are the most likely to know what materials are valuable enough to steal.

When FBI agents evaluate foreign agents to determine whether they will be amenable to committing treason, they look for weaknesses, reasons they don't fit into their own society. Why not admit that those same signs are potential problems when identified in a fellow FBI agent? What does it take to get an FBI counterintelligence supervisor to admit that an agent under his command is a security risk? Occasional polygraphs won't substitute for field and headquarters management creating an atmosphere in which aberrant behavior is identified and not tolerated. And when I say not tolerated, I mean getting rid of harassers and criminals. FBI agents are well paid, and the job is a great opportunity, and everyone is replaceable.

Other potential security risks are the agents who openly refuse to do their jobs—"deadwood" or "retired in place" as they are called in the Bureau. These highly demotivated employees often claim they've been screwed by the Bureau at some point in their careers and hold the Bureau responsible for their lack of performance. "Deadwood" employees are security risks, who should be counseled by their supervisors in an attempt to bring their work up to standards. If after counseling they still cannot perform adequately, they should be fired. The FBI owes the taxpayers that much. It is well known that R. W. Miller, the first FBI agent to be arrested for espionage, was a "deadwood" agent. The OIG report on the Bureau's performance in the Robert Hanssen investigation echoes my opinion on this: "Hanssen received minimal supervision in most of his positions, was not required to produce significant work product, and had ample time to plan and commit espionage while on duty."

While the Bureau has initiated periodic polygraphs, the polygraph is not the be all, end all in security. It is a useful interview tool, but throughout past decades, traitors from the CIA, the National Security Agency (NSA), and the military have taken regular polygraphs, and yet the tests didn't reveal their crimes or stop them from their spying activities. An example is the CIA's Aldrich Ames, who passed two polygraphs in 1991 when he was already under suspicion of committing espionage, but wasn't arrested and charged as a spy until 1994.

The reason polygraph tests are not universally accepted court in is that they only reveal that a person is reacting with anxiety to a particular question, but they cannot determine exactly why. In short, the test cannot actually prove that an individual is lying. Also, mental illness is a strong variable in polygraphs. Sociopaths and others with personality disorders feel no guilt when they lie, which allows them to pass a polygraph with ease. If a person who is committing espionage feels no guilt, the polygraph is of little value. On the other hand, a person, who feels guilty about everything or overanalyses every question, may show a reaction while giving a truthful answer. In the end, it is the polygrapher, not the machine, who decides whether the subject is telling the truth. And polygraphers are fallible humans.

Finally, polygraphs are worth nothing if the system covers problems. When problems are uncovered on a polygraph—alcohol, extramarital affairs, petty theft, and other known security vulnerabilities—there has to be a system in place for dealing with them. Employee assistance programs and mental health resources must not be viewed as career-ending alternatives.

TREAT CRIMES AS CRIMES

Finally, agents who break the law by pilfering government property, as did Gary Harlow, who stole thousands of rounds of ammunition and a truck full of weaponry, are major security risks. Crimes committed by agents should be treated as crimes, not as unpleasant administrative matters. Falsifying a government record is against the law, and it is not acceptable for an agent to fake records and remain on duty, especially if the agent is a manager. Breaking into another person's computer is against the law. Stealing evidence from a crime scene is against the law. Zero tolerance for FBI lawbreakers must be the rule.

When I was a trainee in the Dallas Police Academy, we were told: If you find anyone, even the chief of police, with his hand in the cookie jar, cuff him and say, "Tell it to the judge." Dallas Police Academy instructors made it clear from the first day that there was a strict code of behavior on the job.

The FBI Academy left no such impression. In fact, the message I got from people's actions was quite the opposite: that fudging the rules and getting away with things was something of a game, and that attitude had a tremendous impact on my future work life. By the time I left the academy, I knew that I'd have to tolerate vile remarks and sexist actions from my male coworkers in order to survive in the Bureau. I also knew that I would have no redress. In my entire time with the FBI, only two supervisors, neither of whom were my direct supervisors, ever intervened, despite the hundreds of times I was harassed in their presence. Aside from those two occasions, I never witnessed a single supervisor object to any form of harassment that occurred in his presence. This failure to act, this acceptance of illegal and offensive behavior as the norm, is not acceptable.

OVERCOMMITTED

Over its history, FBI responsibilities have expanded beyond its ability to keep up, especially since taking on the mission of preventing terrorism. Its priorities are currently to:

1. Protect the United States from terrorist attack
2. Protect the United States against foreign intelligence operations and espionage
3. Protect the United States against cyber-based attacks and high-technology crimes
4. Combat public corruption at all levels
5. Protect civil rights
6. Combat transnational and national criminal organizations and enterprises
7. Combat major white-collar crime
8. Combat significant violent crime
9. Support federal, state, local and international partners
10. Upgrade technology to successfully perform the FBI's mission

While reviewing FBI field office press releases for 2003, I noticed there are certain violations that are still worked by the FBI, such as bank robberies, that have been competently handled by police departments for a long time. In fact, when a bank robbery takes place, it is almost inevitably the police who arrive on the scene and start the investigation. FBI agents do not ride around in patrol cars and are not in a position to investigate a bank robbery until after the fact. Police now have state-to-state communications and are able to cooperate with law enforcement all over the country. The Bureau's involvement in bank robbery investigations is also a point of irritation with many police officers. Motor vehicle theft and illegal drugs are other violations that are handled by either local police or many other federal agencies. It's time for Congress to start a serious review of FBI jurisdictions and reapportion such responsibilities and the resources to go with them. The truth is that the Bureau can only do so much with the manpower that is available; absorbing responsibilities and then expecting personnel to work harder to meet each new responsibility is a setup for failure.

REORGANIZATION

In 210 B.C., Roman author Petronius Arbiter wrote:

> We trained hard . . . . but every time we formed up teams we would be reorganized. I was to learn that we meet any new situation by reorganizing. And a wonderful method it can be for creating the illusion of progress while producing confusion, inefficiency and demoralization.

11 Coleen Rowley's disclosures to Congress, there has been a massive reorganization under way at the FBI, which of course, is a reorganization of Director Freeh's reorganization. Unfortunately, reorganizations are often window dressing that last as long as the current political appointee. A major cultural transformation is the only way to pull the Bureau out of its stodginess and allow it to function in an effective, lawful, and judicious manner. And when I refer to a cultural transformation, I mean a change that reaches from the executive ranks to the newest agent in the field and demands that all FBI employees be treated with respect and that all of the Bureau's employees' talents be leveraged, whether they are agents or not. If an individual can't con-

form to this, he or she should be fired, so the rest of the employees can do their jobs.

BUREAU FAMILY

The FBI should concentrate less on the Bureau family euphemism and more on building and sustaining a professional work environment. Psychologists who study retaliation and violence on the job say that setting up a workplace as a family is not always positive. The reason is that when a member is rejected or unhappy, they may feel that their family is turning against them, which provokes a deeper hurt than not liking a job. It would be a rather ugly metaphor to describe my career in terms of family. If so, it was definitely child abuse. As long as this legacy continues, it will be a legacy of decline.

Pride does not come from mere association with a group. Pride, as the Marine Corps and Army Rangers know, comes from consistent achievement. Thus, concentrating on creating a professional work environment where the goal is to achieve, rather than complain and blame, is a healthier goal than giving lip service to the concept of a fantasy FBI family.

CULTURAL CHANGES BEGIN AT THE ACADEMY

The tone for agent behavior is set in the academy, and the academy can drive cultural change. Since a relatively small number of agents teach at the academy, it would be a manageable task to monitor what is taught and how it is presented. Teaching at the academy should be a prestigious and coveted assignment and never a job for employees with a history of low performance or disciplinary actions. Never should an employee be "demoted" to the academy, as happened with Larry Potts of Ruby Ridge infamy.

THE FUTURE

The FBI has what it needs to create its own bright future. The resources are there, and from all indications, Director Mueller is a sincere and intelligent man who is trying to wrench the Bureau from the grasp of its self-destructive culture. The Bureau has the potential to be an exhilarating place to work, and I have fond memories of dear friends and hardworking colleagues who are so dedicated that they risk their lives fighting for what they believe. They deserve better and so does the nation.

AFTERWORD

You matter because you are you. You matter to the very last moment
of your life.

Dr. Cecily Saunders
St. Christopher's Hospital
London, England

For the nearly ten years I worked as a government consultant, I
also served as a patient-care volunteer at a Virginia hospice, providing emotional and physical attention to the dying and their
family members. That experience felt so right for me that I quit my job
and went to nursing school.

As a hospice nurse, death has a place in my life that's not all bad, but
some days are more difficult than others. I recall one particular day. I
was exhausted and dreaded what the shift might bring. It was a new job,
but it stirred up familiar old memories: memories of children, their
faces, their questions, their pain. A child's anguish is the same whether
a parent dies at hospice or is killed in the line of duty.

A fellow FBI agent once observed that there is something about a
catastrophe that made me glow, and he was right. The shouting, running, physical outbursts of arrests or even the pressure of organizing an
onslaught of raw data during a terrorist attack into a logical case presentation that the attorney general's office wants *right now*—those things
sharpened my senses and honed my concentration to the point that I

believed I could achieve the impossible. Hospice emergencies are not the driving, pushing, pounding kind. They're poignant and intimate confrontations you don't brag about to the guys over a beer. Even the famous dark humor so common to law enforcement and medical personnel doesn't cut it at hospice. Death and grief are to be faced and discussed openly, honestly, yet with compassion. This requires a special kind of bravery that comes from deep in the soul, not from the adrenal glands.

I am often asked: What was the most frightening moment in your law enforcement career? I've yet to come up with an answer that satisfies the movie-trained imagination. Juiced on the excitement of emergencies and confident in my undercover assignments, I never felt true fear until Doug Abram was killed in the line of duty. At that point, my perspective on life and death changed forever.

If you ask me the most frightening thing about hospice work, the answer is easy: facing a six-year-old child whose mother is dying and explaining that, though no one ever told him how sick mommy truly is, her death will occur within minutes or hours, then answering a few questions, and taking his hand, and standing with him while it happens.

At hospice, I sometimes get a glimpse of heaven when I am privileged to share that most intimate passage from this world to the next. It is much different from death in the context of law enforcement where life was brutally snatched away leaving me empty and unsettled, doomed to an eternity of "what ifs." What if I'd been there when he kicked through the door and the bullet lodged in his head? What if I'd been there to hold his hand through those final minutes when the doctors withdrew life support? It's not that the "what ifs" don't occur to people whose loved ones die after lengthy illness. It's just that sudden, unexpected death guarantees "what ifs."

When I was an FBI agent, I never knew what a day would bring. At hospice, there is a certain amount of predictability. I begin every morning in the same way, with a quick check of each room to determine whether a patient is in crisis. If not, I draw the morning meds and begin physical assessments. On the day I'm remembering, the patient in the first room was sleeping peacefully. His breathing was rhythmic and his color good, so I closed the door and moved on down the hall where a woman in her seventies was actively dying. She was pale and exhibiting Cheyne-Stokes breathing, a pattern that alternates rapid breaths with periods of apnea, during which the person doesn't breathe at all. Her husband sat beside her bed, with her hand in his, and I could see that the tips of her fingers were blue, often a prelude to death. Holding my voice to a whisper, I asked whether he needed anything. He looked up and shook his head. "We're fine," he said sadly, not taking his hand from hers.

I closed the door and moved on. Next was a man I'd come to know and enjoy over the weeks he'd been my patient. Only a year younger than I, he had pancreatic cancer and a grossly swollen belly. This man had lived a hard life, and in our younger days, he might have been someone I arrested. But times change, and he changed. He'd become religious and now lived his days with faith and hope. This morning, his labored breathing could be heard from the door. It bubbled and rolled as if he were breathing through water. When I laid my stethoscope on his chest, I couldn't hear his heart over the clatter of his respiratory system. The pulses in his arms and feet were weak, and his feet had a blotchy bruised look that had begun to spread up the back of his legs. I knew he could die at any time; at most he'd last a few more hours.

I was prepared for his passage from this life to the next, somewhat glad even, because his immense physical pain would end. However, on the roll-away bed beside him was the reason that day razored my heart: his teenaged son. It was my job to wake him and guide him through his last good-byes. When I called his name, the boy sat bolt upright and turned toward his father's bed.

"Is he dying?" the boy asked, looking at me like the son of every cop killed in the line of duty.

"Not right this minute, David, but I think he could at any time."

By now David was standing, so I moved to his side. I'd keep the father comfortable, but the son was now my patient, too.

"David," I began as gently as I could, "here's what I see."

I showed him the mottled feet and legs, then explained that when the body is in extreme crisis it can close off the blood supply to nonessential areas, such as the hands, feet, and bowels, shunting circulation to the vital organs and brain. This causes the blotchy-bruised look of mottling. It's not like in the movies, I told him. His father would likely breathe slower and slower, sometimes holding his breath for long periods, until at last he breathed no more. It is the body's process of slowing down, which would make his father appear to be falling into an increasingly deeper sleep. I assured him it wouldn't be frightening and that his father wouldn't look much different, although his face might move after death in a reflex action.

I asked David whether he had any questions, and he shook his head. Tears rolled from the corners of his eyes, and he sank to his father's bed. I sat beside him with my arm around him. I said nothing, but I, too, wept.

Children in grief—for me their faces fade, only to be recalled at the oddest times. There was a cute little girl, eight or nine years old, dressed in a shade of pink that accented her milky white skin and blond hair. She wrote an unforgettable poem for her father, a police officer now dead from a criminal's bullet. When she stood to read it for the grief counseling group, she was adorably chubby and squeezable, feminine and a little flirty. Her giggle charmed the room of children and adults. That's one thing about children in grief: they can laugh one minute and cry the next.

"My daddy was fun," she read. "He made me laugh. My daddy got shot, and now he's dead." Suddenly her shoulders tightened and without looking up, she raised the paper to cover her face and whimpered until someone put an arm around her shoulder and guided her back to her seat.

My spirit is not always tough. I cry when my hospice patients die and when their families hurt but, for me, it's better than the mask I wore as a special agent of the FBI.

BIBLIOGRAPHY

NEWSPAPERS AND PUBLICATIONS
Christian Science Monitor
Fort Wayne News-Sentinel
IEEE Spectrum
The New York Times
The Denver Post
The Nation
The Rocky Mountain News
Time Magazine
The Washington Post

SELECTED INTERNET SITES
Anarchy Archives Online Research Center on the History and Theory of Anarchism: http://dwardmac.pitzer.edu/anarchist_archives
CBS News online: www.cbsnews.com
Chicago Historical Society online projects, The Dramas of Haymarket: www.chicagohistory.org
CNN online: www.cnn.com
ECK online: www.eck.com
Federal Bureau of Investigation: www.fbi.gov
Federation of American Scientists: www.fas.org
Findlaw: www.findlaw.com
FortWayne.com: www.fortwayne.com/mld/newssentinel
Geocities, What is Anarchism?: www.geocities.com
Government Accountability Project online: www.whistleblowers.org
MSNBC online: www.msnbc.com
Newsmax: www.newsmax.com
Proquest: www.proquest.com
Public Broadcasting System online: www.pbs.com
Socialism and Man in Cuba: http://chehasta.narod.ru/socman.htm
Southern Poverty Law Center: www.splcenter.org
The New York Times: www.nytimes.com
The Washington Post online: www.washingtonpost.com

Time Online Edition: www.time.com
United States Department of Defense Security Service online: www.dss.mil
United States Department of Justice: www.usdoj.gov
United States Government Accounting Office: www.gao.gov
United States Immigration and Naturalization Service: www.ins.usdoj.gov
United States Office of Personnel Management: www.opm.gov
Yale University Law web: www.yale.edu/lawweb

BOOKS AND CITED REFERENCES:

Paul Avrich. *Anarchist Portraits.* Princeton, New Jersey: The Princeton University Press, 1988.

Paul Avrich. *Sacco and Vanzetti The Anarchist Background.* Princeton, New Jersey: The Princeton University Press, 1991.

Paul Avrich. *The Haymarket Tragedy.* Princeton, New Jersey: The Princeton University Press, 1984.

Dietrich Bonhoeffer. *Letters and Papers from Prison.* New York: Collier Books, 1953.

Allen W. Dulles. *The Craft of Intelligence.* Westport, Connecticut: Greenwood Press, 1963.

Hugh Heclo. *A Government of Strangers: Executive Politics in Washington.* Washington, DC: Brookings Institution, 1977.

J. Edgar Hoover, *A Study of Communism.* New York: Holt, Rinehart and Winston, 1963.

Intelligence Activities And The Rights of Americans Book II, Final Report of The Select Committee To Study Governmental Operations With Respect To Intelligence Activities United States Senate Together with Additional, Supplemental, and Separate Views, Part II. The Growth of Domestic Intelligence: 1936 to 1976. United States Government Printing Office, 1976.

Robert J. Lamphere, Tom Shachtman. *The FBI-KGB War: A Special Agent's Story.* New York: Random House, 1986.

George Orwell. *1984.* New York: Signet Classic, 1961 (Harcourt, Brace, Jovanovich, Inc., 1949).

Duško Popov. *Spy/Counterspy.* New York: Crosset and Dunlop, 1974.

Katherine Anne Porter. *The Never-Ending Wrong.* Boston, Massachusetts: Little, Brown and Company, 1977.

Richard Gid Powers. *Secrecy and Power: The Life of J. Edgar Hoover.* New York: The Free Press, 1987.

Eugenia Semyonovna Ginsburg. *Journey Into the Whirlwind.* New York: Harcourt, Brace & World, Inc., 1967.

Joseph L. Schott. *No Left Turns: The FBI in Peace & War.* New York: Praeger Publishing, 1975.

Athan G. Theoharis, Tony G. Poveda, Susan Rosenfeld, Richard Gid Powers. *The FBI: A Comprehensive Reference Guide From J. Edgar Hoover to the X-Files.* New York: The Oryx Press, 2000.
Don Whitehead. *The F.B.I. Story.* New York: Random House, 1956.
Weather Underground. *Prairie Fire: The Politics of Revolutionary Ant-Imperialism,* (Communications Co., San Francisco), 1974.

ENDNOTES

Introduction

x "The famed FBI laboratory charged with fabricating findings that impact more than 3,000 criminal cases . . .": "Errors at F.B.I. May Be Issue In 3,000 Cases," *The New York Times*, March 17, 2003. Retrieved from the www.nytimes.com on April 12, 2003.

x "In August 2001, Special Agent John E. Roberts said . . .": George Lardner Jr. and Dan Eggen, "Top FBI Officials Facing Inquiry Retaliation Alleged in Ruby Ridge Probe," *The Washington Post*, August 9, 2001, A1. Retrieved from www.washingtonpost.com on June 30, 2002.

xi "Democratic Senator Patrick J. Leahy of Vermont said, "It appears from this that the 'good old boy' network . . .": George Lardner Jr., "Censure of Freeh Was Secretly Rejected: Review of FBI's Flawed Ruby Ridge Probes had Prompted Disciplinary Recommendation," *The Washington Post*, August 5, 2001. Retrieved from www.washingtonpost.com on June 30, 2002.

xi "in November 2001, he felt it necessary to distribute an agency-wide memorandum extending his personal guarantee of protection . . .": "Congressional Panel to Probe FBI Agent's Claim That HQ Hindered Moussaoui Investigation," Associated Press, May 24. 2002. Retrieved from www.washingtonpost.com on May 24, 2002.

xii "expect to be dismissed . . .": Louis J. Freeh, "A Report to the American People on the Work of the FBI 1993-1998, "Director Chapter 1: Law Enforcement Ethics and Fairness." Retrieved from www.fbi.gov on April 5, 2003.

Chapter 3: Welcome to the FBI

20 "massive holes in the FBI's command structure and in its record-keeping capabilities . . .": "Ashcroft Orders Comprehensive Review of FBI," NewsMax.com Wires, June 21, 2001. Retrieved from www.newsmax.com/archives/articles/2001/6/20/160742.shtml on July 1, 2002.

Chapter 4: Life in the Academy

29 "Sharing exculpatory evidence with the defense . . .": According to the US Department of Justice Office of the Inspector General, "An Investigation of

the Belated Production of Documents in the Oklahoma City Bombing Case," March 19, 2002, retrieved from www.usdoj.gov/oig/special/02-03/chapter4.htm on July 31, 2003.:

> In all criminal trials, the government, which is prosecuting the defendants, must provide certain information to the defense prior to trial. In the federal system, discovery is governed by Rule 16 of the Federal Rules of Criminal Procedure; the Jencks Act, codified at 18 U.S.C. § 3500; and case law, the most significant of which is the Supreme Court decision of Brady v. Maryland, 373 U.S. 83 (1963). In general, these rules and court decisions require that the government provide the defense with all evidence that will be used at trial, the statements of individuals who will testify during the trial, and evidence in the possession of the government that is materially favorable to the defense, including information indicating that the defendant did not commit the crime charged and evidence that could be used by the defense to impeach the government's witnesses. In essence, these rules require the government to disclose some information about its case to the defense, but the defense is not entitled to review the government's entire case file.
>
> Although the broad outlines of discovery are the same in all federal trials, actual discovery practices vary considerably depending on the practices of district courts and the United States Attorneys' Offices. In some areas, federal prosecutors allow the defense to view most of the case file while in other jurisdictions the discovery is limited.
>
> The question of what constitutes exculpatory information required to be disclosed to the defense, commonly referred to as Brady information, is the source of most discovery problems. The main responsibility for reviewing the prosecution file and disclosing Brady information rests with the prosecutors. In certain instances, a judge may review material and make a ruling as to whether it needs to be disclosed to the defense. The government commits prosecutorial error if it fails to disclose information to which the defense is entitled, and the defense may allege that the government has violated its discovery obligations even after a conviction. In some instances, the error may be so egregious that the court determines that the defendant did not receive a fair trial, reverses the conviction, and grants the defendant a new trial.

30 "Strangely, the agent who confirmed this oversight in March 2001, did not report the problem to headquarters until May 7, 2001.": US Department of

Justice Office of the Inspector General, "An Investigation of the Belated Production of Documents in the Oklahoma City Bombing Case," March 19, 2002, retrieved from www.usdoj.gov/oig/special/02-03/chapter4.htm on July 31, 2003.

30 "He claimed that he planned to report the problem, but only after he determined the scope of it.": US Department of Justice Office of the Inspector General, "An Investigation of the Belated Production of Documents in the Oklahoma City Bombing Case," March 19, 2002, retrieved from www.usdoj.gov/oig/special/02-03/chapter4.htm on July 31, 2003.

Chapter 5: My First Field Assignment
37 "The revolution is made by man . . .".: Chè Guevara, Socialism and Man in Cuba, http://chehasta.narod.ru/socman.htm.

42 Each Special Agent must have the confidence . . . FBI memorandum, *Justification for Limiting the Position of Special Agent in the FBI to Males*, May 19, 1971, p. 3.

47 "According to *Prairie Fire: The Politics of Revolutionary Anti-Imperialism , . .*": Weather Underground, Prairie Fire: The Politics of Revolutionary Ant-Imperialism, (Communications Co., San Francisco), 1974, p. 16.

50 "Our intention is to engage the enemy . . .".: "According to *Prairie Fire: The Politics of Revolutionary Anti-Imperialism . . .*": Weather Underground, *Prairie Fire: The Politics of Revolutionary Anti-Imperialism*, (Communications Co., San Francisco), 1974, p. 10.

50 "Remarks prepared for delivery by Robert S. Mueller III, Director, Federal Bureau of Investigation at the Dedication of the Martha Dixon FBI Field Office Pittsburgh, Pennsylvania," November 20, 2001. Retrieved from www.fbi.gov/pressrel/speeches/dixon.htm Wide on May 26, 2002.

51 "she 'was very much an agent. Not a female agent, but an agent . . .".: Steve Twomey, "The Call That Never Came," *The Washington Post*, December 1, 1994, Page d1.

Chapter 6: A New Meaning to Undercover
55 "Doublethink means the power of holding two . . .".: George Orwell, 1984, New York: Harcourt, Brace, Jovanovich, Inc., 1949, p. 176.

59 "officers need to learn when to keep their mouths shut . . .".: Allen Dulles, *The Craft of Intelligence,* Westport, Connecticut, Greenwood Press, p. 173.

60 "Describing the case's twisted details . . .".: Leef Smith, "Defense Says Ex-Agent was Driven Insane by Work, Worry," *The Washington Post*, January 29, 1997. Retrieved from www.proquest.com on August 14, 2001.

Chapter 7: Boys' Clubhouse: No Girls Allowed
61 "the tendency of some female rookie police . . .": Retrieved from www.wordspy.com/words/JaneWaynesyndrome.asp on May 26, 2003.

Chapter 8: Life is Stranger Than Fiction
67 "It's not the large things . . .": Charles Bukowski, *The Shoelace. Retrieved* from http://www.artdamage.com/buk/shoelace.htm on August 24, 2003.
69 "The Ryan assassination fell within the Bureau's jurisdiction . . .": The FBI's prosecutive report that summarizes the FBI's investigation from November 18, 1978 through January 12, 1979, is available online through the FBI's Freedom of Information Electronic Reading Room at www.fbi.gov.

Chapter 9: Back in the USSR
71 "During those years I experienced many conflicting feelings . . .": Eugenia Semyonovna Ginzburg, *Into the Whirlwind*, New York: Harcourt, Brace & World, Inc., 1967, p. 436.

Chapter 13: Cruel Intentions
95 "Once in a while you find yourself in an odd situation. . ." Thor Heyerdahl, *Kon Tiki*, New York: Washington Square Press, 1950, p. 1.

Chapter 14: New Lessons Learned
101 "The thoughts of a prisoner—they're not free either. . .": Alexander Solzhenitsyn, *One Day in the Life of Ivan Denisovitch*, New York: New American Library, 1963, p. 47.

Chapter 15: Smart Woman, Another Foolish Choice
105 "I am amazed and astounded . . ." Joseph Schott, *No Left Turns*, New York: Praeger Publishing, 1977, p. 4.

Chapter 16: Life in Hooverland
117 "The political challenge of communism springs from Lenin's conviction that power, not law, is decisive.": Hoover, J. Edgar, *A Study of Communism*, Holt, Rinehart and Winston, New York, 1962.
121 "The FBI began to suspect that Philby was a traitor in 1951 . . . ": Robert J. Lamphere, Tom Shachtman, *The FBI-KGB War: A Special Agent's Story*, Random House, New York, 1986, p. 239.
122 "The story goes that the Germans had given Popov about $80,000 . . .": Duško Popov, *Spy/Counterspy*, Crosset and Dunlop, New York, 1974, pp. 150-152.

122 "Popov took up residence in the United States . . . ": Du_ko Popov, *Spy/Counterspy*, Crosset and Dunlop, New York, 1974, center photo insert.

122 "transporting a woman across state lines for immoral purposes . . .": Duško Popov, *Spy/Counterspy*, Crosset and Dunlop, New York, 1974,, pp. 166-167. The FBI had jurisdiction in the Mann Act, which is also known as the White Slavery Act.

Chapter 17: Terrorism: A Walk on the Wild Side

123 "The U.S. Government continues its commitment to use all tools necessary . . .": United States Department of State, Patterns of Global Terrorism: 1999. Retrieved from http://www.state.gov on June 13, 2001.

124 "The PLF had splintered into three groups . . .": Associated Press, "Eccentric Force Claims Hijacking" *The Washington Post*, October 9, 1985.

127 "Abu Abbas, who was carrying an Iraqi diplomatic passport . . .": "Achille Lauro Hijacker Nabbed in Iraq," April 16, 2003. Retrieved from www.cbsnews.com on May 1, 2004.

127 "to board a waiting Yugoslav JAT Airways plane, despite the U.S. warrant for his arrest . . .": Loren Jenkins, "U.S. Protests Abbas' Departure After Issue of Arrest Warrant," *The Washington Post*, October 13, 1985.

128 "The United States warrant against Abbas for piracy, hostagetaking, and conspiracy . . .": CNN, "U.S. mulls legal options after Abbas capture," April 17, 2003. Retrieved from www.cnn.com on May 4, 2003.

Chapter 18: Rocky Mountain Highlights

129 "There was an atmosphere of endeavor, of expectancy and bright hopefulness . . ." Willa Cather, *My Ántonia*, Boston, Massachusetts: Houghton Mifflin Company, 1918, p. 258.

129 "the Bureau used the Mann Act to arrest and prosecute . . .": "The 'Lawless' Years (1921-1933)." Retrieved from www.fbi.gov/libref/historic/history/lawless.htm on March 7, 2002.

130 "The FBI was not able to arrest Louisiana Klan leader Edward Clarke for murder or racial violence, but they were able to get him on morals charges . . .": Don Whitehead, *The F.B.I. Story*, (Random House, New York), 1956, p. 62.

130 "stirred disunity and resulted in the Klan's decline in political power . . .": Athan G. Theoharis, ed., *The FBI: A Comprehensive Reference Guide*, (Checkmark Books, New York), 2000, p. 47.

131 There are two kinds of FBI offices. The larger offices are known as "headquarters city offices," for example Denver, which covered Colorado and Wyoming, is a headquarters city office. If a territory is large, there are often

smaller offices in outlying areas of the division, which are known as resident agencies. The agents assigned to resident agencies are called resident agents.

Chapter 19: Hate Comes in Many Forms

141 ". . . at night you feel strange things . . .": D.H. Lawrence, Letter from Germany, 1924.

144 An excellent resource on white supremacists and other hate groups is the Southern Poverty Law Center at www.splcenter.org.

145 "in 1985, Denver police had identified 30 skinheads, but by 1991, there were 400 . . .": Lisa Levitt Ryckman, "Episodes of Hatred Pock States History: Skinheads May be Trying to Revive Venomous Revolt," *The Rocky Mountain News*, November 23, 1997.

146 "Thill, then nineteen-years old, confessed to the two shootings during a television interview . . .": Howard Pankratz, "Prosecutors Play Thill Tape," *The Denver Post*, November 20, 1999, Page: B-01.

146-47 "the procedure for use of ricin and DMSO can also be found in the *al Qaeda Jihad Training Manual* . . .": al Qaeda Jihad Training Manual, "Lesson 16: Assassinations." Retrieved from www.usdoj.gov/ag/trainingmanual.htm on May 23, 2003.

The manual was seized by the Manchester (England) Metropolitan Police during a search of an Al Qaeda member's home. It was found in a computer file described as "the military series" related to the "Declaration of Jihad."

Chapter 22: Knowing When to Leave

165 "When you've deliberately suppressed every desire . . .": Dietrich Bonhoeffer, *Letters and Papers from Prison*, (Collier Books, New York), 1953, p. 312.

Chapter 23: The Formative Years

169 "When a reporter from a newspaper here in Maryland . . .": Katherine Anne Porter, *The Never-Ending Wrong*, Boston, Massachusetts: Little, Brown and Company, 1977, Foreword.

171 "the government inserted provisions into the Immigration Act of March 3, 1903 . . .": *Immigration Act of March 3, 1903*. Retrieved from www.ins.usdoj.gov/graphics/aboutins/statistics/LegisHist/457.htm

172 "of the 45 million people who comprised the 1877 U.S. population . . .": Paul Avrich. *The Haymarket Tragedy*, (The Princeton University Press, Princeton, NJ), 1984, p. 16.

172 "Anarchist philosophy was propagated by 19th century French writer . . .": Pierre Joseph Proudhon, *What is Property*, 1840, p. 264. Retrieved from www.geocities.com/CapitolHill/1931/secA1.html#seca11 on May 10, 2002.

172 "Anarchist rhetoric was violent, with dynamite touted as the great equalizer. . . .": Retrieved from www.chicagohistory.org/hadc/artifacts.html on May 13, 2002.

173 "Some newspapers advocated using grenades to clear the crowds, and it was during this period that armories were established in the center of U.S. cities . . .": Paul Avrich, op. cit., pp. 35-37.

173 "Before the month was over, a grand jury had indicted 31 people. . . .": Paul Avrich, op. cit., p. 279.

175 "Due to the war, President Wilson revived the July 6, 1798, Act Respecting Alien Enemies . . .": *An Act Respecting Alien Enemies*, Sections 1-3, United States, 1798, www.yale.edu/lawweb/avalon/statutes/alien.htm.

175 "resulted in detentions that are reminiscent of the anarchist era . . .": United States Department of Justice Office of the Inspector General, *The September 11 Detainees: A Review of the Treatment of Aliens Held on Immigration Charges in Connection with the Investigation of the September 11 Attacks*, April, 2003. Retrieved from www.usdoj.gov on June 7, 2003.

175 "This is because the guidelines for processing illegal aliens . . .": United States Department of Justice Office of the Inspector General, *The September 11 Detainees: A Review of the Treatment of Aliens Held on Immigration Charges in Connection with the Investigation of the September 11 Attacks*, April, 2003. Retrieved from www.usdoj.gov on June 7, 2003.

176 "Historians disagree as to whether he was, at the time, an attorney or a special agent of the Bureau of Investigation (BOI). . . .": Richard Gid Powers, *Secrecy and Power: The Life of J. Edgar Hoover*. (New York, NY: The Free Press, 1987), pp. 42-43.

176 "where his job was investigating suspected anarchists and communists . . .": "FBI Directors," retrieved from www.fbi.gov/libref/directors/directmain.htm on May 22, 2002.

176 "Hoover entered on duty with the Department of Justice . . .": "FBI Directors," retrieved from www.fbi.gov/libref/directors/directmain.htm on May 22, 2002.

176 "The wartime BOI augmented its forces with a group of citizen volunteers known as the American Protective League . . .": Richard Gid Powers, *Secrecy and Power: The Life of J. Edgar Hoover*. (New York, NY: The Free Press, 1987), p. 43.

176 "the Bureau gave 260,000 citizens badges . . .": Richard Gid Powers, *Secrecy and Power: The Life of J. Edgar Hoover*. (New York, NY: The Free Press, 1987), p.44.

176-77 "Repressive practices during World War I included . . .": *Intelligence Activities And The Rights of Americans Book II, Final Report of The Select Com-*

mittee To Study Governmental Operations With Respect To Intelligence Activities United States Senate Together with Additional, Supplemental, and Separate Views April 26 (legislative day, April 14), 1976, Part II. The Growth of Domestic Intelligence: 1936 to 1976, Footnote 1, p. 21.

177 "the leading, organizing detective of America . . .": "FBI Directors," retrieved from www.fbi.gov/libref/directors/directmain.htm on May 22, 2002.

177 "massive raids by law enforcement officials in several cities . . .": Athan G. Theoharis et al, *The FBI: A comprehensive Reference Guide,* (Checkmark Books, New York), 2000, p. 9.

178 "Did you see what I did with those anarchistic bastards the other day?" . . .": *The Sacco-Vanzetti Case: Transcript of the Record of the Trial of Nicola Sacco and Bartolomeo Vanzetti in the Courts of Massachusetts and Subsequent Proceedings, 1920-7,* 6 vols. (Henry Holt, New York), 1928-1929, V, 5065. Quoted in Paul Avrich. Sacco and Vanzetti: The Anarchist Background. (The Princeton University Press, Princeton, New Jersey), 1991, p.1.

Chapter 24: Crucibles

181 Constitution of the United States, First Amendment. "Congress shall make no law respecting an establishment of religion, or prohibiting the free exercise thereof; or abridging the freedom of speech, or of the press; or the right of the people peaceably to assemble, and to petition the government for a redress of grievances."

182 " . . .": *Intelligence Activities And The Rights of Americans Book II, Final Report of The Select Committee To Study Governmental Operations With Respect To Intelligence Activities United States Senate Together with Additional, Supplemental, and Separate Views April 26 (legislative day, April 14), 1976, COINTELPRO* Annex, p. 1.

182 "forbid or proscribe advocacy of the use of force . . .": *COINTELPRO* Annex, p. 2.

183 "The unexpressed major premise of the program . . .": *COINTELPRO* Annex, p. 3

183 "they defended the use of the classic four-letter-word . . .": *COINTELPRO* Annex, p. 3.

183 "In short, the programs were to prevent violence . . .": *COINTELPRO* Annex, p. 10.

183 "President Roosevelt gave the FBI the power to wiretap individuals . . .": *Intelligence Activities And The Rights of Americans Book II, Final Report of The Select Committee To Study Governmental Operations With Respect To Intelligence Activities United States Senate Together with Additional, Supplemental, and Separate Views April 26 (legislative day, April 14) , 1976, p. 4.*

184 "Hoover's account of a 1936 meeting . . .": *Intelligence Activities And The Rights of Americans Book II*, p. 6.

184 "In 1939, for instance, field offices were told to investigate . . .": *Intelligence Activities And The Rights of Americans Book II*, p. 6.

184 "The USA PATRIOT Act requires that . . .": Public Law 107-56, Uniting and Strengthening America by Providing Appropriate Tools Required to Intercept and Obstruct Terrorism (USA PATRIOT Act), Section 905A.

185 "The language inserted by the Act now permits wiretaps, surveillance . . .": Public Law 107-56, Section 218.

186 "the Israelis estimated that about 95 percent . . .": John Kifner, "Roots of Terror: A special report: Alms and Arms: Tactics in a Holy War," *The New York Times*, March 15, 1996. Retrieved from www.nytimes.com on June 8, 2003.

186 "In fact, in 2003, the Justice Department's Office of the Inspector General reviewed . . .": United States Department of Justice Office of the Inspector General, *The September 11 Detainees: A Review of the Treatment of Aliens Held on Immigration Charges in Connection with the Investigation of the September 11 Attacks*, April, 2003, p. 2. Retrieved from www.usdoj.gov on June 7, 2003.

187 "The FBI cleared less than 3 percent . . .": OIG, *The September 11 Detainees*, p. 51.

188 "A Muslim man in his 40s, . . .": OIG, *The September 11 Detainees*, pp. 71-72.

Chapter 25: Most Unwanted
192 "through GS-13 within five years, the total grows to a minimum of $76,564 . . .": Office of Personnel Management, "2003 General Schedule." Retrieved from www.opm.gov/oca/03tables/html/gs.asp on May 26, 2003.

193 "She further charged that he put her in a chokehold . . .": Athan G. Theoharis, et al, et al, *The FBI: A comprehensive Reference Guide*, (Checkmark Books, New York), 2000, p. 137.

193-94 "Another tragic example is the case of . . .": Richard Lacayo, "Bad Habits Die Hard: The FBI is accused of political snooping and racial harassment," *Time*, Feb. 8, 1988.

194 "One agent summed it up as: "These guys like to goof around . . .": Richard Lacayo, "Bad Habits Die Hard: The FBI is accused of political snooping and racial harassment," *Time*, Feb. 8, 1988.

194 "To the Bureau's shame, a federal mediator had to be appointed in 2001 . . .": Bill Miller, "FBI Settlement Gives Black Agents Access to Mediator," *The Washington Post*, May 1, 2001; Page A21

195 "a system that minority agents have frequently said was slow . . .": David

Johnston, "Five Minority Agents File Bias Lawsuit Against Bureau September 26, 2002," *The New York Times*, September 26, 2002. Retrieved from www.nytimes.com/2002/09/26/national/26BURE.html?ex=1034085835&ei=1&en=10633cd75749a656

Chapter 26: Three Who Lost Their Way

202 "According to the affidavit for his arrest, he was sworn in . . .": United States of America v. Edwin Earl Pitts, Affidavit in Support of Criminal Complaint, Arrest Warrant and Search Warrants, filed in The United States District Court for the Eastern District Of Virginia, Alexandria, Virginia, December 17, 1996.

202-3 "According to a joint press release of the FBI and United States Attorney's Office . . .": Joint press release of the FBI and United States Attorney's Office, Eastern District of Virginia, December 18, 1996. Retrieved from www.fas.org/irp/offdocs/pitts_nr.htm on May 26, 2003.

203 "When you give a lesson in meanness to a critter or a person . . .": "The Wisdom of Will Rogers." Retrieved from www.eck.com/personal/will-rogers.html on June 21, 2003.

203 In CIA terminology, an "agent" is an informant, not a CIA employee. Although the term "CIA agent" is synonymous with CIA officer in colloquial usage, officer is the correct designation for the employee. The FBI's and Secret Service's sworn law enforcement corps are called "special agents," not officers. Special agent of the government is a legal term that means someone who is authorized to act in the government's behalf in carrying out specifically stated duties. We had to memorize this definition in the Academy as a response to a common defense attorney trick, which was to get a rookie special agent on the stand and fire off the question, "What makes you so special?", hoping to make them fumble around for an answer and lose credibility.

203 "In a 1998 CNN interview, Aldrich Ames called his own acts banal and greedy . . .": "Rationalizing Treason." Retrieved from www.cnn.com/SPECIALS/cold.war/episodes/21/interviews/ames/ on July 18, 2002.

204 "Aleksandr Karpov, became a cooperating witness for the FBI . . .": Defense Security Service Security Research Center, *Recent Espionage Cases: 1975-1999: Summaries and Sources*, September 1999, p. 6. Retrieved from www.dss.mil/training/espionage on January 10, 2003.

204 "The Bureau also learned of Pitts' involvement from his wife . . .": United States of America v. Earl Edwin Pitts, Affidavit in Support of Criminal Complaint, Arrest Warrant, and Search Warrants, filed in the Untied States District Court Eastern District of Virginia on December 17, 1996.

204 "In May 2003, the Smith was indicted on six counts of fraud by wire . . .":

United States of America, Plaintiff, v. James J. Smith, Defendant. United States District Court for the Central District of California, June 2002 Grand Jury.

204 "Also indicted was Katrina Leung, a naturalized U.S. citizen . . .": United States Attorney, Central District of California, "'Double Agent' Arrested, Former F.B.I. 'Handler' Charged For Allowing Access to Classified Documents," April 9, 2003. Retrieved from www.usdoj.gov on May 23, 2003.

206 "The James J. Smith indictment describes proper storage . . .": *United States District Court for the Central District of California Grand Jury June 2002 Indictment, United States of America v. James J. Smith, Defendant.*, p. 4. Retrieved from news.findlaw.com/hdocs/docs/fbi/ussmith50703ind.pdf on June 20, 2003.

206 "In November 2000, three months before his arrest, . . .": U.S. Department of Justice Commission for Review of FBI Security Programs.

207 "Any clerk in the Bureau could come up with stuff . . .": U.S. Department of Justice Commission for Review of FBI Security Programs.

207 "*Recommendation No. 14: Detecting Improper Computer* . . .": U.S. Department of Justice Office of the Inspector General, "A Review of the FBI's Performance in Deterring, Detecting, and Investigating the Espionage Activities of Robert Philip Hanssen," August 2003, p. 31. Retrieved from www.usdoj.gov on August 15, 2003.

Chapter 27: Master Spy? I Think Not.

210 "Over the years, he held a number of responsible positions in the FBI . . .": United States of America v. Robert Philip Hanssen,)a/k/a "B" , a/k/a "Ramon Garcia" , a/k/a "Jim Baker" , a/k/a "G. Robertson", Affidavit in Support of Criminal Complaint, Arrest Warrant and Search Warrants, filed in The United States District Court for the Eastern District Of Virginia, Alexandria, Virginia, February 16, 2001.

210 "a company in New York run by an officer in the Soviet military intelligence service . . .": United States Department of Justice Commission for the Review of FBI Security Programs, *A Review of FBI Security Programs*, March 2002. Retrieved from www.usdoj.gov on May 23, 2003.

210 "One agent who knew him said Hanssen . . .": Tom Mangold, "When Betrayal and Paranoia Are Part of the Job," *The New York Times*, editorial, January 2, 2002.

211 "Hanssen's work responsibilities at OFM consumed no more than a few hours a day . . .": U.S. Department of Justice Office of the Inspector General, "A Review of the FBI's Performance in Deterring, Detecting, and Investi-

gating the Espionage Activities of Robert Philip Hanssen," August 2003, p. 8. Retrieved from www.usdoj.gov on August 15, 2003.

212 "In the period spanning 1985-1987 alone, he . . .": U.S. Department of Justice Commission for Review of FBI Security Programs.

212 "Examples from the OIG review of the Hanssen case . . .":

213 "An internal FBI report issued in this period [1985-1987] . . .": U.S. Department of Justice Commission for Review of FBI Security Programs.

214 "After learning that its two most important KGB assets had been arrested . . .": U.S. Department of Justice Office of the Inspector General, "A Review of the FBI's Performance," p. 18-19.

214 "In 1987, Hanssen was assigned to the Soviet Analytical Unit . . .": U.S. Department of Justice Office of the Inspector General, "A Review of the FBI's Performance," p. 8.

214-15 "Shortly after his return to the Unit, Hanssen committed a serious security breach . . .": U.S. Department of Justice Office of the Inspector General, "A Review of the FBI's Performance," p. 8.

215 "his brother-in-law FBI agent Mark Wauk attempted to file a report . . .": U.S. Department of Justice Office of the Inspector General, "A Review of the FBI's Performance," p. 14.

215 "The field offices complained . . .": U.S. Department of Justice Office of the Inspector General, "A Review of the FBI's Performance," p. 7.

216 "Hanssen installed unauthorized software on his office computers . . .": U.S. Department of Justice Office of the Inspector General, "A Review of the FBI's Performance," p. 8.

216 "As with Hanssen's other security violations . . .": U.S. Department of Justice Office of the Inspector General, "A Review of the FBI's Performance," p. 9.

217 "Hanssen's personality traits set him apart from his FBI colleagues . . .": U.S. Department of Justice Office of the Inspector General, "A Review of the FBI's Performance," p. 6.

217 "he did not know of other spies with certainty . . .": U.S. Department of Justice Commission for Review of FBI Security Programs.

218 "Finally, on January 13, 2001, Hanssen was promoted to SES . . .": United States of America v. Robert Philip Hanssen, a/k/a "B" , a/k/a "Ramon Garcia" , a/k/a "Jim Baker," a/k/a "G. Robertson", Affidavit in Support of Criminal Complaint, Arrest Warrant and Search Warrants, filed in The United States District Court for the Eastern District Of Virginia, Alexandria, Virginia, February 16, 2001.

218-19 "Between 1987 and 1991, the FBI suffered continuing losses of Soviet human assets . . .": U.S. Department of Justice Office of the Inspector General, "A Review of the FBI's Performance in Deterring, Detecting, and Investigating the Espionage Activities of Robert Philip Hanssen," August 2003, p. 20-22. Retrieved from www.usdoj.gov on August 15, 2003.

Chapter 28: Lack of Candor

222 "an edict that violated both FBI guidelines . . .": FBI Deadly Force Policy: "FBI Special Agents may use deadly force only when necessary—when the Special Agent has a reasonable belief that the subject of such force poses an imminent danger of death or serious physical injury to the Special Agent or another person. If feasible, a verbal warning to submit to the authority of the Special Agent shall be given prior to the use of deadly force." Retrieved from www.fbi.gov on June 15, 2003.

222 "Fourth Amendment restrictions on police power . . .": The use of deadly force to apprehend a suspect is considered to be a seizure under the Fourth Amendment. The Fourth Amendment states that "[t]he right of the people to be secure in their persons, houses, papers, and effects, against unreasonable searches and seizures, shall not be violated, and no Warrants shall issue, but upon probable cause, supported by Oath or affirmation, and particularly describing the place to be searched, and the persons or things to be seized."

223 "The denouement of the Potts saga was an FBI Academy training course . . .": United States General Accounting Office, GAO-02-189R, "FBI Investigation of Alleged Improper Conduct," December 21, 2001, p. 3.

224 "that three special agents in charge be issued letters of censure . . .": GAO-02-189R, p. 4.

224 "In January 1999, the deputy director adopted the SES Board's recommendations . . .": GAO-02-189R, p. 4.

224 "A fair and reasonable reading of the final OPR . . .": GAO-02-189R, p. 4.

225 "In a 2002 *60 Minutes* interview . . .": Ed Bradley, *FBI Whistleblower Harassed?* November 25, 2002. Retrieved from www.cbsnews.com on May 31, 2003.

225 "The Department of Justice's Office of the Inspector General (OIG) investigated . . .": U.S. Department of Justice Office of the Inspector General, *A Review of the FBI's Response to John Roberts' Statements on 60 Minutes*, February 2003, Conclusion. Retrieved from www.usdoj.gov on June 22, 2003.

226 "Roberts's troubles began when he concluded . . .": U.S. Department of Justice Office of the Inspector General, *A Review of the FBI's Response to John Roberts' Statements on 60 Minutes*, February 2003, Conclusion. Retrieved from www.usdoj.gov on June 22, 2003.

227 "Early on Monday, April 19 . . .": John C. Danforth, *Final Report to the Deputy Attorney General Concerning the 1993 Confrontation at the Mt. Carmel Complex Waco*, "D. Hostage Rescue Team," November 8, 2000, p. 9.

228-29 "Special counsel John C. Danforth stated in his preliminary report . . .": John C. Danforth, *Final Report to the Deputy Attorney General Concerning the 1993 Confrontation at the Mt. Carmel Complex Waco*, "D. Hostage Rescue Team," November 8, 2000, p. ii.

229 "HRT commander Rogers did, however, sit silently . . .": John C. Danforth, *Final Report to the Deputy Attorney General Concerning the 1993 Confrontation at the Mt. Carmel Complex Waco*, "D. Hostage Rescue Team," November 8, 2000, pp. 57-58.

230-232 "This is Director Freeh's "bright line" policy in his own words . . .": Louis J. Freeh, *A Report to the American People on the Work of the FBI 1993 - 1998, Chapter 1: Law Enforcement Ethics and Fairness*. Retrieved from www.fbi.gov/publications/5-year/1993-98/report4.htm on June 7, 2002.

Chapter 29: The Thin Line Between Cops and Criminals

233 "special agent Jane Turner, who was assigned the task of investigating thefts . . .": Jerry Seper, "Senators Warn FBI against retaliation," *The Washington Times*, October 23, 2002. Retrieved from www.whistlblowers.org on May 27, 2003.

234 "In an April 29, 2003, interview with Lisa Myers of NBC News . . .": Lisa Myers, "FBI agent under fire—from agency: Turner blew whistle on Ground Zero Theft." Retrieved from www.msnbc.com/ on May 27, 2003.

234 "contrast to that of Special Agent Halbert Gary Harlow, who served as a firearms instructor at the FBI Academy from 1980 to 1991 . . .": Charles W. Hall, "FBI Says it Fired Agent for Falsifying Reports," *The Washington Post*, December 16, 1995. Retrieved from www.proquest.com on August 14, 2002.

235 "falsifying findings in big-name cases, such as the Oklahoma City bombing . . .": John Solomon, "Probe of FBI Lab's DNA Analysis Expanded; Officials Say Inquiry Has Already Led to Changes," Associated Press, April 27, 2003.

235-36 "protected and (in Flemmi's case) participated in a criminal enterprise . . .": FBI Boston press release, "Superseding Indictment Charges Former Agent Connolly and Former FBI Informant Flemmi," Retrieved from boston.fbi.gov/pressrel/2000/superseding.htm on June 14, 2003.

237 "Presented as part of Connolly's defense . . .": Denise Lavoie, "Ex-FBI Agent Convicted of Aiding Mob," Associated Press, May 28, 2002. Retrieved from www.fortwayne.com/mld/newssentinel/3352854.htm on June 14, 2003.

237 "You can get friendly with them . . .": Denise Lavoie, "Ex-FBI Agent Convicted of Aiding Mob," Associated Press, May 28, 2002. Retrieved from www.fortwayne.com/mld/newssentinel/3352854.htm on June 14, 2003.

237-38 "James J. Bulger is being sought for his role . . .": Retrieved from www.fbi.gov/mostwant/topten/fugitives/bulger.htm on June 1, 2003.

Chapter 30: No Justice from Justice

240 "We concluded that the FBI has not effectively managed . . .": U.S. Department of Justice Office of the Inspector General Audit Division, "Federal Bureau of Investigation's Management of Information Technology Investments," December 2001, p. 3.

244 "As Hugh Heclo points out . . .": Heclo, Hugh. *A Government of Strangers: Executive Politics in Washington.* Washington, DC: Brookings Institution, 1977, p. 143.

244 "an April 2003 Institute of Electrical and Electronics Engineers *Spectrum* . . .": Jean Kumagai, "Mission Impossible?" *IEEE Spectrum*, April 2003, p. 29.

244 "The fact that handwritten notes scanned as images are not electronically searchable . . .": Jean Kumagai, "Mission Impossible?" *IEEE Spectrum*, April 2003, p. 29.

244 "Today, more than two years after Hanssen's arrest, . . .": OIG, p. 24.

Chapter 31: Why the FBI Can't Play Well With Others

248 "Rowley wrote in her letter that Minneapolis had identified two potential criminal violations . . .": Coleen Rowley, Memo to FBI Director Robert Mueller, May 21, 2002.

248 "While FBI headquarters found the evidence presented . . .": Coleen Rowley, Memo to FBI Director Robert Mueller, May 21, 2002.

249 "Also intertwined with my reluctance in this case . . .": Coleen Rowley, Memo to FBI Director Robert Mueller, May 21, 2002.

249 "Among the evidence that agents found during the search . . .": The United States District Court for the Eastern District of Virginia Alexandria Division, 2002 Term Grand Jury Superceding Indictment of Zacarias Moussaoui, a/k/a "Shaqil," "Abu Khalid al Sharawri," Defendant. The counts of the indictment were Conspiracy to Commit Acts of Terrorism Transcending National Boundaries (18 U.S.C. §§ 2332b(a)(2) & (c)), Conspiracy to Commit Aircraft Piracy (49 U.S.C. §§ 46502(a)(1)(A) and (a)(2)(B)), Conspiracy to Destroy Aircraft (18 U.S.C. §§ 32(a)(7) & 34), Conspiracy to Use Weapons of Mass Destruction (18 U.S.C. §§ 2332a(a)), Conspiracy to Murder United States Employees (18 U.S.C. §§ 1114 & 1117), Conspiracy to Destroy Property (18 U.S.C. §§ 844(f), (1), (n)). Retrieved from www.findlaw.com on June 21, 2003.

250 "A November 9, 2001, *New York Times* article . . .": W. J. Broad, D. John-

ston, J. Miller and P. Zielbauer, "Experts see F.B.I. missteps hampering anthrax inquiry," *New York Times*, November 9, 2001.

250 "After being interviewed by the FBI, laboratory officials asked . . .": W. J. Broad, D. Johnston, J. Miller and P. Zielbauer, "Experts see F.B.I. missteps hampering anthrax inquiry," *New York Times*, November 9, 2001.

251 "The Bureau opened the National Infrastructure Protection Center (NIPC) . . .": "Presidential Decision Directive 63 Fact Sheet." Retrieved from www.fas.org/irp/offdocs/pdd-63.htm on May 23, 2002.

251 "telecommunications, energy, banking and finance, transportation, water systems and emergency services . . .": "White Paper on The Clinton Administration's Policy on Critical Infrastructure Protection: Presidential Decision Directive 63," www.fas.org/irp/offdocs/paper598.htm, May 22, 1998. Retrieved from the World Wide Web on July 18, 2002.

251 "The General Accounting Office (GAO) conducts continuing analyses . . .": General Accounting Office, *Critical Infrastructure Protection: Significant Challenges in Developing Analysis, Warning, and Response Capabilities* (GAO-01-1005T), July 25, 2001, p. 1.

252 "the key assets recorded may not be the ones that infrastructure owners consider . . .": General Accounting Office, *Critical Infrastructure Protection: Significant Challenges in Developing Analysis, Warning, and Response Capabilities* (GAO-01-1005T), July 25, 2001, p. 8.

252-53 "The FBI's penetration efforts in the late 1970s . . .": U.S. Department of Justice Office of the Inspector General, "A Review of the FBI's Performance in Deterring, Detecting, and Investigating the Espionage Activities of Robert Philip Hanssen," August 2003, p. 16. Retrieved from www.usdoj.gov on August 15, 2003.

253 "During the Task Force effort [1986-1987], the FBI . . .": U.S. Department of Justice Office of the Inspector General, "A Review of the FBI's Performance in Deterring, Detecting, and Investigating the Espionage Activities of Robert Philip Hanssen," August 2003, p. 18-19. Retrieved from www.usdoj.gov on August 15, 2003.

253 "Ineffective oversight by FBI management and poor . . .": U.S. Department of Justice Office of the Inspector General, "A Review of the FBI's Performance in Deterring, Detecting, and Investigating the Espionage Activities of Robert Philip Hanssen," August 2003, p. 17. Retrieved from www.usdoj.gov on August 15, 2003.

253 "Even the investigative arm of Congress, the General Accounting Office . . .": Government Accounting Office, GAO-01-888T, "GAO's Work at the FBI: Access to Data, Documents, and Personnel," Government Accounting Office, June 20, 2001, p. 1.

254 "Concern about access to records and people at the . . .": GAO-01-888T, op. cit., p. 1.

254 "One of the greatest problems is delay . . .": GAO-01-888T, op. cit., p. 3.

254 "Another problem relates to the quality of documentation . . .": GAO-01-888T, op. cit., p. 5.

255 "One of the ways he expanded his Bureau . . .": "FBI History: A Timeline." Retrieved from www.fbi.gov/libref/historic/history/historicdates.htm on May 22, 2002.

256 "If you're ridin' ahead . . .": "The Wisdom of Will Rogers." Retrieved from Retrieved from www.eck.com/personal/willrogers.html on June 21, 2003.

Chapter 32: Scared of Changes

263 "In fact, members of the Society of Former Agents of the FBI . . .": "Charles George, then president of the Society of Former Special Agents of the FBI, compared her to convicted spy Robert Hanssen, calling her behavior 'unthinkable' in the society newsletter; instead of going to the Russians, she went to Congress." "Persons of the Year 2002," *Time Inc.* Retrieved from www.time.com/time/personoftheyear/2002/poyrowley2.html on August 15, 2003.

263-64 "If you work for a man, in heaven's name work for him . . .": Elbert Hubbard quoted in Richard Gid Powers. Secrecy and Power: the Life of J. Edgar Hoover (The Free Press, New York), 1987, p. 356.

264 "As an article in the FBI's *Law Enforcement Bulletin* pointed out . . .": FBI, "Law Enforcement Bulletin," Volume 71, Number 5, May 2002, p. 18.

267 "Consider this finding from the Judge Webster's 2002 commission . . .": U.S. Department of Justice, Commission for Review of FBI Security Programs.

268 "Hanssen received minimal supervision in most of his positions . . .": U.S. Department of Justice Office of the Inspector General, "A Review of the FBI's Performance in Deterring, Detecting, and Investigating the Espionage Activities of Robert Philip Hanssen," August 2003, p. 5. Retrieved from www.usdoj.gov on August 15, 2003.

268 "An example is CIA's Aldrich Ames, who passed two polygraphs in 1991 . . .": "Secrets, Lies, and Atomic Spies." Retrieved from www.pbs.org/wgbh/nova/venona/dece_ames.html on October 22, 2002.

270 "Its priorities are currently . . .": "FBI Priorities." Retrieved from www.fbi.gov on June 15, 2003.

INDEX